ZWINGLI AND THE ARTS

Da Capo Press Music Reprint Series

MUSIC EDITOR
BEA FRIEDLAND
Ph.D., City University of New York

ZWINGLI AND THE ARTS

Charles Garside, Jr.

Da Capo Press · New York · 1981

Library of Congress Cataloging in Publication Data

Garside, Charles.
  Zwingli and the arts.

  (Da Capo Press music reprint series)
  Reprint. Originally published: New Haven: Yale
University Press, 1966. (Yale historical publications.
Miscellany; 83)
  Bibliography: p.
  Includes index.
  1. Zwingli, Ulrich, 1484-1531. 2. Christianity and
the arts — History of doctrines — 16th century. I. Title.
II. Series: Yale historical publications. Miscellany;
83.
  [BR345.G3 1981]   246   81-4277
  ISBN 0-306-76018-5   AACR2

This Da Capo Press edition of
Zwingli and the Arts is an unabridged
republication of the first edition published
in New Haven in 1966. It is reprinted by
arrangement with Yale University Press.

Published by Da Capo Press, Inc.
A Subsidiary of Plenum Publishing Corporation
233 Spring Street, New York, N.Y. 10013

ZWINGLI AND THE ARTS

Charles Garside, Jr.

NEW HAVEN AND LONDON, YALE UNIVERSITY PRESS, 1966

*To the Memory of
My Father
and for
My Mother
First and Best of Teachers*

ACKNOWLEDGMENTS

This essay in its earliest form was submitted in 1956 in candidacy for the degree of Doctor of Philosophy in Yale University. I am grateful to the Graduate Faculty for the award of a Sterling Fellowship for the year 1955–56; to my director, Franklin LeVan Baumer; and to my readers, Hajo Holborn, Beekman C. Cannon, Charles Seymour, Jr., and Roland H. Bainton. To Professor Bainton in particular I am profoundly indebted for advice and constant encouragement. The award of a Morse Fellowship during the year 1958–59 enabled me to travel to Zurich and finish an intermediate draft. Chapter 4 has benefited from the criticism of François Bucher of the Department of the History of Art in Princeton University. Gustav Reese of New York University kindly read the entire manuscript, thereby sparing me several errors in the first three chapters. Of the many friends who have assisted me during the writing of this essay I must mention especially Montgomery Angell, Jr., Robert R. Porter, Jan G. Deutsch, and above all my colleague Martin I. J. Griffin, Jr., who read closely, and greatly improved, every page of the final version. I am also deeply grateful to the Brewer Prize Committee of the American Society of Church History for awarding the manuscript a special commendation in 1963.

Portions of Chapters 1 and 3 first appeared in the *Archiv für Reformationsgeschichte, 48* (1957), 56–74. The translation of Hätzer's pamphlet was earlier published in the *Mennonite Quarterly Review, 34* (1961), 20–36. They are reprinted here by the kind permission of the editors. For permission to quote the Cappel Song in the translation of John T. McNeill and the Plague Song in the translation of D. G. Sear, I have to thank the Oxford University Press and the Philosophical Library respectively.

The present essay grew out of my senior thesis on Calvin and Music for the Special Program in the Humanities in Princeton University, and I should like here to acknowledge my enduring debt to three great teachers and friends who guided me then in my first researches into the problem of the relationship of Protestantism and the arts: the late Roy Dickinson Welch, the late Theodor Ernst Mommsen, and the late Elmore Harris Harbison.

My debt to my parents is such that it can only be recorded, not explained.

C. G., Jr.

Timothy Dwight College
New Haven, Connecticut
November 1965

CONTENTS

Contents

SHORT TITLES

Bullinger: *Heinrich Bullingers Reformationsgeschichte,* ed. Johann Jakob Hottinger and Hans Heinrich Vögeli, 2 vols., Frauenfeld, 1838–1840.

Die Vokalmusik: Arnold Geering, *Die Vokalmusik in der Schweiz zur Zeit der Reformation,* Schweizerisches Jahrbuch für Musikwissenschaft, 6, Aarau, 1933.

Egli: *Actensammlung zur Geschichte der Zürcher Reformation in den Jahren 1519–1533,* ed. Emil Egli, 2 vols., Zurich, 1879. References are to the number of the document.

Farner, *1:* Oskar Farner, *Huldrych Zwingli, Seine Jugend, Schulzeit und Studentenjahre 1484–1506,* Zurich, 1943.

Farner, *2:* Oskar Farner, *Huldrych Zwingli, Seine Entwicklung zum Reformator 1506–1520,* Zurich, 1946.

Farner, *3:* Oskar Farner, *Huldrych Zwingli, Seine Verkündigung und ihre ersten Früchte 1520–1525,* Zurich, 1954.

ME: *The Mennonite Encyclopedia,* 4 vols., Scottdale, Pennsylvania, 1955–1959.

ML: *Mennonitische Lexicon,* Frankfurt am Main und Weierhof (Pfalz), 1913–

S: See *Z.*

Wyss, *Chronik:*   *Die Chronik des Bernhard Wyss,* ed. Georg Finsler,
Quellen zur Schweizerischen Reformationsgeschichte, *1,*
Basel, 1901.

Z: *Huldrych Zwinglis Sämtliche Werke,* Berlin-Zurich,
1905– . References are to volume, page, and line number. In quoting Zwingli the scriptural references sup-
plied by the editors have been retained. The edition
edited by Melchior Schuler and Johannes Schulthess (8
vols., Zurich, 1828–1842) is referred to as *S.* Unless
indicated to the contrary, all translations are my own.

INTRODUCTION: *The Great Wheel of the Church*

*But in Divinity I love to keape the road, and, though not
in any implicite, yet an humble faith, follow the great wheele
of the Churche, by which I move.*

                                        Sir Thomas Browne

"In the entire history of European art it is difficult to name any one fact more momentous than the admission of the graven image by the Christian Church." [1] That fact is illustrated by such various achievements in ecclesiastical art and architecture as the Isenheim Altar and the mosaics of Ravenna, the cathedral of Naumburg and Hagia Sophia, the roof of Beauvais and the dome of St. Peter's. The admission of the image gave rise to the iconoclastic ferocities of the Reformation in the West, as it had earlier to the more sophisticated theological and political controversies in the East. It divided Eastern Christendom for almost two centuries, and very nearly destroyed the Byzantine Empire. There have thus always been Christians, theologians and laymen both, who have doubted strongly or denied strenuously the propriety of the use of visual arts in Christian worship. Their debate with the Church began long before the Church admitted the image; it continued thereafter up to the Reformation. With the dissolution of the one Western Church into Roman and non-Roman Churches in the sixteenth century, the history of the debate entered upon a decisively new phase, now exacerbated and further

---

1. Ernst Kitzinger, "The Cult of Images in the Age before Iconoclasm," *Dumbarton Oaks Papers,* 7 (Cambridge, 1954), 83.

I

complicated by confessional and liturgical animosities both between Triden-
tine Catholicism and Protestantism, and within Protestantism itself.

It is today being conducted in a more lively and significant fashion than
perhaps at any time in the past four hundred years. Indeed, under the
pressures of two interrelated twentieth-century developments, the revival of
scholarly study of the liturgy and the increasing acceptance of a contemporary architectural setting for the liturgy, the history of the debate is entering
another phase. Not since the liturgical changes wrought by the Reformation
has there been so intense and so extensive a re-examination of Christian lit-
urgies, Roman and non-Roman.[2] Not since the Reformation destroyed the
many reciprocal ties between artist and Church has so strenuous and so self-
conscious an effort been exerted by each to come to creative terms with the
other without compromising their respective values.[3] Within the Roman
Church bitter dissension has been exhibited recently over the propriety of
contemporary architecture and liturgical art; so, too, among the several
denominations of Protestantism.[4] Now, however, Roman and non-Roman
Churches increasingly share a concern for a better understanding of the
liturgy and a more appropriate liturgical and ecclesiastical art. The debate
has become international, nondenominational, more and more markedly
ecumenical, and may be said to have entered yet another phase with the Second Vatican Council and the wide-ranging artistic and musical implications
of the Constitution on the Sacred Liturgy.[5] We cannot yet understand
deeply or assess with any precision the significance of this new phase, but the
fact of its existence is undeniable. In this mid-twentieth-century context of
the debate it is therefore more necessary than ever to put the question again:
how did Protestantism affect the arts?

2. See, for example, the brief but admirably balanced essay by Massey Hamilton Shepherd, Jr.,
"The History of the Liturgical Renewal," in *The Liturgical Renewal of the Church,* ed. Massey
Hamilton Shepherd, Jr. (New York, 1960), pp. 21–52; cf. the more extended study of Ernest
B. Koenker, *The Liturgical Renaissance in the Roman Catholic Church* (Chicago, 1954), passim.

3. See, most recently, the important symposium in which four Roman Catholics, one Presby-
terian minister, and five Anglicans participated: *Towards a Church Architecture,* ed. Peter
Hammond (The Architectural Press, 1963), as well as Hammond's earlier work, *Liturgy and
Architecture* (New York, 1961).

4. See William S. Rubin, *Modern Sacred Art and the Church of Assy* (New York, 1961), esp.
pp. 45–63; cf. Basil Spence, *Phoenix at Coventry: The Building of a Cathedral* (New York,
1962), passim.

5. For the text of chapters 6 and 7, dealing respectively with "Sacred Music" and "Sacred
Arts," see J. D. Crichton, *The Church's Worship: Considerations on the Liturgical Constitution
of the Second Vatican Council* (New York, 1964), pp. 212–15, 224–27.

PROTESTANTISM AND THE ARTS: LIMITATIONS AND PROCEDURE

If the historian is to pursue this inordinately complex question, he must return to a progressively more exacting consideration or reconsideration of that period in which Protestantism radically altered and expanded the frame of reference for the debate. The Reformation of the sixteenth century was not simply Lutheran. It was Zwinglian, Calvinist, and Anglican as well. It was also Anabaptist and Socinian. It was, in fact, as multipartite as it was monolithic, to such a degree that discrimination between migrating movements and contentious factions was frequently as difficult in the sixteenth century as it is for scholars of the twentieth. Not only "Protestantism," but also "Reformation" must therefore be rigorously qualified for purposes of historical analysis. History progresses not by finding answers but rather by constant clarification and refinement of the questions put to the past. Accordingly, the present study restricts itself to the origins of the Reformed as over against the Lutheran tradition, concentrating primarily on Zwingli, and directing itself more to as close an examination as possible of Zwingli's attitude *toward* the arts than to the subsequent impact of that attitude *on* the arts in Zurich after his death. The context of the city, however, cannot be ignored; for twelve years Zwingli and Zurich were inseparable. Indeed, the development of Zwingli's attitude, especially toward the visual arts, can be understood only with continuing reference to the artistic and social life of the city. By the same token, full account must be taken as well of Zwingli's personal experience of the arts, particularly music.

To these limitations there must be added the problem of procedure. Luther, Zwingli, and Calvin were neither professional artists nor professional aestheticians: they were theologians. Any endeavor to derive from their works an independent aesthetic, in the present sense of the word, is to measure them by standards alien to their time, indeed, to look in them for something which did not then exist.[6] Again, to judge their personal experience of the arts by any standards other than those applicable to them within

---

6. Cf. Ernst Cassirer, *An Essay on Man: An Introduction to a Philosophy of Human Culture* (New York, 1953), p. 76: "Up to the time of Kant a philosophy of beauty always meant an attempt to reduce our aesthetic experience to an alien principle and to subject art to an alien jurisdiction. Kant in his *Critique of Judgement* was the first to give a clear and convincing proof of the autonomy of art. All former systems had looked for a principle of art within the sphere either of theoretical knowledge or of the moral life." See also Paul Oskar Kristeller, "The Modern System of the Arts," *Journal of the History of Ideas, 12* (1951), 496–527; *13* (1952), 17–46.

the context of the sixteenth century is similarly misleading. Of such distortion one example must suffice.

In a study of Luther's attitudes toward the arts, Paul Lehfeldt criticizes the Reformer's behavior during his visit to Rome in 1510. Lehfeldt is aware that during his brief sojourn in the city Luther ran feverishly from church to church, from relic to relic, from Mass to Mass, intent on acquiring as many as possible of the vast numbers of spiritual benefits which Rome then afforded. But at the same time he complains that Luther took no direct interest in the artistic activity then currently under way in the city, reproaching him for being concerned only with spiritual matters. Indeed, "so completely was he filled with these thoughts and observances that he stood apart to a certain degree from everything which we today consider worth seeing." [7] Lehfeldt would have Luther come to Rome as a twentieth-century secular connoisseur; the fact is that he came to Rome as a sixteenth-century monk. He came not to a museum but to "Holy Rome," whose treasures were for him spiritual and not aesthetic. Heinrich Boehmer, to the contrary, does not lose sight of that fundamental fact, and rightly argues that "one cannot conclude from this that he was by nature wanting in taste for the plastic arts. It simply means that he was wandering through the Eternal City with the eyes of a pilgrim." [8] The importance to the historian of these conflicting judgments lies simply in the fact that Boehmer and Lehfeldt start from decisively different points of view: the former is faithful to historical context; the latter is not.

Thirteen years after the Rome journey, Luther asserted in the *Formula Missae* of 1523 that "there is scarcely one of the handicrafts in all the world which does not contribute a great part of its activity to, and derive its gain from, the Mass." [9] Thereby he gave expression to the central fact of preReformation culture in the West, namely, that its vital center, the heart of all its multiform creativity, was the liturgy:

In fact the art of Christendom in both its Byzantine and medieval phases was essentially a liturgical art which cannot be understood with-

7. Paul Lehfeldt, *Luthers Verhältniss zu Kunst und Künstlern* (Berlin, 1892), 21; for other statements as inaccurate as they are unjust, see pp. 32, 93.
8. Heinrich Boehmer, *Martin Luther: Road to Reformation,* trans. John W. Doberstein and Theodore G. Tappert (New York, 1957), p. 71; cf. Roland H. Bainton, *Here I Stand: A Life of Martin Luther* (New York, 1951), p. 49.
9. *Formula Missae et Communionis,* trans. Paul Zeller Strodach, *Works of Martin Luther* (Philadelphia, 1932), 6, 86.

out some knowledge of the liturgy itself and its historical origin and development. And the same is true to a great extent of popular and vernacular culture. The popular religious drama, which had such an important influence on the rise of European drama as a whole, was either a liturgical drama in the strict sense, like the Passion plays and Nativity plays, or was directly related to the cult of the saints and the celebration of their feasts. For the cult of the saints, which had its basis in the liturgy, was the source of a vast popular mythology and provided a bridge between the higher ecclesiastical and literary culture and the peasant culture with its archaic traditions of folklore and magic.

In the same way the church itself—I mean the liturgical edifice—was at the same time the organ of both the higher and the lower culture, and consequently a great instrument of social integration. On the one hand it was the temple in which the liturgy was celebrated in the common language of educated Christendom, and, on the other, in the village and the pilgrimage place it was the center of the common people for whom it was at once school and theater and picture gallery.[10]

For public worship in general, for the celebration of the Mass above all else, the Church for centuries had ceaselessly created a total art bound to it by liturgy. Even on the eve of the Reformation the public worship of the Church continued to be the major focus for artistic activity, especially in Northern Europe, for there life still was "encompassed and measured by the rich efflorescence of the liturgy: the sacraments, the canonical hours of the day, and the festivals of the ecclesiastical year."[11] Accordingly, any consideration of Zwingli's attitude toward the visual arts and music must turn on the fundamental question: how does he understand the relationship of these arts to Christian worship?

The procedure for the following essay will therefore be to examine Zwingli's understanding of the arts in terms of their applicability to, and value for, Christian worship, and the arts to be examined will in turn be limited to the visual arts and music, for they are pre-eminently the arts of the liturgy. Limitations and procedure will thus be united by liturgy, the only point of departure faithful to the sixteenth century.

10. Christopher Dawson, *The Historic Reality of Christian Culture: A Way to the Renewal of Human Life* (New York, 1960), pp. 72–73.

11. Jan Huizinga, *The Waning of the Middle Ages: A Study of the Forms of Life, Thought and Art in France and the Netherlands in the XIVth and XVth Centuries* (New York, 1949), p. 233.

1. MUSICAE AMATOR

Musicae pertinax amator
Vita Conradi Celtis

THE EARLIEST YEARS: 1484–1496

Huldrych Zwingli, from his earliest days, seems to have been musically gifted as well as musically inclined. Among the several towns in the Toggenburg valley, Wildhaus, where he was born on January 1, 1484, was by tradition exceptionally musical, so that his first environment contributed to his interest and enthusiasm for the art.[1] Not until 1494, however, was he formally instructed in music; he was sent away to study under Gregor Bünzli[2] at the Latin school of St. Theodor in Klein-Basel. Since there, as in all other such *Trivialschulen,* the curriculum consisted of Latin, dialectic, and music, Zwingli's first education in music was both literally and figura-

1. As late as 1819, Johann Friedrich Franz reported that "if a traveler to Wildhaus joins a group of young people, say about twenty, he may then surely count on the fact that twelve or fourteen of them will be musical. Some will be able to play the violin, others will be good singers, some will play the organ, some the zither, several the clarinet, and others the flute, and they will be able thus to put on the most delightful concert. . . . One seldom enters a house in which some sort of musical instrument is not found, particularly the zither, with which the father of the house and his wife, accompanied in song by their children, while away the time on beautiful summer evenings or on Sundays; one may therefore count on fifty zithers and from ten to twenty house organs in Wildhaus alone. People who in their whole lives have enjoyed nothing more than the inadequate musical training of school, often play the organ or the piano with considerable ability." *Zwinglis Geburtsort* (St. Gall, 1819), pp. 134–35.

2. On Bünzli, about whom little is known, see the literature cited by Fritz Schmidt-Clausing, "Johan Ulrich Surgant, ein Wegweiser des jungen Zwingli," *Zwingliana, 11* (1961), 318, n. 92.

7

tively a matter of course. But he doubtless had taught himself the rudiments before then, a supposition strongly borne out by his intimate friend and first biographer, Oswald Myconius, who says that at the school in Basel, though he was only ten years old, "he distinguished himself in music far beyond his years, as is the rule with those to whom any art whatever comes easily." [3] At Basel, also, Zwingli gave evidence, apparently for the first time, of the lovely voice soon to play so significant a role in his career. Another friend— eventually to be his successor in Zurich—Heinrich Bullinger, himself a practicing musician and amateur composer,[4] records that while at St. Theodor's school "he was well instructed by this Bünzli, and since the youth had a good voice and enjoyed music, he therefore was well trained in it." [5]

BERN: 1496-1498

Zwingli proved to be a brilliant student and in two years had quite outgrown the *Trivialschule* in Basel. He was sent in 1496 to Bern, where he continued to study Latin and the Latin classics under the personal direction of the man "who was the first one in Switzerland to adopt in their entirety the educational ideas of the Renascence," [6] the celebrated humanist scholar and poet Heinrich Wölflin. Like many other northern humanists of that time, Wölflin was passionately devoted to music; he was even a composer of sorts.[7] Thus there can be little doubt that he encouraged and furthered the young Zwingli's musical interests. It is possible, too, that Zwingli may have received training in formal composition from the distinguished and learned professional musician Bartholomäus Gotfrid Frank, at that time the Cantor of St. Vincent's Church in Bern.[8] Charged with the general education of the young choristers as well as their special musical training, Frank was regarded both as a fine teacher and as an authority in all matters musical. Doubtless he and Wölflin knew each other; it has even been suggested that

3. Oswald Myconius, "Vita Huldrici Zwinglii," in *Vitae Quatuor Reformatorum* (Berlin, 1841), p. 4.
4. See Fritz Blanke, *Der junge Bullinger* (Zurich, 1942), pp. 17, 25–26; for the music and text of the song Bullinger wrote for his wife Anna on their wedding day, pp. 113–15.
5. Bullinger, *1*, 6.
6. Samuel Macauley Jackson, *Huldreich Zwingli, The Reformer of German Switzerland 1484–1531* (New York, 1901), p. 56; cf. Farner, *1*, 164–68.
7. The three extant songs by Wölflin attest to his ability as a composer: see Albert Büchi, "Eine Motette des Berner Kantors Bartholomäus Frank, 1494–1495," *Zeitschrift für schweizerische Kirchengeschichte, 8* (1914), 241–51.
8. On Frank, see *Die Vokalmusik*, pp. 116–26.

Frank set some of Wölflin's verses to music.[9] That Wölflin did not introduce his gifted pupil to Frank is therefore highly improbable, and the latter may well have taught Zwingli musical composition, if not officially then at least informally.[10]

Regardless of who taught him, the young Huldrych was rapidly becoming an excellent musician, of such extraordinary talent in fact that his musicianship was directly responsible for the first crisis of his life. During the year 1496–97 the Dominican monks, attracted by his musical achievements and promise, and particularly by his beautiful voice, urged him to enter their monastery in Bern for a probationary year. There he could pursue his musical studies and more especially sing in the chapel choir, a point on which Bullinger is most emphatic: "While he was in Bern and could sing well, the prayer monks of Bern lured him into the cloister with the intention that he should remain there up to the end of the year of probation." [11] Wölflin was sympathetically inclined toward the order,[12] and Zwingli's love for music was at this time so intense that he accepted the offer and entered the monastery.[13] Almost immediately thereafter, he was withdrawn by his family. The precise reasons for this abrupt move are not now known, but in all probability they strongly disapproved of Zwingli's taking a step merely for the sake of music which might have resulted in a radical decision at too early an age.[14] Huldrych was thus removed from Bern and sent in 1498 to Vienna, a transfer from monastery to university which the contemporary chronicler Johann Stumpf described as follows: "His uncle Bartholomew Zwingli, deacon and pastor at Wesen, did not want to leave him in the cloister, took

9. The suggestion was made in the article on Wölflin in Edgar Refardt, *Historisch-biographisches Musikerlexicon der Schweiz* (Zurich, 1928), p. 344; in *Die Vokalmusik*, p. 118, Geering categorically denies any necessity for it. He dismisses the possibility too lightly, however, and the question ought properly to remain open.

10. Büchi, *Eine Motette*, pp. 241–51; cf. Walter Köhler, *Zwingliana*, *3* (1913–20), 224, and Farner, *1*, 171–72.

11. Bullinger, *1*, 7.

12. Farner, *1*, 172.

13. Zwingli's actual entry into the monastery has occasonally been denied, as, for example, by John Thomas McNeill, *The History and Character of Calvinism* (New York, 1954), p. 20. Nevertheless the evidence from Bullinger seems to assert this beyond doubt, as does the testimony of Zwingli himself, Z, *3*, 486, 3–4; cf. further Johann Stumpf, *Chronica vom Leben und Wircken des Ulrich Zwingli*, ed. Leo Weisz, Quellen und Studien zur Geschichte der Helvetischen Kirche, *1* (Zurich, 1932), p. 17, and Farner, *1*, 172–73.

14. Cf. the penetrating observation of Jaques Courvoisier, *Zwingli, Soldat de Dieu* (Geneva, [1957]), p. 19. Farner, *1*, 173, suggests that the unsavory reputation of the Bernese Dominicans at that time may have contributed to the family's decision.

him out before he could take orders, and sent him to Vienna in Austria where he practiced in the liberal arts." [15]

The removal to Vienna did not bring an end to either Zwingli's passion for music or his resolution to study it, for as Stumpf, continuing the chronicle, added significantly, "in particular he was basically grounded in all instruments, such as harp, lute, viol, flute, reedpipe, and cornett, completely educated, a good composer, and so forth." [16] That Zwingli should continue his musical studies is no surprise, considering the love for them he had thus far consistently shown. Moreover, music was still considered central to a humanistic education, for "no one supposed to be learned in the liberal arts was thought that unless he had been taught music." [17] But most important of all for Zwingli was the fact that during these years at Vienna he was taught by a man who was the most spectacular personality on the university faculty, the "German archhumanist," in fact the greatest organizer of German humanism, Conrad Celtis Protucius (1459–1508).[18] Celtis had been crowned poet laureate in 1487, the first German to receive this singular honor, and after a decade of wandering and lecturing throughout Europe had come to Vienna in 1497 at the particular insistence of the Emperor Maximilian, who was himself a humanist and an enthusiastic amateur musician, as well as a lavish patron of professionals.[19]

The University of Vienna had already a considerable humanistic and musical tradition. It continued to maintain the long-established and close connection between music and mathematics; since 1449 lectures on music

15. Stumpf, *Chronica*, p. 17.

16. Ibid.

17. Rodoricus Zamorensis, *Der Spiegel des menschlichen Lebens* (1488), a contemporary book on the liberal arts which Zwingli may even have known and read; cf. Georg Schünemann, *Geschichte der deutschen Schulmusik* (2d ed. Leipzig, 1931–32), 2, p. 7.

18. Cf. Markus Jenny, "Zwinglis mehrstimmige Kompositionen, Ein Basler Zwingli-Fund," *Zwingliana, 11* (1960), 173, who also proves untenable the argument in *Die Vokalmusik*, p. 43, that Zwingli received the greater part of his musical training at Basel. On Celtis, in addition to the still useful essay by Friedrich von Bezold, "Konrad Celtis, 'der deutsche Erzhumanist,'" *Aus Mittelalter und Renaissance* (Munich and Berlin, 1918), pp. 82–152, see the biography of Lewis W. Spitz, *Conrad Celtis, The German Arch-Humanist* (Cambridge, 1957), esp. pp. 72–82, and Heinrich Hüschen, "Celtes," *Die Musik in Geschichte und Gegenwart* (Kassel and Basel, 1952), 2, cols. 950–54.

19. Nan Cooke Carpenter, *Music in the Medieval and Renaissance Universities* (Norman, Okla., 1958), p. 228.

had been required for all students in the Arts Faculty. Members of that faculty even seem to have given private instruction in practical music.[20] But Celtis' arrival in 1497, and later the foundation of the exclusively humanistic College of Poetry and Mathematics in 1501, made the university for a while a revolutionary center of experimentation in musical theory and practice. Profoundly interested in music, Celtis, throughout his career at Vienna, concentrated on what were to be his most exciting and significant innovations in the new learning. He taught both rhetoric and poetics, using for his models those who were then considered the most perfect masters of the two arts, Cicero and Horace respectively. At that time Horace's Odes posed a vexing problem, for Celtis, like other contemporary humanists, believed as "an established fact that the ancients had not read their odes, but had sung them to the accompaniment of the cithara." [21] Yet none of this music survived. The humanists, who so ardently longed not only to revive classical poetry but to reconstruct it in a manner approaching that of the ancients, were therefore compelled to admit that what were for them the world's greatest lyric poems could not be appreciated as they knew they ought to be and as they wanted them to be.[22] Celtis, a professional poet and an amateur musician, was not content to rest in such a quandary. His combined talents afforded a solution: to compose music for the odes. He began at once to direct one of his musical pupils, a certain Petrus Tritonius, in the composition of such music.

The most fascinating aspect of these settings is that in order to preserve the complex meters of Horace's lines, which was, after all, Celtis' intent, the music was throughout rigidly subordinated to the text, the time values of the musical notes following and underscoring the various metrical patterns of the lines. Celtis' decision to compose music for the odes marked the initial step toward the musical humanism and measured music which were to function so decisively in the cultural life of the sixteenth century. But although he was profoundly concerned for the restoration of the supposed classical union of music and poetry, these musical settings were designed principally to assist his students in their study of the various classical meters. He had them sing the odes at the close of his lectures so that the lesson of

---

20. Carpenter, p. 226; see pp. 224–30 for an account of music in the curriculum at Vienna. For a brilliant survey of humanism in the university see Werner Näf, *Vadian und seine Stadt St. Gallen* (St. Gallen, 1944), *1*, 123–34, as well as the older, more comprehensive study by Gustav Bauch, *Die Reception des Humanismus in Wien* (Breslau, 1903).

21. Rochus von Liliencron, "Die Horazischen Metren in deutschen Kompositionen des 16. Jahrhunderts," *Vierteljahrsschrift für Musikwissenschaft*, *3* (1887), 35.

22. Ibid.

Horatian poetics might be more imaginatively and permanently fixed in their minds. Later, indeed throughout most of the sixteenth century, when composers wrote music in the style of these odes they did it as a rule either because they were themselves teachers or because they had been commissioned to do so by other teachers of classical poetry.[23] Celtis initiated and maintained throughout his life the primarily educational motivation and character of musical humanism in the north. Its aims were always to be didactic and professionally pedagogical.[24]

Finally, Celtis' influence was to be felt in yet another direction. Once Tritonius' four-voiced musical settings for the Horatian Odes and Epodes were published in Augsburg in 1507, the new technique of composition was immediately appropriated by other composers, especially for the purposes of religious music. Tritonius' original publication had, in fact, contained some hymns, and soon whole collections of them appeared which were written in the musical style of the humanistic choral ode. Thus music which was the direct outgrowth of exclusively classical and philological research, the product of a secular institution and secular ideas, came eventually to exert an extraordinarily pervasive influence on the religious music of the sixteenth century.[25]

For the two years that Zwingli was consecutively at Vienna (1500–02),[26] Celtis was working intensely on the odes, as was Tritonius. Zwingli, together with others of the master's students, probably even sang them at the end of

23. Carpenter, p. 229.

24. D. P. Walker, *Der musikalische Humanismus im 16. und frühen 17. Jahrhundert* (Basel, 1949), pp. 6–7, n. 9.

25. On the spiritual odes see Hellmuth Christian Wolff, "Die geistlichen Oden des Georg Tranoscius und die Odenkompositionen des Humanismus," *Die Musikforschung,* 6 (1953), 300–13; 7 (1954), 39–53; Eduard Bernoulli, *Aus Liederbüchern der Humanistenzeit: Eine bibliographische und notentypographische Studie* (Leipzig, 1910), Beilage XVI, a-b-c; and Hans Joachim Moser, *Paul Hofhaimer, ein lied- und orgelmeister des deutschen Humanismus* (Stuttgart-Berlin, Cotta, 1929), pp. 162–67, examples 112–28. Celtis' experiments also profoundly affected Protestant musical development. If the complicated meters of the classical text were to be distinctly audible to students, the melody had to be lifted from the middle of the voices to the soprano. For this revolution in musical thinking Celtis is without doubt responsible. When the idea was transferred to spiritual song it made possible the eventual joining together of choir and congregation because a musically untrained congregation could hear the melody above, rather than within, the counterpoint and unite in singing it: see Rochus von Liliencron, "Die Chorgesänge des lateinischdeutschen Schuldramas im XVI Jahrhundert," *Vierteljahrsschrift für Musikwissenschaft,* 6 (1890), 309–387, passim.

26. Zwingli matriculated at Vienna in 1498, but against his name in the register for that year is written "exclusus." Whether he withdrew or was expelled is not precisely known; for the most recent discussion of the problem, see Farner, 2, 184–94. He matriculated again in 1500.

his classes. He was receiving finer musical supervision, and living and study-ing in the midst of musical developments far more exciting and challenging, than he could have experienced in the Dominican monastery at Bern. Fur-ther stimulus to his musical studies must also have been provided by his fel-low student Heinrich Glareanus, a young scholar soon to become known throughout Europe as the leading musical humanist of Switzerland, to whom Zwingli dedicated his first poem. He and Glareanus became such close friends while at the university that they corresponded for several years afterward.[27] And all the while the young Huldrych "practiced music in his spare time, with singing and string-playing; also piping, but with modera-tion,"[28] so that musical practice was consistently accompanied by musical theory.

BASEL: 1502–1506

Zwingli returned to Switzerland in the spring of 1502 to enter the Univer-sity of Basel, where he received his bachelor's degree in 1504, and then a master's degree in 1506, for which, as a result of the university statutes of 1492, music, together with mathematics, was one of the required subjects.[29] His enthusiasm for music continued quite naturally, since Basel, like Vienna, was more and more becoming an intensely musical community. Bullinger is careful to note that "he learned also to play a variety of musical instruments, especially the lute, of which he was a famous master,"[30] and a singular fragment of evidence from Zwingli himself confirms that his musical inter-ests and activity persisted: at some time after 1511 the young scholar pur-chased an edition of the works of Pico della Mirandola, in which he subse-quently wrote the following marginal note: "When a young messenger, whom I sent home from the university, commended my manner of life to my father, what I was doing and my studies, and at the end recounted my love for music and instruments, including the parties, my father, however, answered: 'I would rather have a philosopher than a jokester.'"[31]

The autobiographical fragment has additional significance. Zwingli's fam-ily had withdrawn him from the monastery at Bern for reasons now un-

27. See, for example, Z, 7, 9, 16–18.

28. Bullinger, *1*, 31.

29. Carpenter, p. 300; see pp. 300–08 for a general description of music in the curriculum at Basel.

30. Bullinger, *1*, 7.

31. Walter Köhler, *Das Buch der Reformation Huldrych Zwinglis* (Munich, 1926), No. 23, p. 16; cf. Farner, *1*, 202–05.

known, although one reason may have been disapproval of their son's study of music because it was not a sufficiently serious pursuit. This disapproval is certainly evidenced in the father's reply and particularly in the words of Zwingli himself, who cites music and parties in one and the same breath. What he refers to as "parties" may have been simply groups of his friends joining together to play and sing concerted music privately. Nevertheless, whether they were musical gatherings or social functions or both, Zwingli was many years later to be charged openly with the very musical-social activity to which he himself confesses here—an accusation which almost prevented his appointment to the position of people's priest at the Great Minster in Zurich.

In addition to studying at the university, he now began to teach at St. Martin's church-school in Basel. His strenuous schedule demanded occasional relaxation, and Myconius describes how he continued to turn to his dearly beloved music: "He mixed serious things with jest and sport, for he was of a pleasing talent and his voice was delightful beyond description. Thereafter he learned thoroughly and practiced every kind of musical instrument only in order that, his mind having been tired out by serious things, he might both be refreshed and return to them more readily." [32]

Zwingli apparently also recommended such musical relaxation to his pupils at St. Martin's school, for he "most carefully urged all students of letters to cultivate [music] on the same plan with him." [33] Myconius was so familiar with the accusations hurled at his intimate friend, and so anxious to explain this facet of Zwingli's personality, that he defended the Reformer's intense love for music with a splendid Ciceronian flourish: "For since there is nothing which more honestly exhilarates the mind of man, by whatever sorrow disturbed, which more pleasantly calms [the mind of man], by whatever blow cast down, why should he not have urged men thus?" [34]

GLARUS: 1506–1516

Having received his master's degree in 1506, Zwingli left Basel, was ordained, and in December was appointed pastor to the community of Glarus,

32. Myconius, "Vita," p. 4; cf. Bullinger, *1*, 306: "he was of an open and cheerful disposition which enabled him to sustain great and diverse tasks, particularly through God's grace and especial help; after which he had recourse to music; thereby his burdened spirit would be refreshed and delighted."
33. Myconius, "Vita," p. 4.
34. Ibid.

there to remain as parish priest until 1516. In addition to his pastoral duties, he continued his humanistic and theological studies, began to learn Greek, founded a school for the children of the community, and taught in it. He must have thoroughly enjoyed his teaching, for since the curriculum was no doubt much like that of St. Martin's school at Basel or St. Theodor's school at Bern, the two principal subjects were Latin and music,[35] those in which he had been longest and most carefully trained and was most proficient. He used to play both lute and trumpet with his students on their holidays, and on one occasion is supposed to have quieted a classroom of unruly boys by playing a melody on his lute for them.[36] Since Bullinger records that he was already an acknowledged master of that instrument, the story is not entirely improbable. Indeed, that he may have been more successful teaching music than Latin is suggested by the conclusion of a letter written to him by one of his former students, Johannes Dingnauer, who hails him first as "most eloquent performer on the Apollinian lyre," and only secondly as "the Cicero of our time, undoubted master, Huldrych Zwingli" (7, 31, 20–21). In his later years Zwingli reveals his delight in teaching music, as well as his love for it, through reference to a peculiarly apt story from Quintilian. He cites it in a tract written against the Anabaptists in 1525, beginning with a pedagogical simile:

Just as when one has learned to play the lute, but not in the correct manner, and afterward one learns the right way, so must one allow much more time to disaccustom oneself of the previous wrong way than to learn the new method; for something of the old will always remain. For this reason a lute player, Timotheos of Miletos, demanded a double fee to teach someone who could already play the lute, and reckoned one [half] to get rid of old habits and the other [half] for the teaching of the new.[37]

35. Farner, 2, 68–69. For a description of the ideally educated student of the time, who, in addition to Latin, had to be "musicus studiosissimus," see Z, 7, 126, 9–14.
36. McNeill, *The History and Character of Calvinism*, p. 21.
37. Z, 4, 269, 14–21. The classical source is Quintilian, *Institutio Oratoria* 2. 3. 3. Farner, 1, 171, suggests that the passage has autobiographical implications, and that Zwingli is recalling here the fact that he had taught himself music at Wildhaus only to have to learn the art again at Basel under the guidance of Bünzli; the suggestion has been adopted by Courvoisier, *Zwingli*, p. 20. Moreover, Zwingli's citation of the anecdote may have further significance. He must have been fully aware that many of his learned contemporaries pointed to Timotheos of Miletos as one of the most conspicuous reformers and innovators in ancient music, so that the religious reformer of Switzerland, a passionate lover of music, may thus have felt a very

EINSIEDELN: 1516–1518

In 1516 Zwingli was called from Glarus to the monastery at Einsiedeln, where he was to remain until his call to Zurich two years later. His enthusiasm for music must surely have remained undiminished despite his new duties there, for it almost prevented him from taking the most momentous step of his entire career. When late in October of 1518 the office of people's priest in the Great Minster at Zurich fell vacant, Oswald Myconius wrote to Zwingli from the city asking him if he would consent to be a candidate for the post. Zwingli agreed, and Myconius evidently labored mightily in his friend's behalf. But on December 3, 1518, he wrote again to Zwingli, this time confessing to his difficulties in a most illuminating letter, the significant portion of which follows:

> You have friends here, you have critics also; the latter, however, are in the minority, and the former numerous and worthy. There is no one, moreover, who does not praise your teaching to the heavens. I shall tell you everything candidly. There are some whom your ready talent for music offends; as a result they say, to use their words, that you are worldly and sensual. There are some also who censure your past because you have been too much influenced by those who have devoted themselves to sensual pleasures. These criticisms I restrain as much as I can; indeed I have subdued them so that they will injure you in no way.
>
> [7, 107, 6–12]

Myconius was able to quiet the charges pertaining to music, but he implored his friend to clear himself of the more formidable charge of an illicit love affair. Of this Zwingli did clear himself, in an immediate reply to Canon Heinrich Utinger, one of his most influential supporters in the cathedral chapter. Significantly, however, he returned also to the former charge, even though Myconius had said that he had given sufficient explanation to his enemies: "Some have charged me with supporting music; assuredly they are worthless fools and unworthy of any consideration . . . for whenever mention is made of an actor or a musician, they think of a fee. I, as they say, play for myself and listen to the pleasing harmony without compensation" (7, 113, 12–16).

---

real kinship with him; cf. Erwin Panofsky, "Who Is Jan van Eyck's 'Timotheos'?", *Journal of the Warburg and Courtauld Institutes, 21* (1949), 84, and *Early Netherlandish Painting; Its Origins and Character* (Cambridge, 1953), *1*, 435–36, n. 2.

The implications of this reply are twofold. First of all, he denies, in his love for music, any associations that are worldly or immoral. His musical activity is restricted exclusively to his private life, to singing and instrumentalizing in his own home with his family and friends. Just as significantly, he does not once suggest that he will relinquish his private music-making, even were he not to be called to the Great Minster if he continued it. Music was clearly playing a decisive role in Zwingli's personal life.

Despite his detractors, he was called to Zurich, and on January 1, 1519, he preached officially for the first time as people's priest of the Great Minster.

ZURICH: ECCLESIASTICAL MUSIC

The city in which Zwingli was to live for the remaining twelve years of his life, and whose spirit he was to transform completely, was, ironically enough, less musical than any other in Switzerland. This is not to say that it was wholly devoid of any musical culture, but rather that music, like the visual arts, played a distinctly secondary role in the life of the city. Unlike Vienna or Basel, what formal musical activity Zurich maintained was associated exclusively with its churches and cloisters and, above all, with the two minsters.

Ever since the late fourth century a church had crowned the steep hill rising up from the right bank of the Limmat, the swiftly flowing river that divides the city. According to a much-beloved legend, Saints Felix and Regula had been beheaded on the hill, and Charlemagne himself commanded that a church be erected there to house their relics. Not long after the middle of the ninth century, Berta, the younger daughter of Charlemagne's grandson Ludwig the German, transferred these relics to the other side of the Limmat, where she built another church, far more splendid, close to the left bank.[38] In 874 this Carolingian basilica of the Fraumünster was consecrated, and for that occasion, at the suggestion of Ratpert, a monk from St. Gall, both the canons and canonesses of the church sang together in mixed choirs, a phenomenon which was at that time without precedent.[39] The ecclesiastical-musical culture of Zurich may be said to date, then, from the last quarter of the ninth century and to have centered at first around the

38. Konrad Escher, *Die beiden Zürcher Münster* (Frauenfeld and Leipzig, 1928), pp. 7–8.
39. Leo Weisz, "Kirchengesang und Kirchenmusik im alten Zürich," *Schweizerische Musikzeitung und Sängerblatt, 73* (1933), 4–5.

liturgy of the Fraumünster. The old church on the hill which Berta had left was destroyed eventually by fire in 1078; but not until almost a century had elapsed did the construction of what was later to be Zwingli's church, the Great Minster, begin. Yet long before the vaulting was finally completed in 1285, the new church on the right bank of the Limmat had become as much a center of musical activity as the older Fraumünster. The entire cultural life of thirteenth-century Zurich, in fact, moved between the poles of the two minsters, the former under the leadership of the poet-musician and Cantor of the Great Minster, Konrad of Mure, and afterward, under its dynamic provost Johannes; the latter under the great Abbess Elizabeth of Wetzikon, a patroness of musicians as well as poets.[40]

The canons of the Great Minster had at first simply copied the liturgy of the Fraumünster, substituting boys' voices for the women who were not allowed in the chapter; the office of Cantor was established, in fact, for the very purpose of training such a choir. But inasmuch as Charlemagne, the legendary founder of the Great Minster, had been canonized in 1165, the chapter determined to acquire for his church in Zurich the liturgical music used for the cult of the great king at Aachen. The anniversary of his death was celebrated every year after 1233 with the music brought from Aachen, into which was incorporated a long sequence in praise of Zurich.[41] The Fraumünster, too, possessed its own festival hymns and its own office, which dated from 1334, likewise containing a special sequence honoring Zurich, in celebration of the feast of the patrons of the city, Saints Felix and Regula.[42] And once every year after 1260, the two minsters combined their musical resources for the feast of Saint Fides. Since her altar was in the Fraumünster, on the appointed day the canons of the Great Minster marched out of their church in solemn procession down the hill to the Limmat and crossed the river, where they were met by the canonesses of the Fraumünster. The two processions then marched together into the church, where alternatively and in mixed choirs they sang Mass with a sequence written especially for the occasion.[43] Aside from these liturgical curiosities, almost nothing else is known about the musical life of the city in the high Middle Ages.[44]

40. Escher, *Die beiden Zürcher Münster*, pp. 40–42.
41. Weisz, *Kirchengesang*, p. 8; cf. also Jacques Handschin, "Die Musik," in *Zürich: Geschichte, Kultur, Wirtschaft* (Zürich, 1933), p. 224.
42. Weisz, *Kirchengesang*, p. 5.
43. Handschin, "Die Musik," pp. 224–25.
44. Only four musical documents are extant from pre-Reformation Zurich; cf. Weisz, *Kirchengesang*, pp. 6, 8, 49. The remainder were destroyed in October 1525; see esp. the

The Great Minster apparently began to expand its musical resources early in the fifteenth century, at least to the point of acquiring an organ,[45] and when polyphony was introduced into the Zurich churches somewhat later, the performance of the liturgy at the Great Minster became famous for the unusually fine quality of the singing, especially now that the choir was accompanied by an organ. This artistic pre-eminence was due to a particularly brilliant Cantor, one Felix Hemmerlin, who was in close contact with, and considerably under the influence of, the musical activities of nearby St. Gall. He raised the standards of musical performance to such a height that contemporaries referred to him as the "King of the Chorus," and in 1448 he himself admitted modestly that "it is a truth, and a fact generally acknowledged by public acclaim, that in Southern Germany there is no church in which, as well by day as by night, the divine service is celebrated with such magnificence and such splendor as in the Great Minster of Zurich." [46] The example that was set evidently stimulated the other religious establishments of Zurich to improve their musical standards. Of the orders represented within the city—Augustinian, Franciscan, and Dominican [47]—the Dominicans especially became conspicuous for both the quality and the ostentation of their singing, as did also the Dominican nuns of the Oetenbach convent.[48]

The musical facilities of all these churches were further amplified somewhat more than a quarter century later, but within the realm of instrumental rather than choral music, and from a wholly secular impetus. Hans Waldmann, the last great pre-Reformation burgomaster of Zurich, had been patron of the Fraumünster for two years when he decided in 1478 that he would be buried there.[49] Wishing, doubtless, to satisfy his ambitions for the

---

detailed report of Canon Felix Fry in Leo Weisz, "Quellen zur Reformationsgeschichte des Grossmünsters in Zürich," *Zwingliana,* 7 (1939), 82–83, n. 13, as well as *Gerold Edlibachs Chronik,* ed. J. M. Usteri, Mitteilungen der Antiquarischen Gesellschaft in Zürich, 4 (Zurich, 1846), 275. For a similar situation in the visual arts, see below, p. 80, n. 14.

45. An organist at the Great Minster is mentioned for the first time in 1418; see Salomon Vögelin, *Das alte Zürich, historisch und antiquarisch dargestellt* (Zurich, 1878), p. 312.

46. Both quotations from Weisz, *Kirchengesang,* p. 10.

47. Handschin, "Die Musik," p. 224, suggests that one of the reasons why Zurich was never comparable to the other cities of Switzerland as a center of musical culture, at least during the Middle Ages, was the fact that the Benedictines, who were pre-eminently interested in the cultivation of music, were never represented by an establishment within the city.

48. Weisz, *Kirchengesang,* p. 10.

49. Escher, *Die beiden Zürcher Münster,* p. 46. On Waldmann, see below, p. 78, n. 4.

church under his care, as well as to enrich his burial place, and knowing, too, that the Great Minster already possessed an organ, he determined that the Fraumünster should not be without one. Accordingly, in 1479 he presented fifty gulden for that purpose, and that same year a beautiful organ, built by Konrad Sittinger of St. Blasien, was installed in the church, a musical event of such significance that Gerold Edlibach took care to record the fact in his chronicle of the city.[50] Six years later, in 1485, Sittinger constructed another organ on Waldmann's commission, this one for the burgomaster's new Water Church,[51] and not long afterward all three religious orders likewise had organs built for the churches in their cloisters.[52] Finally, almost as if they were not to be outdone, the canons of the Great Minster in 1507 installed a magnificent new instrument which Edlibach praised highly for its "charming and good work, with its many registers."[53] Indeed, the mid-fifteenth century proved to be the high point in the musical history of Zurich before the Reformation.

Choral polyphony is infinitely more taxing than Gregorian chant; consistently satisfactory performance demands not only an expert choir but also an exceptionally talented musician to train and direct it. Felix Hemmerlin and his gifted pupil Nikolaus von Wyl were just such musicians, but their successors in the Cantorate of the Great Minster clearly were not so able. The Fraumünster, on the other hand, had never attained quite to the musical excellence of its rival across the Limmat, and by the last quarter of the century the standards of musical performance in both churches had begun to decline markedly, a deterioration to be observed as well in the cloisters and convents that took their lead from the two minsters.[54] Indeed, Myconius, who taught in the city from 1516 to 1520, shortly thereafter characterized not only the music but its presentation by the church choirs:

> One can occasionally hear nothing but a single sound which is drawn out through modulations of a hundred kinds without words, such as would be thought ridiculous even in an amorous air. All this provides no advantages, in that neither singers nor listeners can understand what

50. Escher, *Die beiden Zürcher Münster*, pp. 46–47. Edlibach, *Chronik*, p. 174. Vögelin, *Das alte Zürich*, pp. 531–32.
51. Vögelin, *Das alte Zürich*, p. 227.
52. Weisz, *Kirchengesang*, p. 9.
53. Ibid.
54. Weisz, *Kirchengesang*, p. 10.

is sung because the musical racket drowns out everything, and the words are made incomprehensible.[55]

Bullinger, perhaps because he was the more sensitive musician, was more laconic but no less devastating. "The music in parishes and monasteries," he remarked, "was for the most part idolatrous."[56] Zwingli spoke acidly of the "song which one sings off-key in the churches" (2, 788, 21), and the common people also objected. Ever since the fourteenth century, German "spiritual songs" had become increasingly popular with the laity of Zurich. Not only were these songs in the vernacular, which all could understand; they were written for only one voice, which anyone could sing. But the Church had set itself resolutely against them. The Council of Constance, for example, had expressly stated that "as it is forbidden to laymen to preach and to expound Scripture, so is it forbidden to them even more to sing in public congregations, for as it is with the former, so is it with the latter."[57] To eradicate such popular religious music entirely proved impossible, however, and the more the common people objected to the poor performance of the music officially sanctioned by the Church, the more they wanted to sing vernacular spiritual songs instead.[58]

Thus Zwingli came to a city whose musical life was thoroughly unlike what he had known at Vienna or Basel. The learned music for the classical odes and the choral dramas to which he had been exposed under Celtis was unknown at Zurich. Its musical life was centered not around a university but around its churches. Far from being predominantly humanistic, it was almost exclusively ecclesiastical. The various church choirs were no longer capable of adequate performance of intricate polyphonic music. Furthermore, under existing ecclesiastical conditions, the possibilities for acceding to the laity's desire to sing the spiritual songs were, to say the least, dim. For any sensitive musician the prospect was uninviting; for one trained not only in the old chant and polyphony of the Church but in the radically new humanistic choral odes, it was especially so. And yet this very situation was

55. Oswald Myconius, "Guter Rath an die Priester der Schweiz, welche die Zürcher verlästern, ihr Lästern einzustellen" (1524), in K. R. Hagenbach, *Johann Oekolampad und Oswald Myconius, die Reformatoren Basels,* Leben und ausgewählte Schriften der Väter und Begründer der reformirten Kirche, 2 (Elberfeld, 1859), 392.

56. Bullinger, *1, 3.*

57. Quoted in Fritz Schmidt-Clausing, *Zwingli als Liturgiker: Eine liturgiegeschichtliche Untersuchung* (Göttingen, 1952), p. 82. The Council of Basel also forbade these spiritual songs; cf. Weisz, *Kirchengesang,* p. 9.

58. Weisz, *Kirchengesang,* p. 11.

soon to furnish a significant context for the extraordinary success of Zwingli's liturgical-musical revolution.

THE PLAGUE SONG: 1520

Neither the deterioration of what musical life the city had to offer him nor the criticism of his own superb musicianship appears to have affected Zwingli. After his arrival in Zurich he maintained an active, if not increased, interest in the private music-making of which he had written to Canon Utinger. Under the rubric 1519, another contemporary chronicler, Bernhard Wyss, records the most extensive and enthusiastic catalogue of Zwingli's musical virtuosity to come from a contemporary pen:

> I have never heard about anyone who, in the musical arts—that is, in singing and all the instruments of music, such as lute, harp, large viol, little viol [*rabögli*],[59] pipes, German flute—as good as any Swiss—the trumpet, dulcimer, cornett, and waldhorn, and whatever else of such like had been invented and which he saw, could take it to hand as quickly as he and in addition was so learned as was shown above.[60]

Whether Zwingli was able to play all these instruments with equal facility, or whether he could actually play all of them, cannot of course be proved. But the evidence from contemporary sources, above all from Wyss, is so overwhelmingly unanimous with regard to the range of his talent that he must certainly have been if not a creative then at least a performing musical genius.[61] Moreover, his creative gifts as a composer of both music and poetry were very shortly to be called forth, and in most significant fashion.

During August of 1519 a terrible plague broke out in Zurich. Zwingli at the time was at Bad Pfäfers, since the waters there were considered bene-

59. On the identification of the *rabögli*, see Georg Finsler, "Das Rabögli, ein von Zwingli gespieltes Musikinstrument," *Zwingliana*, *1* (1901), 191–93, and *Die Vokalmusik*, p. 43.

60. Wyss, *Chronik*, pp. 3–4.

61. Walter Köhler, in an earlier biography of Zwingli (Leipzig, 1923), p. 22, made the extreme claim that "Zwingli was a musical genius." A. E. Cherbuliez, in "Zwingli, Zwick und der Kirchengesang," *Zwingliana*, 4 (1926), 355, n. 1, dryly suggested that this judgment was "perhaps euphemistically phrased." Köhler's final estimate, tempered by that of Cherbuliez (p. 355), was as follows: "Zwingli's abundant musical talent was a natural gift. One would not call him a musical genius, but he possessed an astonishing skill in playing almost a dozen musical instruments. Of the three great Reformers, he was musically the most gifted; technical knowledge and power brought to fruition his native ability, and he played the lute with especial fluency"; *Huldrych Zwingli* (Leipzig, 1943), p. 13; cf. the contradictory judgments in *Die Vokalmusik*, pp. 43, 47.

ficial for gallstones. Notwithstanding his own poor health, and despite the danger to his person, he repaired at once to the stricken city. Throughout the remainder of that month he was tireless in the performance of his pastoral duties, daily exposing himself to the disease. Finally in September he fell a victim to it. For a time he was so desperately ill that his recovery was considered hopeless; indeed, by November, rumors of his untimely death were being circulated in both Constance and Basel. He was spared, however, and though he did not recover fully until the close of the summer of 1520, in January of that year he was able again to preach at the Great Minster.

That he had come so close to death and yet had been saved by God was the most devastating psychological and religious experience that Zwingli had thus far undergone. He regarded both the illness and his recovery from it wholly in terms of the new religious feelings which had been deepening within him since his days at Einsiedeln. But this was not so much a conversion experience as the climax of the long personal development in process since 1516, when he had begun to immerse himself in the religious thought of Erasmus. From his illness he emerged triumphant, absolutely dedicated to the task of proclaiming and establishing the cause of the sovereign God, who, through Christ, had delivered him out of death to be His instrument. Perhaps no other experience in his life was to affect him quite so profoundly or quite so completely. Under such circumstances it was natural that he should feel an overwhelming desire to give some form, some external expression to the impact of this tremendous inner experience, and thus to write the following long and intensely personal poem:

A Christian Song, Written by Huldrych Zwingli
as he was Attacked by the Plague

[1]   *At the Beginning of the Illness.*
Help, Lord God, help
    In this distress!
I think that Death
    Is at the door.
Come, Christ, before!
    For Thou hast conquered Death.

To Thee I call:
    Be it Thy will,
Pluck out the dart

That wounds my heart.
Allow me not
    One hour of peace, to pause for breath.

And if Thou yet
    Wouldst have me dead,
Amidst my earthly days,
    Yet may I still Thee praise.
Thy will be done!
    Nought can me stun.
Thy tool to make
    I am, or break!

For takest Thou
    My spirit now,
From earth away,
    Thou dost so, lest it go astray
And others' state
    And pious lives contaminate.

[2]   *In the Midst of the Illness*
Comfort, Lord God, comfort!
    The illness grows;
I am in throes
    Of agony and fear.
Therefore draw near
    To me, in grace and mercy.

Thou dost redeem
    Him who can trust,
As all men must,
    And his hopes place
In Thine own grace,
    And for Thee all else set aside.

Relief has come;
    My tongue is dumb,
I cannot speak one word.
    My thoughts are dark and blurred.

Therefore 'tis right
    That Thou the fight
Shouldst carry on
    For me, Thy son.

I am too weak,
    Dangers to seek;
Nor can I fight
    The devil's taunts and evil might;
Yet will my soul
    Be Thine for aye, complete and whole.

[3]   *In Convalescence*
Healed, Lord God, healed!
    I do believe
The plague does leave
    My body now.
And lettest Thou
    The sinner's scourge depart from me,

Then shall my mouth
    Through all my days
Show forth thy praise
    and wisdom more
Than e'er before,
    Whatever dangers may beset me.

And though I must
    Become as dust
And suffer death, I know,
    Perhaps with greater woe,
Than did befall
    And me appall,
As I did lie
    To death so nigh,

Yet will I still
    My part fulfill

In this our world
And all things bear, for Heaven's reward,
With help from Thee,
Who art alone to life the key.[62]

Words by themselves were not enough, however. Zwingli had written poetry before, but the occasions for it had not been remotely comparable to the experience of the plague.[63] Something more expressive than words was needed, something more deeply characteristic of Zwingli's personality, and to that need his lifelong love for music and his many years of training in the art responded. He composed a polyphonic setting in four voices for the poem.[64] Music, and music alone, could answer his desire to shape and record the immensity of the experience that he had undergone. Thus the Plague Song constitutes a natural, if not ineluctable, musical epitome of the profoundly aesthetic aspects of Zwingli's personality, just as does the fact that he chose to present the experience itself in a poetic form. "Scarcely anywhere else has Zwingli, who was so reserved in such matters, drawn back the veil so completely from the arcanum of his prayer-life as he does here now under the fresh impression of his violent plague experience . . . the nerve of his innermost attitude is here laid bare." [65]

Yet three years later Zwingli insisted that music be prohibited completely from public worship. That so sensitive a musician and composer should make such a demand at all, not to speak of his intransigence on the subject, poses an apparent paradox which has long perplexed both his biographers and historians of music. Far from being a paradox, however, such an opposition to the use of music in the liturgy was for Zwingli as natural and indeed as inevitable in 1523 as his recourse to music had been in 1520.

62. Z, *1*, 67–69. The translation is that authorized by Oskar Farner in his *Huldrych Zwingli, der schweizerische Reformator*, trans. D. G. Sear as *Zwingli the Reformer* (New York, 1952), pp. 35–37; cf. Farner, *2*, 367–72, for the texts of the "plague songs" of Heinrich Bullinger and Théodore de Bèze, both of which bear a marked resemblance to that of Zwingli, although dependence of the former two on the latter's text cannot at present be definitively established. See also the important discussion of the plague song by Arthur Rich, *Die Anfänge der Theologie Huldrych Zwinglis* (Zurich, 1949), pp. 104–19.

63. Z, *1*, 11–22; 53–60.

64. Bullinger, *2*, 182.

65. Farner, *2*, 372. For earlier scholarly comment on the plague song see Farner, *2*, 374–75, and Rich, *Die Anfänge*, pp. 105–06. For Zwingli's setting of Psalm 69, perhaps composed at this time, see Jenny, *Zwinglis mehrstimmige Kompositionen*, pp. 170–72. Cf. Hannes Reimann, "Huldrych Zwingli-der Musiker," *Archiv für Musikwissenschaft, 17* (1960), 132–35, for the music of the plague song and the setting of Psalm 69, the composition of which, however, Reimann places probably in 1525.

2. THE TRUE STILLNESS

Sometimes I go to the point of wishing that all the melodies of the pleasant songs to which David's Psalter is adapted should be banished both from my ears and those of the Church as well.

St. Augustine

With silence one sings beautifully.

Angelus Silesius

On January 19, 1523, Zwingli published for the first time a full-scale program for the reform of the Church. It consisted of sixty-seven *Conclusions* [1] intended for public discussion at the First Zurich Disputation. The course of that debate was such, however, that the greater part of their contents was disregarded for more immediately controversial matters. Zwingli therefore began almost immediately afterward to prepare an extensive written commentary on the *Conclusions* in vernacular Swiss-German, and somewhat over six months later, on July 14, the monumental *Interpretation and Substantiation of the Conclusions* was published by Froschauer in Zurich.[2] In it Zwingli attacked in varying detail all manner of current ecclesiastical practices, comparing and contrasting them relentlessly with the substance of the Gospel, understood now primarily as the "Law of Christ." Among such practices was that of liturgical music, to which he addressed himself in Conclusions 44, 45, and 46 under the rubric "Prayer." The commentary on

1. *Z, 1,* 458, 1–465, 21.
2. *Z, 2,* 14, 1–457, 22. The English rendering of the title is that of Sear in *Zwingli the Reformer,* p. 51.

27

these three *Conclusions* is of paramount importance; it is Zwingli's lengthiest statement on the problem of music in worship. His conclusion as well as the complex of arguments employed are the most radical to come from a major reformed theologian in the sixteenth century.

The question of the relation of music to worship had already been raised by Andreas Bodenstein von Karlstadt, who, during the late summer of 1521, somewhat less than two years before Zwingli completed his commentary, had drawn up a *Disputation on Gregorian Chant* in fifty-three theses, constituting the earliest critique of the use of music in worship from within the ranks of sixteenth-century Protestantism. Karlstadt believed that the newly discovered spiritual content of the Gospel posed an acute problem with respect to its outward expression in liturgical forms. He anticipated the radicalism of Zwingli: frequently there are notable similarities between the Wittenberg theses and the Zurich *Conclusions,* although the difference between the documents in thought and expression is ultimately substantial. Consequently, Karlstadt's *Disputation* must be examined first, not only because it is intrinsically important but also because comparison and contrast with Zwingli's *Conclusions* provide a necessary and invaluable means for evaluating the two points of view, as well as the revolutionary significance of the latter.

THE DISPUTATION ON GREGORIAN CHANT

Karlstadt's opening theses maintain that with respect to prayer, "the chant which we call Gregorian puts a distance between the mind and God," [3] because if performance of the chant is to be of a high order, the singer must concentrate so intently on the music that by necessity he must first of all be a musician and only secondarily a human being at prayer. Further, he argues that the psychological necessity for concentration on the music to be played rather than the prayer to be said obtains with equal force for instrumentalists as well, so that together with the chant, organs and all other instruments should be banished from the service of worship. He proposes that in their stead the psalms should be sung by the congregation in the vernacular, since he can imagine almost no greater hindrance to true prayer than the barrier of a language which the people do not understand.[4]

3. For the Latin text of the theses see Hermann Barge, *Andreas Bodenstein von Karlstadt* (Leipzig, 1905), *1, Exkurs V,* 491–93.
4. Theses 9, 16, 18, 32, 35, 36.

These criticisms and proposals are peripheral, however, to Karlstadt's central argument against Gregorian chant. In Theses 11, 12, and 13 he contrasts sharply the behavior of the deacons in the Church of the sixteenth century with that of the deacons in an earlier period of the Church's history which he designates simply as "formerly":

> In this age deacons are judged by the melodiousness of their voices; formerly they were judged by the honesty of their lives. In this age deacons roar throughout the churches; formerly they gave alms liberally to the poor. In this age it is the task of the deacons to relieve the sluggards for leisure, whereas formerly they relieved the apostles, so that they might be free more abundantly to preach the Word of God.

By exalting the institutional practices of an earlier age, apparently that of the apostles, over against those of the present, he discloses both an emotional attitude and a pattern of thought which have been designated as "primitivism." [5] As widespread and well-defined as this notion was in the sixteenth century, humanists and reformers alike were fond of drawing just such invidious comparisons. Either the Golden Age of classical antiquity or the Apostolic Age of the Christian Church was idealized at the expense of the contemporary world. The former was predominantly a cultural concept, the latter almost wholly religious. They were not always mutually exclusive, however; they are blended, for example, in the Erasmian ideal of a *Christianismus renascens*. Karlstadt's historical comparison between two types of churches from the point of view of the general framework of religious primitivism is thus not altogether surprising. On the other hand, only in Theses 37 and 38 does the precise bearing of this argument from history on the total structure of the *Disputation* become clear, for in them he argues that "the Church of which Gregory was head instituted these mumblings. But not the Church of which Christ is head."

To emphasize the disparity between the Pope and Christ was scarcely an innovation; idea and illustration both reached back by way of Hus at least to the fourteenth century and John Wyclif. But rather than say simply "the Pope," thereby making the contrast a general and timeless one, Karlstadt is at pains to stipulate a particular historical person, and by doing so he lays bare the nerve center of the entire *Disputation*. Beneath the various and

---

5. See Franklin Hamlin Littell, *The Anabaptist View of the Church: A Study in the Origins of Sectarian Protestantism* (Boston, 1958), pp. 46–55.

seemingly chaotic theses against music in worship lies in fact a single premise, one superintending point of view—namely, the fall of the Church.[6]

This was one of the great thematic ideas of the later Middle Ages. For
sects such as the Waldensians and the Cathari, for men such as Marsilio of
Padua and Joachim of Fiore, for orders such as the Franciscan Spirituals,
and for pre-Reformation churches such as the Bohemian Brethren, a radical
distinction between the true Church of Christ and His Apostles, on the one
hand, and a Church fallen away from them, on the other hand, had provided not only the fundamental basis for their criticism of the existing
church but also the major foundation for their conception of history itself.
In this historical scheme there was a specific period in which the Church had
initially fallen and to which the majority of these men and groups adverted:
When Constantine the Great legitimized Christianity, was baptized, and
later made his Donation to the Pope, the Church entered upon its millennial
course of corruption and decay. As it grew into an ever more worldly and
powerful institution, it became correspondingly less and less like the true
Church of Christ. This monumental threnody, not to speak of countless variations on it, was enthusiastically adopted by both humanists and reformers
in the sixteenth century, so that from one point of view its appearance in
Karlstadt's *Disputation,* like that of the note of primitivism, is conventional.

Yet the fall was not assigned invariably to the Constantinian period.
There is some evidence, for instance, that the Waldensians had placed it
earlier, at some time during the Apostolic Age. Consequently, Karlstadt's
placing the initial fall squarely within the Gregorian pontificate is quite unconventional.[7] Even more of an innovation is the fact that—possibly for the
first time—ecclesiastical music is accounted one of the distinctive marks of
the fall of the Church, a point which explains the true significance of Karlstadt's earlier historical contrast. That period which Karlstadt had described
vaguely as "formerly" is not, in fact, as it seemed to be, the Apostolic Age; it

6. Ibid., pp. 55–78; cf. esp. Erich Seeberg, *Gottfried Arnold, die Wissenschaft und die
Mystik seiner Zeit: Studien zur Historiographie und zur Mystik* (Meerane i. Sa., 1923),
pp. 257–75, for the idea of the fall in the later Middle Ages; for its adoption by Erasmus
and the humanists, pp. 280–90.

7. Although Sebastian Frank assigned the fall of the Church to the first generation immediately after Christ's apostles, he pointed to the Gregorian Pontificate as the beginning of
the specifically "Roman Tyranny." Significantly enough, he considered the marked increase
at that time in the ceremonial life of the Church as one of the explicit indications of this
tyranny: see his *Chronica / zeÿtbuch und geschÿchttbibel von anbegyn biss inn diss gegen-
wertig m.d. xxxj. jar. . .* (Strassburg, 1531), 506a.

is rather that of the pre-Gregorian Church. When he turns for the last time to a violent diatribe against the use of music in worship, he is arguing likewise from the premise of the fall. The post-Gregorian era has witnessed an increasing variety of ecclesiastical chants, all of which in their multiplicity and their senselessness testify to the Church's fallen state, and all of which must be categorically abandoned.

Karlstadt's constructive proposals for music in worship are ambigious, however, and ambiguous precisely because he is arguing from the idea of the fall. He regards the musical forms of the sixteenth-century Church, with which he had daily contact, simply as post-Gregorian. But what were the musical forms of the pre-Gregorian Church, of the "true Church" before the fall? Here he is manifestly unclear and is forced, as a result, from generality into a mere indeterminateness which is made obvious in the concluding thesis, his only positive statement on the role which music should play in worship: "If, therefore, you wish chant to remain in the Church, you should desire none except that which is one, so that there may be one God, one baptism, one faith, and one chant." True church music, then, can only be unaccompanied unison singing of the psalms in the vernacular by the whole congregation. Yet even here Karlstadt's conclusion is not precise, because he says, *"if* you wish chant to remain in the Church." That one conjunction makes it impossible to determine whether or not he was in favor even of such congregational singing as he proposes; possibly he wanted a service from which all music was excluded. Clearly, the *Disputation* ends on an equivocal note. On the other hand, all Karlstadt's theories were conspicuously at variance with his practice, for despite the vigorous theses against Gregorian chant, the Mass he prepared for Wittenberg in 1522 retained virtually all the traditional musical forms and practices of the post-Gregorian Church, including Latin and the use of a choir.[8] Furthermore, there is no evidence that church music was ever discontinued at Wittenberg.[9]

Hermann Barge, the only scholar thus far to have given the *Disputation* careful attention, has identified correctly the intention behind the writing of the theses when he says that Karlstadt "recognized the incompatibility of the traditional ecclesiastical-Catholic singing practices with the new evangelical

8. Leonhard Fendt, *Der lutherische Gottesdienst des 16. Jahrhunderts, sein Werden und sein Wachsen* (Munich, 1923), pp. 93–101; for the text of the mass, pp. 99–101.

9. James Mackinnon, *Luther and the Reformation* (New York, 1929), *3,* 71; for a survey of music in the University of Wittenberg see Carpenter, *Music in the Medieval and Renaissance Universities,* pp. 260–71.

consciousness." [10] Karlstadt was indeed concerned with the problem of the formal expression of the "restored" Gospel, and believed that eventually either the old liturgical forms would have to be reshaped to the newly understood content of Scripture or that entirely new forms would have to be evolved. From the point of view of form and content both, however, not to speak of practical application, his theses fail to grapple directly with the problem, because his fundamental approach is historical. His criticism of the musical abuses of the post-Gregorian Church is essentially conventional. His attack on organs and other musical instruments, because of their secular, immoral, or theatrical connotations, is by no means unique. Erasmus, for example, in his annotations to 1 Corinthians 14, had complained bitterly that

> We have introduced into churches a type of laborious and theatrical music, a confused chattering of diverse voices, such as I do not think was ever heard in the theatres of the Greeks or the Romans. They perform everything with slide-trumpets, trombones, cornetts, and little flutes, and with these the voices of men contend. Amorous and foul songs are heard, songs to which prostitutes and actors caper. People assemble in the sacred edifice as in a theatre, for the sake of degrading their ears.[11]

Cornelius Agrippa von Nettesheim was equally vituperative. He expressed himself as follows in his *Declamatio:*

> Nowadays, however, there is in the churches so much license and liberty regarding music that even during the singing of the mass vile songs are played on the organ, and so they do no honour to the sacred office, but with their frivolous minstrels, bought for money, they give occasion not for devotion and worship but for whoring, not with human voices but with a bestial howling.[12]

These are not isolated protests; one has only to recall the condemnation of the ecclesiastical music in Zurich by Myconius, Bullinger, and Zwingli. In fact, the Church councils and synods of the late fifteenth and early sixteenth

---

10. Barge, *Karlstadt, 1,* 371; the evaluation of the *Disputation* by Hans Joachim Moser, *Die evangelische Kirchenmusik in Deutschland* (Berlin-Darmstadt, 1953-54), p. 28 is both superficial and misleading.

11. *Opera omnia,* ed. J. LeClerc (Leyden, 1703–06), *6,* 731 F.

12. Cited by Wilhelm Fränger, *The Millennium of Hieronymus Bosch: Outlines of a New Interpretation,* trans. Eithne Wilkins and Ernst Kaiser (Chicago, 1951), p. 91.

centuries throughout Western Europe exhibit ample criticism of musical abuses within the Church [13] comparable in tone as well as content to that of Karlstadt's *Disputation*. Both were arguing from an *institution* rather than from the *Gospel*. In consequence, although the *Disputation* began auspiciously by discussing the content of man's relationship to God in and through prayer, a subject in which the relationship of liturgical forms to the new evangelical consciousness might well have been extensively developed, the liturgical problem was soon submerged in historical considerations. The premise of a fall in the Church guiding the *Disputation* thus deflected Karlstadt's thought so that he was actually unable to explore effectively the problems he obviously intended to treat: Is there a valid role for musical forms in worship now that both worship generally and prayer specifically have been newly understood in the light of the Gospel?

Zwingli addresses himself to that same problem in the *Interpretation and Substantiation of the Conclusions,* but unlike Karlstadt he does not deviate from the subject nor shrink from its implications. As a result, his analysis leads finally to a profoundly wrought statement of the relationship between music and worship and prayer which is consistently informed by the new evangelical consciousness. Zwingli's achievement owes no small part of its success to the fact that, unlike Karlstadt, he had been steadily preoccupied with the problem of liturgical forms since 1516.

THE PRECONDITION OF HUMANISM

Zwingli was a humanist. He had been trained in Vienna and Basel at schools and universities that were vigorous and self-conscious centers of humanism. He was the pupil of Bünzli, Wölflin, and Celtis, all of them notable humanist scholars. Throughout the decade 1506–16, during which he was parish priest at Glarus, he continued not only to pursue his classical and musical studies but to engage constantly in learned correspondence with leading members of the Basel circle, intellectuals and erudite men of affairs such as Glareanus, Vadianus, Froben, and Beatus Rhenanus. Finally, while serving at the convent of Einsiedeln under Gerold von Dieboldseck, a humanist himself, Zwingli was to all intents and purposes a thoroughgoing disciple of Erasmus. This long course of humanistic training, culminating in his two years of virtually complete immersion in Erasmian thought, had the

13. For numerous examples of such criticism see K. G. Fellerer, "Church Music and the Council of Trent," *The Musical Quarterly,* 39 (1953), 576–94 passim.

most far-reaching consequence not only for Zwingli's theology as a whole but also for his attitude toward music and the visual arts.

Erasmus yearned for a revival of Christianity. Through the *sacrae litterae* of the New Testament and the early Fathers, the original *Christianitas* was to be restored to the world. But parallel with this ideal was his longing, equally intense, for a revival of the *humanitas* of classical antiquity through the restoration of the world of *bonae litterae*.[14] The specifically Christian content of Erasmian humanism was thus at once determined and limited by the fundamentally secular ideal of *humanitas,* with which the ideal *Christianitas* was inextricably linked. Consequently, Zwingli was first exposed to a vast program for a *Christianismus renascens* which was as much sociocultural as religious.[15] The basic aspects of this world of thought, as they were initially appropriated by Zwingli, including its opposition to the established ecclesiastical tradition, were nowhere more compactly set forth than in a letter written to him in 1518 by Beatus Rhenanus:

Nothing grieves me more than that I see a Christian people everywhere weighed down by ceremonies that do not pertain to the matter at hand, nay more, weighed down by mere trifles. And I find no other cause than that the priests, deceived by those mule-driving sophistical theologians, teach heathen or Jewish doctrines. I am speaking now of the rank and file of the priesthood. For it does not escape me that you and those like you place before the people the pure philosophy of Christ from its very sources, not corrupted by the interpretation of Scotist or Gabrielist, but expounded by Augustine, Ambrose, Cyprian, and Jerome, faithfully and correctly. But standing in that place where whatever is said the people think is most true, those people bleat out nonsense about the power of the Pope, remission of sins, purgatory, fabricated miracles by the saints, restitutions, contracts, vows, pains of hell, Anti-Christ. [7, 115, 5–17].

14. On the richness and complexity of Erasmus' concept of *humanitas* see the brilliant essay by Rudolph Pfeiffer, *Humanitas Erasmiana,* Studien der Bibliothek Warburg, 22 (Leipzig-Berlin, 1931), 1–24.

15. For the most penetrating and detailed discussion of Zwingli's encounter with the form and substance of the Erasmian *Christianismus renascens* see Arthur Rich, *Die Anfänge der Theologie Huldrych Zwinglis* (Zurich, 1949), pp. 9–72, esp. 9–24, and the earlier literature cited throughout; see further Farner, 2, 152–72, as well as Courvoisier, *Zwingli, Soldat de Dieu,* pp. 50–58, and J.-V.-M. Pollet, "Zwinglianisme," *Dictionnaire de Théologie Catholique, 15²* (Paris, 1950), cols. 3749–54.

Scripture and the Fathers of the Church are unconditionally espoused against medieval philosophy and theology. But Rhenanus does not condemn simply the substance of the ecclesiastical tradition; the entire structure of its external forms, all those "ceremonies that do not pertain to the matter at hand," are likewise condemned when contrasted with "the pure philosophy of Christ." The return to the *sacrae litterae* of early Christianity thus forced the Erasmian humanists from purely philological considerations to historical ones. Considerations of substance became inseparable from those of form, so that the program for a *Christianismus renascens* ultimately meant nothing less than an attempt to get out of the whole ecclesiastical environment created by medieval Christianity and to return to the religiocultural environment of the early Church and antiquity as they conceived it.

When Erasmus stated that "the history of Christianity is the history of its degeneration," [16] he shared with Karlstadt the idea of a corrupted Church. But agreement between the two stops there. Karlstadt was arguing from within the ecclesiastical environment as well as from within the institution that had molded it. Erasmus, on the other hand, was not deeply involved in either the external or the internal life of the medieval Church. Furthermore, he was arguing not from the ecclesiastical tradition but from *sacrae litterae,* Scripture and the Fathers, interpreted philologically and historically, not philosophically and theologically. His was a point of view self-consciously apart from and outside the institutional forms and the traditional content he was criticizing. And it is this aspect of Erasmian humanism, this want of involvement, this consciously maintained distance from the medieval ecclesiastical environment which so powerfully influenced Zwingli. He was a parish priest; he was also an Erasmian. He came finally to an evangelical understanding of Christ; he came to it, however, not from within the established theological tradition, as had Luther, but from the humanist "philosophy of Christ." The religious conscience that precipitated Luther's personal struggle for the assurance of his soul's salvation, as well as the weapons by which the struggle itself was fought, were formed within the philosophical and theological tradition of the late medieval Church. Thus when Luther fought his way through to a new and transforming understanding of the relationship of his soul to God, despite the many years of personal anguish involved, his profoundest instinct was to conserve as much as possible the tradition in which he had attained his victory. His initial concern was directed solely to spiritual reformation within the given structure of that exist-

16. Cited by Seeberg, *Gottfried Arnold,* p. 258.

ing ecclesiastical tradition. He did not at first contemplate a reformation of the liturgical and institutional forms through which the tradition expressed itself. By contrast, Zwingli's fundamental intellectual and psychological separation from the ecclesiastical environment [17] not only enabled him to criticize it more readily and as a whole, but made it virtually impossible for him to disengage questions of substance from those of form. As a result of his conditioning by the humanist idea of a total program for *Christianismus renascens,* Zwingli could not entertain thoughts of a spiritual reformation without an institutional and liturgical reformation at the same time.

The inseparability of the two in Zwingli's mind derives from yet another aspect of Erasmian humanism, to which he was also profoundly indebted. The "philosophy of Christ" posited a radical distinction between the flesh and the spirit. Outward observance in worship was without value, because it was corporeal; true Christian discipleship meant the spiritual life, an almost exclusively inner experience, whose external expression in public worship was in itself relatively insignificant. The entire corporate liturgical structure of medieval Christianity was thus at the least implicitly threatened, because true worship was internal rather than external, individual rather than communal. Such an antinomy between flesh and spirit was early absorbed by Zwingli—not from Erasmus alone, to be sure, but certainly his influence in this respect was extensive and lasting.

For that fact Zwingli's edition of Erasmus' *Lucubrationes* provides ample testimony.[18] Purchased by him while still at Glarus, and obviously read closely and intensely, it is full of underlinings, as well as marginal and interlinear glosses. Erasmus, for example, had asked: "But is not Christianity the spiritual life?" Zwingli underscored the question in the text, and replied by writing beside it in the margin: "Christianity is the spiritual life." [19] Such comments and underscorings point to his enthusiastic response to the Erasmian point of view. One such gloss, however, must be singled out especially, for it indicates how wholeheartedly Zwingli had adopted the Erasmian understanding of the tension between form and substance in wor-

17. S, 5, 548; cf. Farner, 2, 219–20; Courvoisier, *Zwingli,* p. 49, and Pollet, *Zwinglianisme,* col. 3748. See also Walter Köhler, "Luther und Zwingli," *Zeitschrift für Theologie und Kirche,* neue folge 6 (Tübingen, 1925), 456.

18. Farner, 2, 158; cf. the authoritative study by Walter Köhler, *Huldrych Zwinglis Bibliothek,* Neujahrsblatt zum Besten des Waisenhauses in Zurich, *84* (Zurich, 1921), passim.

19. Quoted in Abel E. Burckhardt, *Das Geistproblem bei Huldrych Zwingli* (Leipzig, 1932), p. 131.

ship. In the margin opposite a passage in which Erasmus had derided the foolishness of a merely external worship, Zwingli jotted the following:

> The common people think that God is placated by victims of cattle and by corporeal things. But even since God himself is spirit: mind: not body, it is obvious that like rejoices in like: doubtless he [i.e. God] is above all to be worshiped by purity of mind. And today the mass of Christians worship God through certain corporeal ceremonies: whereas the piety of the mind is the most pleasing worship. For the father seeks such worshipers as will worship him in spirit, since he is spirit.[20]

This radical Erasmian antinomy between flesh and spirit, form and content, was to become one of the assumptions controlling Zwingli's systematic commentary on music in worship, as well as his later critique of images. That it is not immediately apparent in the later context is due to the fact that it was an assumption with which Zwingli had lived for several years before 1523.

How aware he was before 1515 of the problem of form in a strict liturgical sense is impossible to say. But in that year, as a field chaplain to the Swiss mercenary army in Italy, he uncovered evidence for variations in the celebration of the Mass which impressed him considerably.[21] A year later his interest in the history of the development of the liturgy was further aroused when he found in the little village of Mollis an old liturgical manual in which instructions were given to administer the sacrament in both kinds to children immediately after baptism.[22] The discovery was of the greatest significance for his intellectual development. Already he had begun to steep himself in Erasmian spiritualism, with its attendant denigration of the flesh and corporeal forms of worship. Now Zwingli found that the ceremonial legalism of the Church was open to question from a purely historical point of view. Thereafter, the problem of giving external form to the substance of the "philosophy of Christ" was to assume an increasingly prominent role in

---

20. Ibid.: "Vulgus existimat deum placari victimis pecudum rebusque corporeis. Verum etiam cumque deus ipse sit animus: mens: non corpus, consentaneum est simile gaudere simili: nimirum potissimum colendus est puritate mentis. Et hodie vulgus Christianorum corporeis quibusdam caerimoniis colit deum: cum gratissimus cultus sit animi pietas. Tales enim adoratores quaerit pater, qui in spiritu adorent, cum ipse sit spiritus." Cf. the illuminating commentary on Mark 6:46 (S, 6¹, 501): "Observa hic duplicem esse orationem, hoc est, orationem bifariam posse considerari: est enim in oratione caro et spiritus."
21. Schmidt-Clausing, *Zwingli als Liturgiker*, p. 35.
22. Z, 2, 133, 11-20; cf. the comment of Schmidt-Clausing, p. 37.

his thinking, until at length he constructed his own liturgy for the Great Minster in Zurich and put it into practice after 1523.

Once arrived in Zurich, Zwingli began to preach openly against the ceremonial piety of the Church.[23] His teaching bore practical fruit when in March 1522 Christopher Froschauer and some members of his staff ate meat during Lent. Zwingli defended their action in a notable sermon, during the course of which he maintained that "if Christ by His death freed us from all sins and burdens, then we also are in baptism, that is, in belief—released from all Jewish or human ceremonies" (*1*, 130, 28; 131, 1–3; cf 129, 7–13). The statement sets forth the underlying theme not only of the sermon itself but of Zwingli's whole formal liturgical program. By 1522 he had won his way through to an evangelical understanding of Christianity. The intellectualized abstractions of the "philosophy of Christ" had been replaced by concrete reality of action and an utter obedience to God's will which was thoroughly alien to Erasmus. During the process of transformation in the nature of his belief, Zwingli had come to the conviction that Scripture alone was to be the norm, *normam evangelicae* (*1*, 284, 32–33), for the outward expression of the tremendous reality of the Christian experience. "The question," he wrote, "was not whether Lent should be abolished, but whether at that time it was permissible according to the law of Christ to eat meat" (*1*, 151, 22–24; cf. 107, 20; 108, 1; 132, 15). Thus for Zwingli the tension between form and content in religion, inherited from the Erasmian antinomy between flesh and spirit, had become merged with a tension between the ceremonial laws of the Church and "the law of Christ," in which the latter only was to be binding.

Accordingly, when Zwingli later in April defended the position he had adopted in the letter to Erasmus Fabricius, he wrote:

> I will confess frankly that I wish to see a considerable portion of the ceremonies and prescriptions abolished. . . . I demonstrated that simple people could be led to recognition of the truth by means other than ceremonies, namely, so far as I was able to learn from Scripture, by those with which Christ and the apostles had led them without ceremonies.
> [*1*, 148, 35–36; 149, 39; 150, 1–2; cf. 151, 33–34; 153, 4–10]

His fundamental position with regard to worship was thus made patently clear. The whole structure of the ceremonial life of the existing Church is

23. On Zwingli's preaching see Farner, *3*, 29–187.

challenged simply by setting it against the fact that Christ demanded none at all. And in the *Archeteles,* which he wrote at the close of 1522, the disparity between form and substance is yet more incisively drawn:

> If ceremonies are to be retained for a time, they are to be abolished sometime. What prevents their abolition now, especially since the world is looking to this, and all the pious and learned are moving toward this . . . what evil, now, is going to befall us if the rubble of ceremonies is cleared away in its entirety, in as much as God declares that He is worshiped in vain by these things?
>
> [*1*, 308, 5–7; 271, 29–30; cf. 276, 8–11; 318, 4–9]

Seen from the point of view of the problem of the relation of form to substance, the *Archeteles* is the necessary link between the marginal gloss on Erasmus and the *Interpretation and Substantiation of the Conclusions* of 1523. Zwingli's denial of validity to outward ceremony as well as his critique of existing ceremonial piety and practice denote the continuing relationship with Erasmian humanism. On the other hand, Zwingli's evangelical understanding of Christ and his realization of the absolute sovereignty of Scripture, his replacement of the philosophy of Christ by the law of Christ, mark a complete break with the humanistic culture ideal of a *Christianismus renascens.* But the gradual transformation in his understanding of the substance of Christianity is paralleled consistently, first by a continuing awareness of the problem of form, and then by a transformation in his understanding of the forms by which that Christianity expresses itself. The observation has been made that "Zwingli proceeds from the periphery, Luther moves out from the center." [24] It would be more accurate to say that Zwingli moves from center and periphery simultaneously, for his fundamental insistence on an inextricable relationship between the forms and content of religion remains constant. Only against this background can the import of Zwingli's *Conclusions* on music in worship be fully understood.

THE NATURE OF TRUE PRAYER

The forty-fourth *Conclusion,* which Zwingli originally proposed for debate, read as follows: "True worshipers call upon God in spirit and in truth without clamor before men" (*1*, 463, 13–14). To that *Conclusion* he subsequently appended the *Substantiation* below:

24. Schmidt-Clausing, p. 41.

No prayer is more pleasing to God than that which recognizes Him truly and calls on God truly with heart free from doubt, not with hypocrisy, but with right, true acknowledgment and recognition. Thus [Ex. 14:15] Moses calls earnestly on God within his heart and does not move his lips. So also Hannah did not cry aloud [1 Sam. 1:13]. So, too, Christ [Matt. 6:7] prohibited much babbling and has taught that we should pray in spirit and in truth [John 4:24] where He frees us also from particular localities; that not in one locality better than another may God be well and correctly called upon, but in all localities where God is called upon in spirit and in truth, there does He say: Here am I.[25]   [2, 348, 5–16]

This commentary, although brief, contains matter of far-reaching significance not only for Zwingli's analysis of the relation between music and prayer but also for his fundamental approach to all forms of the liturgy.

Two conceptions of worship are presented here in stark contrast: one is a matter exclusively of external forms involving "clamor before men"; the other is a matter exclusively of internal content involving "spirit and truth." The latter is an expression of the life of truth—obedience, therefore, to the law of Christ; the former, an expression of the life of hypocrisy—acquiescence, therefore, to the ceremonial piety of contemporary Catholicism. Between two such completely divergent conceptions there can be no middle ground. Zwingli will admit no compromise, and his attitude toward church music can be fully comprehended only within the context of these antipodal modes of worship, implicitly adumbrated in his glosses on Erasmus: one true and one false, one external and corporeal, the other internal and spiritual.

Like Karlstadt, Zwingli regards the definition of prayer as the central problem of worship; in fact, worship and prayer are for him synonymous terms. Like Karlstadt, too, he seems at first sight to be working toward a definition of true prayer as unconditionally silent. In addition to the citation from Exodus, he adduces as evidence the same prayer of Hannah to which Karlstadt had also referred.[26] The question whether it should be silent is put aside for the moment; first he will make clear that prayer is definitely not

25. Unless indicated to the contrary, all references in the text will be to Vol. 2 of Zwingli's works. Whether Zwingli knew Karlstadt's *Disputation* is at present impossible to ascertain.

26. Theses 3–4: "For within the heart the soul is poured forth in the sight of God. Thus prayed Hanna, the wife of Elkanah"; cf. Z, *3*, 853, 17–21.

"babbling." The words of Christ must be observed literally, so that "empty phrases" are not to be tolerated, nor are there to be "many words." When these exist, worship at once lapses into an hypocrisy, a ceremonial display before men; and it must be borne in mind that for Zwingli "hypocrisy" and "display before men," like "worship" and "prayer", are synonymous. Thus liturgical activity of any kind which entails empty phrases, many words and babbling, clamor of any sort, is a false worship which cannot long be tolerated.

Although Zwingli has not yet specifically mentioned music, the implications already to be drawn from such a position are patently clear. The choral and instrumental music of the contemporary Catholic Church was full of the repetition of many words. Furthermore, it had become increasingly a matter of display before men, frequently a dazzling display of the technical abilities not only of the performers but of the composer. Within the framework of Zwingli's two opposing types of worship, such performances are inevitably false and hypocritical, because they stand in open defiance of the instructions for worship which Christ Himself had given to men. But all this is as yet inference; Zwingli reserves explicit discussion of music for the commentary on the forty-fifth *Conclusion:* "Hypocrites do their work so that they may be seen by men as well as taking their reward in this life" (*1*, 463, 15–16).

FREEDOM FROM LITURGY

Zwingli's *Substantiation* of the forty-fifth *Conclusion* opens by continuing the discussion of that hypocrisy which pretends to be worship. Indeed, his primary aim is to make so clear the total disparity between hypocrisy and worship that the two will be forever dissociated. His argument is drawn entirely from Scripture, in fact from the words of Christ Himself: "And these are the true words of Christ which He spoke concerning the scribes and the Pharisees [Matt. 23:5]: They do all their work that they may be seen by men" (348, 22–25). To which Zwingli pointedly adds: "Christ paints them in these colors, not I" (348, 25–26). Grounding his argument on this passage and the verses on hypocrisy in Christ's Sermon on the Mount, he proceeds ruthlessly to denounce alms-giving and fasting as hypocritical, and stresses, above all, as the worst of all displays before men, the worship of those who "perform their prayers where they know that most people congregate" (348, 28–29). Thus Zwingli presents an unmistakably clear idea of what worship and prayer should not be. Yet if the implications of that negative definition are pursued logically, true worship and prayer could not be public at all. Zwingli is not unaware of this conclusion; in fact, recognition as well as complete acceptance of its inevitability is actually the climax of his argument thus far: "But when we wish to pray we should withdraw into our chamber and close the door after us and there, in secret, call upon our heavenly Father" (348, 29: 349, 1-2).

With that sentence Zwingli reveals the extremity of his reach. What he seeks is nothing less than an irreducible purity of worship—in other words, an absolutely private prayer: the individual withdrawn from the world and from his fellow men, absolutely alone in communion with his heavenly Father.[27] The Father's Son has commanded such worship. Therefore, ideally, no other form should be considered, for no other form would accord so literally with the law of Christ. Thus Christ's instructions stand at the very core of Zwingli's liturgical thinking, from out of which all else radiates and without which the external forms in which his liturgy was finally cast cannot be comprehended. Within the framework of the two antipodal modes of worship adumbrated in the forty-fourth *Conclusion,* private prayer is now seen to be unconditionally the prototype of true worship as set forth by the law of Christ; all other forms, above all the plethora of ceremonial forms in use by the contemporary Church, are by necessity antitypes of varying inadequacy.

Adherence to the prototype, however, if strictly observed, would abolish all forms of formal congregational worship. There would be no liturgy at all, for Christ's instructions, in fact, make any such public liturgy impossible. True worshipers would, as individuals, whenever and wherever they desired, simply withdraw into solitude and pray by themselves to God in spirit and in truth. The real import of Zwingli's sentences on locality of worship at the close of the *Substantiation* of *Conclusion* 44 now becomes apparent. If true prayer is bound to no particular time, then Christ has also released men "from particular localities; that not in one locality better than another may God be well and correctly called upon, but in all localities where God is called upon in spirit and in truth, there does He say: Here am I" (348,

---

27. Cf. Antoine.-E. Cherbuliez, *Die Schweiz in der deutschen Musikgeschichte* (Frauenfeld-Leipzig, 1932), p. 177, and "Zwingli, Zwick und der Kirchengesang," *Zwingliana,* 4 (1921–28), 363. See also Oskar Söhngen, "Theologische Grundlagen der Kirchenmusik," in *Leiturgia, Handbuch des Evangelischen Gottesdienst,* 4 (Kassel, 1961), 33. The first version of my essay was completed in 1956; my fundamental conclusions have not changed. It is therefore gratifying to find myself almost entirely in agreement with Söhngen's important essay, which came to my attention only recently. It will be cited hereafter as Söhngen, *Leiturgia.*

13–16). Zwingli recognizes that conclusion; he accepts it, and later, in 1523, reaffirms it. Speaking again on the subject of prayer, he maintained that "just as we are bound by no limits or circumstances, so also not by those things which accompany circumstances. . . . we are freed by Christ from every person, and thus from the order which accompanies the person" (623, 24–25; 26–27). In short, unconditional freedom is required so that the individual Christian may pray when, where, and how he wishes. Worship as such is without external form to the point that ultimately it denies formal liturgy, a condition which Zwingli himself formulates most compactly when he declares: "If you are reverent, then let it be alone" (349, 23).

NECESSITY FOR LITURGY

Such an ideal could scarcely be realized, however, if the communal worship of the visible Church is to be observed and retained, and this for Zwingli was a necessity beyond dispute. The content of prayer must be given some formal, ritual expression in public. Yet once worship is made public, full opportunity is immediately provided for countless varieties of hypocrisy and display. Zwingli reveals himself here, as also in his treatment of the problem of the visual arts, as almost hypersensitive to human weakness. He is acutely conscious of how differently men will act in public than in private, no matter how ideal their intentions may be. He understands the delicacy of the equilibrium between the public and the private person, and so frankly confesses that "worship is corrupted and vitiated by the many" (349, 24). He discloses thereby his own consciousness of the central tension which is never for a moment absent from his liturgical thinking: the permanently irreconcilable conflict between Christ's demand for a private prayer impossible of realization in public worship and his own awareness of the dangers ever present in public worship of any sort. These two principles, *freedom from liturgy* and *necessity for liturgy,* in his mind stand always in opposition to each other.

THE REJECTION OF MUSIC

Zwingli at last turns specifically to the problem of music in worship: "Here no objection will avail with respect to the choral singing of the psalms, the which not the hundredth part understands, to say nothing of the singing fools, the nuns, who in all their lives do not understand one verse of the psalms they mumble" (349, 11-14).

Professional choirs are but one example of that public display which voids the potency of true prayer. The singers—monks, or nuns—are, in Zwingli's own words, "those who perform their deeds to be seen by the world" (349, 7). Music performed by such choirs—professional or amateur—is ostentatious and hypocritical. Consequently, it is one of the first, if not the very first, liturgical observance that can be eliminated in order to ease the tension between ideal freedom and practical necessity.

Yet such a rejection of choral music can be argued on Scriptural grounds only by accepting the absolute seriousness with which Zwingli intends to understand Christ's instructions for the realization of the substance of true prayer. The allusion to the poor performance of the nuns introduces a specific contemporary element suggesting that Zwingli's critique of music in worship is, like that of Karlstadt, based on existing abuses within the Zurich churches and convents.[28] Such is not the case, however. There can be little doubt that Zwingli's extraordinarily developed and sensitive musicianship was pained by the deterioration of the ecclesiastical musical standards in the city. The remark itself, as well as the scathing comments below, attest to that fact. But Scripture alone provides him with his argument for a completely silent worship:

> But should it not be good, they say, for one to sing the praise of God before all men. Answer: Show me that it is good and I will believe it to be good. God alone is good and the sole source of all good things [Matt. 19:17; Jer. 2:13]. If the mumbling of psalms is good, then it must come from God. Show me where God has commanded such moaning, mumbling, and murmuring.   [349, 14-19]

Zwingli's ruthlessly logical biblical exegesis demonstrates itself here. Christ had said: "Why do you ask me about what is good? One there is who is good. If you would enter life, keep the commandments." Where, then, asks Zwingli, has God commanded choral singing in worship? Within his exclusively scriptural frame of reference the answer is clear: nowhere. On the contrary, he continues, "God has commanded you to go into your chamber and speak with your heavenly Father in a secret place and there He will see you,

---

28. Theses 30-31: "Those prayers which are made without attention are either noisy or unintelligible, just as are the murmurings of the untaught and the lamentable incantation of the nuns"; cf. Söhngen, *Leiturgia,* p. 20.

hear you and respond to you" (349, 21–23). The principle of freedom from formal liturgy is thus clearly seen in operation against singing, and the implications for church music suggested by the forty-fourth *Conclusion* are finally made explicit. Because true worship must be private and individual, choral singing, merely by virtue of its public nature, may not be allowed.

Notwithstanding, did not Saint Paul say [Col. 3:16]: "Let the word of Christ dwell in you richly in all wisdom; teaching and admonishing one another in psalms and hymns and spiritual songs, singing with grace in your hearts to the Lord." Zwingli replies at once: "Here Paul does not teach us mumbling and murmuring in the churches, but shows us the true song that is pleasing to God, that we sing the praise and glory of God not with our voices, like the Jewish singers, but with our hearts" (350, 2–6). Two statements of importance are made. First of all, Zwingli is careful to point out that Paul says "with our hearts"; no audible-musical interpretation can be laid upon the text as it stands. Therefore, the apostle's injunction must be strictly observed and all choral music rejected from true worship. Yet there remains the immensity of the Old Testament evidence for the use of music in worship. May not one rest a case for church music on that? Zwingli's second point is directed to just such a rejoinder. To be sure, musical activities existed; Zwingli is too careful an exegete to ignore them. But they were nowhere instituted by God, and consequently they were invalid for true worship. If one must draw on Old Testament evidence, then one should attend to the prototypes previously cited of Moses and Hannah, both of whom prayed silently in their hearts, exactly as Christ later instructed all men to do. The introduction of music into worship in the Old Testament was instituted by man rather than by God. Liturgical music is therefore scripturally indefensible on three closely interrelated, yet distinguishable, grounds:

1.) Music in worship is not explicitly commanded by God in either the Old or New Testament.

2.) Christ instructed men to pray to God individually and in private.

3.) Saint Paul urged men, when together, to worship God and pray to Him in their hearts.

Thus far the principle of freedom from liturgy has dominated Zwingli's argument. Continually pressing against it, however, is the counterprinciple of necessity for liturgy, for Zwingli is fully aware that some kind of public worship is imperative for the life of the visible church within the city. The inner content of worship must have some exterior form; accordingly, he now suggests what form that worship should take: "Worship is corrupted and vitiated by the many, unless the many is taught the word of God, or a few speak with one another concerning the proper understanding of the Holy Word, with respect to which Paul speaks [Col. 3:16]" (349, 24–27). If the ideal freedom from ritual forms prescribed by Christ cannot be realized by a congregation, at least let the form of necessary worship adhere as closely as possible to that prescribed by His apostle. Public worship, therefore, should be reduced to a quite literally Pauline form—namely, an exposition of the content and significance of the psalms, indeed the whole body of Scripture, by men trained for the purpose in biblical exegesis. The service of worship should be such that "we may persuade, teach and warn one another with the psalms and hymns which the prophets have also sung to Him in their hearts and in their chambers" (350, 6–9). Zwingli intimates his tremendous inclination toward a private worship by reiterating his contention that such worship was not unknown in the Old Testament. Moses and Hannah, and the prophets as well, worshiped as Christ and Paul commanded. All the more reason, then, to reject the "Jewish singers" and their unauthorized singing aloud to the Lord, and to insist that within the proposed structure of the Pauline liturgy music have no place. "Therefore," he concludes, "it is my earnest advice that instead of the mumbling of psalms, one read them, and that they be explained, in order that the beautiful spirit of the Holy Ghost which lies therein may be seen" (350, 9–11).

It should now be apparent that Zwingli is not at all objecting to music per se. That he should reject it from worship because he did not understand it or was insensitive to it or because he was ignorant of its technicalities is, as has been shown, simply not true.[29] Equally false is the assertion that he rejected singing and instrumental music "because they profane the Church through their worldly character."[30] Such thinking is characteristic of Karlstadt but alien to Zwingli. The importance of the distinction between the two arguments cannot be overestimated. Karlstadt dismissed instrumental music primarily on the grounds of its worldly and theatrical character.[31] Zwingli, on the other hand, does not even mention the organ, although there were sev-

29. Söhngen, *Leiturgia*, p. 24.

30. Rudolph Staehelin, *Huldreich Zwingli: Sein Leben und Wirken nach den Quellen dargestellt, 1* (Basel, 1895), 294.

31. Theses 16–18: "On the grounds that it is everywhere a hindrance to devotion, we completely reject the measured chant from the church. To be sure, rising to the heights of Hylanus, the Taratantara blares forth, whilst descending at the same time to the depths. Therefore, together with it and the organ, we relegate trumpets and flutes to the theatre of entertainments and the halls of princes."

eral in Zurich, nor does he extensively detail the musical abuses within the city churches. The structure of his thought is wholly different; its foundation is at a deeper level, in which music is conceived virtually as an abstraction. He is being directed by what are for him inescapable facts—namely, that God has not commanded a musical worship, and that the principle of freedom from liturgy was proclaimed by Christ. Music, choral or instrumental, no matter how religiously inspired, artistically beautiful, or superlatively performed, must be prohibited from worship because Scripture has made its existence there impossible.[32] Zwingli the servant of the Word, rather than Zwingli the musician, is prohibiting music from the liturgy. And finally the rejection is complete. Unlike Karlstadt, Zwingli will not tolerate even an unaccompanied unison singing in the vernacular by the congregation. His point of view does not permit him to, because he is not arguing, as had Karlstadt, from the traditions of an existing institution. His humanism, his fundamental psychological detachment from the ecclesiastical tradition, enables him to start not with Gregory and a fallen Church but with Christ and the Word. Because he is trying all things exclusively by "the touchstone of the Gospel and the fire of Paul" (*1*, 319, 7), his argument is, in the strictest sense, scriptural: he is thinking solely in terms of God's Word.

THE FORTY-SIXTH CONCLUSION

"Thus it must follow that church song or clamor without reverence and only for reward is either a search for praise before men or financial gain" (*1*, 463, 17-19). Now at length the forty-sixth *Conclusion* may be understood as Zwingli intended, not as a criticism of church music on two apparently arbitrary grounds but as an intentionally nontheological critique appended to the theological considerations set forth previously in *Conclusions* forty-four and forty-five. That fact understood, what might seem to be the primary grounds for his rejection of church music then properly appear as distinctly secondary. Church music *already* has been proven indefensible on scriptural grounds alone. Nevertheless, those grounds do not necessarily preclude the nonscriptural arguments which Zwingli employs now to support and round out his commentary.

He deals first with the problem of professional choirs. The "singing which one does in churches" is owing either to one, or both, of two states of mind: "The search for praise before men . . . so that one is famous for the fact

32. Söhngen, *Leiturgia*, pp. 20, 22; cf. below, p. 65, n. 21.

that one is pious" (350, 22), or "the fact that one makes money" (350, 22), the desire for "financial gain." If one sings in church without reverence, no matter how well or how badly, then it is certainly an hypocrisy or a display of the kind Zwingli earlier excoriated. But the defenders of church music stubbornly maintain that "if it is done with reverence, then it is not evil" (350, 26–27), to which Zwingli responds: "Have you not heard that you should appraise no deed with respect to how good it is, for if that were permissible, we would appraise our deeds so highly that God would scarcely reward us. Whether a deed is good lies with God alone; it must come from Him" (350, 27–29; 351, 1–2). His rebuttal forces the issue on to the illimitable power of God, as did Christ in the passage from Matthew cited earlier by Zwingli. God alone may judge the merits of men's actions; the latter do not have the right or the ability or the perspective to do so. Music in worship may not be interpreted as a good work, because the entire doctrine of works-righteousness has been voided. Thus professional choirs, even if the most pious of men genuinely consider them good and reverent, may quite possibly not be considered so by a God who has not commanded them. Zwingli does not forget either the fallibility or the finitude of human vision. He is intensely conscious of man's tendency to take excessive pride in his achievements; he knows that this pride is, of all man's spiritual capacities, potentially limitless and infinitely injurious to the majesty of God. "See," he exclaims, "the silly games in the churches cost so much sweat and work and . . . one has to keep up with this hypocrisy . . . and all this does not happen without noticeable sinning, for there is seen either lustful wish for honor or lustfulness" (353, 4–8). Such a drastic malady requires a drastic medicine. Man's opinions must, so far as possible, be summarily dismissed, and the goodness and propriety of a given deed be judged only by God. "Therefore do not bellow the prayer in public as the dumb harlots do; but go and do it in private" (351, 2–3).

Karlstadt had discussed the problem of man's pride in his achievements. He, too, had seen it as a psychological condition which greatly hampered the possibility of true reverence on the part of the professional singer. But because at the last he was willing to allow the possibility of choral singing by the congregation, he evidently did not believe that such psychological difficulties extended to individual members of the congregation. Zwingli is more realistic. For the whole congregation, real concentration in prayer is difficult at all times, but "that one can be pious or reverent in the face of great tumult and noise is against all human reason. Hence the fact that man's reverence is short and quick, that he is not reverent with words and heart for a long period of time" (351, 5–8). A genuine fusion of words and heart in reverence is of perilously short duration. Saint Paul himself [1 Cor. 14:15] entertained similar doubts when he said: "What is it then? I will pray with the spirit and I will pray with the understanding also: I will sing with the spirit and I will sing with the understanding also." It is the one statement he makes in his epistles which seems to permit singing in worship, yet it is sharply qualified by that insistence on an exact correspondence between mouth, understanding, and spirit. Zwingli is too candid to deny that Paul here virtually allows singing; nevertheless, he points carefully to the apostle's qualification: "if you sing a psalm with the mouth, see to it that mouth and mind are in agreement" (352, 16–18). In the light of Zwingli's expressed views on human frailty, it is not surprising that he should then continue: "Now when one prays, mouth and mind are not long on the same track, much less so mind and song" (352, 18–19). Such an observation from a first-class musician is devastating. At one stroke Zwingli epitomizes music's capacity to distract and overwhelm man, as well as man's inherent vulnerability before that mysterious power. Man can barely summon his energy and will to join mouth and mind truly together in prayer; how much more of an effort, then, for a congregation of amateurs to try to sing and pray simultaneously. Those who are unmusical will be distracted by their awkward attempts simply to follow the notes, whereas those who are musically talented, regardless of how much or how little, will be overwhelmed, because they are, by virtue of their competence, the more susceptible to music's power. Music is irresistible; Zwingli would not eliminate it from his private life entirely. Man's nature is unable to sustain the tension between his emotional and intellectual response to music and his imperative to worship God. Either he sings well and prays poorly or sings poorly and prays well or, worst of all, does neither, alternatives which Zwingli himself succinctly formulates as follows: "Those who approve of choral song so strongly are either childish or foolish. Foolish: because they have never learned the right and true prayer, for had they learned it rightly, they would then never allow anyone to interrupt them with mumbling. Childish: because they, like children, like to sing and hear singing, although they do not understand what they are singing" (351, 10–16). Thus an equal concentration on, and attention to, words and music in prayer is impossible for all save the most exceptional. Musical prayer, then, must be rejected for the sake of true prayer, and naturally so, "for as long as the mind is in understanding with the words, I have no doubt that you will never sing again" (352, 13–14). If Zwingli's psychological argument is accepted, his conclusion is irrefutable.[33]

Having supported his theological objections to music with acute psychological analysis, Zwingli moves to the particularities of Zurich, and permits himself at the end a broadside against the musical deficiencies of the liturgy observed there in the only extended statement which is comparable in content and tone to those in Karlstadt's theses:

> Likewise has Amos in the Old Testament also rejected singing [Amos 5:23]. Do away with the murmuring of your songs and I do not want the sound of your lyres. What would the farmer-prophet say to our time if he should see so many kinds of music-making in our churches and so many other kinds of notes, dances, trillers, etc. and in the middle of all this the choristers with their silken shirtings going to the altar for reward. Truly he would cry out so that the whole world could not endure the sound of his noise.   [352, 22–27; 353, 1–3]

Thus Zwingli concludes the negative aspects of the *Substantiation* of the forty-sixth *Conclusion*.[34]

But he is not merely criticizing existing ecclesiastical practice. He is proposing simultaneously the structure for a new liturgy, and to this constructive aspect of his work he returns by way of bringing the whole commentary to a close. As demonstrated earlier, he intends to adhere as strictly as possible to Paul's instructions for worship. Again and again in his epistles the apostle stressed the importance of understanding the Word, and with this stress Zwingli is in complete accord. If freedom from liturgy cannot be realized, then the necessary liturgy, if it is to have value, must contribute to the understanding of the Word that Paul requires on the part of the participants. Thus Zwingli exclaims: "You would do well to read the fourteenth chapter of First Corinthians [1 Cor. 14:19] where you would find that Paul would rather have you read five words with understanding of the

33. Söhngen, *Leiturgia*, p. 21. Theodor Goldschmid, *Das Lied unserer evangelischen Kirche* (Zurich, 1941), p. 79. Alfred Einstein, "The Conflict of Word and Tone," *The Musical Quarterly*, 40 (1954), 329–49.

34. In Thesis 12 Karlstadt raised the social and financial problems of church choirs by implying that the money used for their support should be given instead to the poor. In Theses 22–23 he stated the idea explicitly: "It would be better to give a single penny to a poor man than to give a thousand gold pieces to those howlers and organists, unless they stand together in equal poverty"; cf. Z, 2, 353, 12–16, and the commentary on Matt. 6:6, S, 6¹, 234. See further Erasmus' commentary on I Cor. 14:19 (*Opera, 6,* 732B).

meaning to others than ten thousand words with the tongue" (352, 6–9). If such is to be the foundation of the new liturgy, then Zwingli may rightly say: "Therefore no one should be afraid if noise is expelled from the church and if one ordains in its place well-read men who truly explain the Word of God" (353, 12–14). The intricacies of Latin polyphony and the sonorities of the organ both must submit to the majesty of the Word, and in their stead must be the silence necessary to the hearing, the understanding, and the appropriation of that Word. Zwingli closes the commentary with a last dismissal of his beloved art from the Church and a greeting to the right, true prayer for which he has argued so strenuously and so long:

> Farewell, my temple-murmurings! I am not sorry for you. I know that you are not good for me. But welcome, O pious, private prayer that is awakened in the hearts of believing men through the Word of God. Yes, a small sigh, which does not last long, realizes itself and goes away again quickly. Greetings to you, too, common prayer that all Christians do together, be it in church or in their chambers, but free and unpaid; I know that you are the sort of prayer to which God will give that which He has promised.[35]   [353, 16–21; 354, 1–3]

It is significant that even here at the very close Zwingli attests to the tension in his mind. He speaks of two distinct kinds of prayer rather than one, namely "private" (*innwendigs gebett*) and "common" (*gmeiner gebett*). No two adjectives could be more appropriate, nor correspond more exactly to the two principles of freedom from liturgy and necessity for liturgy between which Zwingli was endeavoring to mediate.

Luther had insisted upon a freedom from ceremony which is fairly comparable to the Zwinglian concept of a freedom from liturgy, in that both reformers shared a thoroughgoing antipathy to the ceremonial legalism of the existing Church. But Luther believed that the traditional external forms as such, the "accidents" of the liturgy, could be retained so long as the "substance" which they expressed was rightly understood.[36] Thus parallel with freedom

35. Surely there is a parallel to Augustine's emotional dilemma in Zwingli's perhaps involuntary aside, "I know that you are not good for me," as there is also in his frank admission that together with his farewell goes "a small sigh." The two sentences taken together suggest that beneath the inexorable theological reasoning with which Zwingli eliminated music from the liturgy there may have lain a disturbing subjective concern for his own reaction to music when joined to worship, which was similar to that of Augustine.

36. See, for example, *The Babylonian Captivity of the Church, Luther's Works,* ed. Jaroslav Pelikan and Helmut T. Lehmann, *36* (Philadelphia, 1959), 52; for contemporary descriptions of

from ceremony ran a freedom *for* ceremony, a freedom, moreover, to maintain and observe virtually all the ceremonies associated with, and sanctioned by, the ecclesiastical tradition. Any other solution to the problem of the relationship between form and content posed by the restored Gospel would, in his eyes, have been merely the substitution of a new ceremonial legalism for the old.

A freedom for ceremony understood along such traditional lines was essentially alien to Zwingli. Over against such a freedom he insisted upon the necessity for liturgy. The *Substantiation* of the three *Conclusions* on prayer is based entirely on Scripture; Zwingli's intention is to realize as thoroughly and consistently as possible the principle he had defended at the First Zurich Disputation: that the Word of God is the norm, at once unconditional and exclusive, for the whole conduct of the Church, from which liturgical forms could under no circumstances be dissociated. This adherence to Scripture alone was rooted in his detachment from, and lack of involvement in, the medieval ecclesiastical tradition. The humanistic concept of *Christianismus renascens* to which he had been exposed so intensely by Erasmus and the Basel circle, and within which form could not in the last analysis be separated from content, here shows its decisive influence. The vast structure of the liturgy of medieval Christianity was to be rejected in its entirety. But what Erasmus had at best only implied Zwingli explicitly preached; moreover, he put it into radical practice. The concept of the necessity for a new liturgy exclusively scriptural in form as well as content is to be understood finally as the product of the humanistic thrust lying deep in Zwingli's theology. Humanism thus constitutes its necessary precondition.[37]

THE APOLOGY ON THE CANON OF THE MASS

Following upon the publication of the *Interpretation and Substantiation of the Conclusions,* Zwingli devoted himself assiduously to his extensive essay on the canon of the Mass, which he issued on August 29, 1523. In that work he criticized every detail of the structure of the Catholic Mass, al-

---

the celebration of a Lutheran mass see Theodor Kolde, *Analecta Lutherana, Briefe und Actenstücke zur Geschichte Luthers* (Gotha, 1883), pp. 216–18; 226–28.

37. For the formal, structural precedents of Zwingli's liturgy of the Word and the Lord's Supper see Julius Schweizer, *Reformierte Abendmahlsgestaltung in der Schau Zwinglis* (Basel, [1954]), passim, and, most recently, Fritz Schmidt-Clausing, "Johann Ulrich Surgant, ein Wegweiser des jungen Zwingli," *Zwingliana, 11* (1961), 287–320.

though permitting the continuance of certain practices, notably vestments and singing, until they could be relinquished, as he had stated positively in his earlier work, "with such discretion that insurrections do not ensue" (353, 15). That retention of these ceremonial observances was intended only for the time being was almost at once misunderstood by some of his more ardent followers, so that on October 9 he published a further brief treatise on the canon in which he made his position clear beyond question.

The singing of the *Introit* and the *Gloria,* although permitted for a while, was to be prohibited as soon as possible, "although here it need not be hurried so anxiously, provided that we proceed without delay as in the annulling of the vestments . . . those sweet nightingales who cannot refrain from singing are to be borne for a while, provided that they sing only heavenly things, until we are able to break through all things with the Word of God" (621, 12–14; 17–19). Zwingli was by no means unaware of the turmoil that had shaken Wittenberg when Karlstadt attempted to put through some of his more extreme reforms, and he was determined at all costs to avoid a similar disturbance in Zurich. The new liturgy had therefore to be put into practice very slowly and very carefully. "But," he added, "wherever it is granted at the beginning, without a quarrel, to omit the swelling of the songs once hateful to the prophet Amos [Amos 5:23], let it be omitted" (621, 19–21). Then he continued by reiterating, but more precisely now, his earlier interpretation of Paul's statements on music in worship. "For we are not unaware that the words of Paul in Ephesians 5 [19] and Colossians 3 [16] concerning psaltery and singing in the heart give no help to those who protect their swan songs by them. For in the heart, he says, not with the voice. Therefore, the psalms and praises of God ought to be treated as if our minds sing to God" (621, 26–30). And in order that the adherents of radical reform may in no wise misunderstand him, he concludes by saying bluntly: "As soon as it can be done, this barbarous mumbling should be dispatched from the churches" (621, 32–33).

Thus Zwingli had every intention of removing all music, instrumental and choral, from the new liturgy, but at the same time he was far-sighted enough to realize to the full that a liturgy wholly devoid of music was an idea so radical that the citizens of Zurich would need to adjust themselves emotionally and intellectually to its novelty. Such an adjustment involved education, and such an education in turn demanded time. His whole attitude is exactly summed up in a speech he delivered during the last day of the Second Zurich Disputation on October 28, 1523:

Everything which is added to the true institutions of Christ is an abuse. But if they are all not done away with at once, then it will be necessary to preach the Word of God firmly and steadfastly against them. Namely, it is a foolish, unnecessary, and indeed an insidious thing concerning the true service that the song which one sings off-key in the churches should exist. . . . As long as song, as well as vestments, is detrimental to the right, true prayer, that is: the lifting up of the spirit to God, then they must be done away with. . . . The people must be educated in the Word of God so that neither vestments nor song have a part in the Mass.   [788, 16–21; 789, 7–10, 13–15]

He is still absolutely insistent that music can have no legitimate function in true Christian worship. But he is just as insistent that the proposed liturgy be implemented only when Zurich was genuinely ready for it. Delay was therefore not only necessary, it was essential for the education of the city. "Therefore," he said, "dear, chosen, true brothers in Christ Jesus, I adjure you, for the sake of God, to take up in hand the Word of God, and stand up for it and preach it . . . in the clearest way possible. . . . Thus the people will be edified; then will these things be done without tumult" (789, 17–23). And with respect to the total elimination of music from worship Zwingli was completely successful.

KARLSTADT AND ZWINGLI

The documents of 1523 analyzed above constitute the sum of Zwingli's major utterances on the problem of liturgical music. In that one year he said all that he believed was necessary on the subject; indeed, any further extended statements would have been superfluous. Why this should be so may be seen best by a final comparison and contrast with the theses of Karlstadt.

Karlstadt's *Disputation* had appealed primarily to history. In consequence, although his argument in one sense moves out from the Word of God in Scripture, the real point of departure for his "protest" is the fall of the Church as an historical institution under Gregory the Great. He is, to say the least, sensitive to the musical abuses of the post-Gregorian Church. He is also conscious, yet neither clearly nor constructively, of some sort of musical-liturgical life within the pre-Gregorian Church. But throughout the theses the character as well as the direction of his thought is conditioned essentially by the fact of the institution. As a result, then, of thinking within this institutional-historical framework, Karlstadt could arrive at a perspective on the problem of music in worship that was only partially new.

For Zwingli, on the other hand, the only possible point of departure was the Word of God in Scripture. By adhering rigorously to this exclusive point of view, he was simply indifferent to the history of the Church as a formal institution after "the touchstone of the Gospel and the fire of Paul." This is not to say that he is unaware of it. On the contrary, events such as the liturgical discoveries in Milan or at Mollis had made him keenly conscious of the historical development of the institutional and liturgical forms of Christianity. But his denial of any validity or significance to all these historical forms was complete notwithstanding, and in this respect he is distinctly ahistorical. The ecclesiastical tradition intervening between the Gospel and St. Paul, on the one hand, and Pope Leo X, on the other, had not conditioned his thought as it had that of Karlstadt. Consequently, Zwingli was able to initiate an entirely new perspective on the problem of music in worship, one that compelled him to ask not the complicated question: What forms of music are legitimate in Christian worship? but the very simple question: Does the Word of God in Scripture permit music in Christian worship at all? Karlstadt's theses resulted finally, although doubtless inadvertently, in an attempt to answer the first of the two questions, precisely because the existence of liturgical music was one of the controlling assumptions of the medieval ecclesiastical tradition, an assumption from which Karlstadt was unable, try as he might, to release himself. In the last analysis, the *Disputation* rests squarely upon it, and the 1522 Mass that he produced for Wittenberg merely confirmed it.

Zwingli, however, argued neither within the traditional assumptions nor from them. He posed the second of the two questions, and the basic novelty of his protest against music in worship derives actually not so much from the several arguments he employs as from the single question on which they rest. And it was in fact the *asking* of that initial question which was of such significance for the future role of music in the churches of Zurich. For twelve hundred years at least the validity and propriety of music's role in the liturgy of the Christian church had never been questioned. Aspects of its performance and the use of certain instruments had often been criticized, to be sure, and since the fifteenth century increasingly so; but never the right *as such* to employ music.

Now, however, Zwingli posed just that question. By doing so he forced

Zurich to the realization that if Scripture was, in fact, to be taken with absolute seriousness as the exclusive norm for Christian behavior, then, according to Zwingli's interpretation of Scripture, music could not be employed in worship. It had never been instituted by God, and Christ's instructions for true prayer made it impossible. Once the scriptural assumption is granted, the theological objections to liturgical music which Zwingli developed out of it so inexorably are as formidable as they are incontrovertible. Whereas Karlstadt was a reformer, Zwingli was a revolutionary.

3. MUSICAE PERTINAX AMATOR

I disturb no one with my music.
Zwingli

Zwingli's intention to eliminate all music from worship in the churches of Zurich was publicly announced in 1523. Not once thereafter did he in any way alter that intention. Yet he was convinced, too, that if such silent worship was to endure at all, if Scripture was indeed to be accepted as an unconditional norm, it would require legal measures in addition to education: the Council would have to decide when it wanted to establish it officially in the city churches. Only through such a legal process could permanence be assured. And so, having made his theological position clear, Zwingli deferred the procedural decision to the city authorities.

He did not have long to wait. In June 1524 the Council issued a series of decrees embodying Zwingli's recommendations which initiated the reconstruction of the Zurich liturgy. The actual texts are no longer extant, but according to Bullinger, "at this time also the authorities in Zurich gave orders that the people were not to play the organ any more in the city and in the churches."[1] Thus, just a little over a year after he had made public his opposition to instrumental and vocal church music, half of that program had been officially enacted by the city. The organs in the Zurich churches were never again to be used. Already the silence so necessary to proper worship had been in part achieved.

There remained the question of vocal music. Zwingli had stated in

1. Bullinger, *1*, 162; cf. Wyss, *Chronik*, p. 56, and Egli, doc. 547.

57

August of 1523 that a minimal singing in worship might be tolerated so long as Mass was celebrated; his intention, of course, was to abolish the Mass as quickly as possible and to substitute for it his new communion liturgy. But implementation of this, his most radical liturgical reform, met with such opposition, first from the canons of the Great Minster and then from the officials of the neighboring cantons, that not until April 12, 1525, did the Council officially enact it. The Roman Mass was sung for the last time on Wednesday of Holy Week. Then, on Maundy Thursday, Zwingli realized the heart of his liturgical reconstruction: The Lord's Supper was celebrated for the first time in Zurich in the Great Minster as a simple communion meal; throughout the service, which the Reformer had prepared himself, the only sound was that of the presiding minister's voice and the occasional spoken response of the congregation.[2] The true stillness of worship had at last been achieved in its entirety.

GREBEL'S LETTER TO MÜNTZER: 1524

That silence was to be an enduring one, just as Zwingli had hoped. There is virtually no evidence that the Reformer was forcing this austere liturgy on a reluctant city. As a matter of fact, Zwingli's opposition to the use of music in worship was defended even by his opponents within Zurich. One of his initial converts and most enthusiastic adherents to the idea of a thoroughgoing reform had been the young patrician Conrad Grebel.[3] Before the Second Disputation was concluded, however, he had realized that he and his master differed fundamentally, indeed irrevocably, on their understanding of how reform was to be implemented. By December 1523 he had broken with Zwingli, although not as yet completely. Grebel had gradually become the leader of a small group of citizens who were likewise disaffected from Zwingli, and in the summer of 1524, sometime after the promulgation of the June decrees, the Brethren, as they came to be called, sought to initiate contact with Luther, Karlstadt, and Müntzer. The most important document surviving from these several attempts was the letter they dispatched to Thomas Müntzer on September 5, 1524.

2. Zwingli had originally proposed an antiphonal spoken response between the men and women of the congregation: see, for example, *Z, 4,* 19, 4–24. The Council forbade it, however (Egli, doc. 684), for reasons not now known; see the comments of Schweizer, *Reformierte Abendmahlsgestaltung,* pp. 66–67, and A.-E. Cherbuliez, "Zwingli, Zwick und der Kirchengesang," *Zwingliana, 4* (1921–28), 369–70. Cf. Erasmus' commentary on I. Cor. 14:19 (*Opera 6,* 731E).

3. On Grebel see the exhaustive biography by Harold Scott Bender, *Conrad Grebel c. 1498–1526, The Founder of the Swiss Brethren Sometimes Called Anabaptists:* Studies in Anabaptist and Mennonite History, 6 (Goshen, Indiana, 1950).

The Brethren heartily endorsed Müntzer's idea of an unconditional obedience to Scripture as a norm for Christian life and worship. Consequently, they were especially disturbed that he evidently was failing to practice this ideal. Significantly enough, the first object of their criticism was his retention of music in worship. Müntzer had, as it were, accepted the challenge implicitly posed by Karlstadt's concluding thesis, and had prepared an extraordinarily powerful choral liturgy to be sung in the vernacular by his congregation at Allstedt.[4] Grebel and the Brethren, however, had absorbed Zwingli's ideas so completely that they objected to this German Mass, because any music in worship "cannot be for the good, since we find nothing taught in the New Testament about singing, no example of it."[5] They criticized Müntzer's practice in eight subsequent points which, in effect, reiterated the arguments Zwingli had proposed in the preceding year. Thus, for example, adverting to Ephesians 5:19 and Colossians 3:16, they stressed the fact that Saint Paul meant that "if anyone would sing, he should sing and give thanks in his heart," echoing Zwingli's exegesis of the same passages: "in the heart, he [Paul] says, not with the voice" (2, 621, 28–29). Again, they pointed out to Müntzer that "whoever sings poorly gets vexation by it; whoever can sing well gets conceit," recalling Zwingli's phrase that church song is "the search for praise before men" (2, 350, 18–19). They concluded their critique by insisting that liturgical music "must be rooted up by the word and command of Christ, for it is not planted by God."[6] Zwingli had publicly maintained such a thesis with regard to ceremonies from at least 1522, but he had given it a particularly prominent formulation during the Second Disputation, when he maintained that "everything which is added to the true institutions of Christ is an abuse" (2, 788, 16–17). This had been asserted, significantly, in response to a direct

4. E. Gordon Rupp, "Luther and Thomas Müntzer," in *Luther Today*, Martin Luther Lectures, 1 (Luther College Press, Decorah, Iowa, 1957), 133–36. On Müntzer's liturgy see Oskar J. Mehl, "Thomas Müntzer als Liturgiker," *Theologische Literaturzeitung* (February 1951), p. 76, and *Thomas Müntzers Deutsche Messen und Kirchenämter*, 1939. Müntzer's liturgical works are to be found in Emil Sehling, *Die evangelische Kirchenordnungen des 16. Jahrhunderts* (Leipzig, 1902), *1*, 472–507. Two earlier studies are E. Jammers, "Thomas Müntzers deutsche evangelische Messen," *Archiv für Reformationsgeschichte, 31* (1934), 121–28, and Karl Schulz, "Thomas Müntzers liturgische Bestrebungen," *Zeitschrift für Kirchengeschichte*, neue folge *10* (1928), 369–401.

5. For the history of the letter and an analysis of its contents see Bender, *Grebel*, pp. 171–83. The translation used here is that by George Huntston Williams, *Spiritual and Anabaptist Writers*, Library of Christian Classics, 25 (London, 1957), 75. For the original text see the *Quellen zur Geschichte der Täufer in der Schweiz, 1, Zürich*, ed. Leonard von Muralt and Walter Schmid (Zurich, 1952), p. 14.

6. All three quotations from Williams, pp. 75, 76. *Quellen*, p. 15.

question from Grebel, and the first example of such abuses to which Zwingli had referred was that of liturgical music. Thus even before church singing was actually abolished from Zurich, Zwingli's ideas on the subject had been wholeheartedly adopted by Grebel and the Brethren, a group of men within the city who in other respects were unquestionably hostile to him.[7]

Their acceptance was on an intellectual level comparable to that of Zwingli, a level which clearly could not be attained by all the citizens of Zurich. Yet it must not be forgotten that ever since the closing decades of the fifteenth century, townsmen generally had been objecting more and more to the disintegration of both the choral and instrumental music of their churches. Zwingli's objections to ecclesiastical music per se, as he had explained them in the *Interpretation and Substantiation of the Conclusions,* were theologically grounded; to such intricate arguments the layman conceivably could be educated through the Reformer's sermons as well as his published writings. But instinctively, the people at large would have agreed with Zwingli's desire to eliminate from the liturgy, if not all music, at least all music sung by professional choirs, even without such intellectual explanation as he gave them, simply because they had no taste either for the music itself or for its mediocre, if not downright bad, performance. Thus the critical state of ecclesiastical music in Zurich, although it did not in itself affect the development of Zwingli's ideas on the role of music in worship, was nevertheless of paramount importance for the implementation of those ideas. Both the comparative speed with which the Council translated them into practice and the absence of any notable opposition to them from the laity is ample testimony that Zwingli spoke to a concrete situation in which his ideas, though radical, were welcome, although not necessarily from his own sophisticated point of view. That the response of the people to the total abolition of the church music they disliked so intensely was in fact wholehearted is indicated, too, by the fact that not only during Zwingli's lifetime but for an extraordinarily long time thereafter no ecclesiastical singing at all was heard in the city. It was not until 1598 that vocal music was once again permitted in the Zurich churches.[8]

7. Bender, *Grebel,* p. 176, observes that with regard to the elimination of music from worship "it is altogether possible that Grebel derived his views from Zwingli." The evidence would seem to support the suggestion; cf. Söhngen, *Leiturgia,* p. 20.

8. On the readmission of singing into the Zurich liturgy see Hannes Reimann, *Die Einführung des Kirchengesangs in der Zürcher Kirche nach der Reformation* (Zurich, 1959), esp. pp. 69–112.

THE DESTRUCTION OF THE ORGANS: 1527

The organs, although unused, still remained as visible witness to the musical violations committed by the old Church against the Word of God. Having stood unplayed for three years after June 1524, they were at last officially destroyed. The contemporary chronicler Bernhard Wyss, himself a musician, recorded (interestingly enough, with neither anger nor dismay) that "in the year 1527 on Monday the 9th of December, that is the last month, the organs at the Great Minster were completely destroyed." [9] For the more astute Bullinger the event took on an almost symbolic significance, in consequence of which he devoted an entire paragraph to it in his history of the Reformation:

When the Organs of Zurich were Broken up in the Minster

The organs in the churches are not a particularly old institution, especially in these parts. Since they do not agree with the apostolic teaching [1 Cor. 14] the organs in the Great Minster in Zurich were broken up on the 9th of December in this year 1527. For from this time forth neither singing nor organs in the Church was wanted. [10]

Bullinger, like Wyss, loved music, but also, like Wyss, he was not at all disturbed by the destruction of the two instruments. On the contrary, he was pleased by this visible demonstration that Zurich, with respect to music at least, had now restored itself entirely to the authentic condition of the Pauline worship advocated by Zwingli. From Pelagius Kaltschmid, who had been the organist at the Great Minster since 1517, there was no objection at all; indeed he seems to have been one of Zwingli's adherents. [11] From the people of Zurich generally no objection seems to have been recorded, either to the decree of 1524 silencing the organs or to their destruction in 1527. [12] Bullinger's observation that "from this time forth neither singing nor organs in the church was wanted" was evidently an accurate description of the

9. Wyss, *Chronik*, p. 86.

10. Bullinger, *1*, 418.

11. Wyss, *Chronik*, p. 33, n. 2. Paul Nettl, in his *Luther and Music*, trans. Frida Best and Ralph Wood (Philadelphia, 1948), p. 5, asserts that when the organ was destroyed, "the organist stood by, helpless and weeping." There is no contemporary evidence for the statement.

12. Gerold Edlibach, *Chronik*, p. 251, concludes his account of the destruction of the organs with the words "gott schicke ess zum besten." The phrase is too ambiguous, however, to support Geering's contention (*Die Vokalmusik*, p. 36) that he was opposed to this decision.

temper of the city. The combination of Zwingli's insistence on a policy of education before legal action, together with the laity's hostility to the old instrumental music of the church, was thus completely successful. Phenomenally so, in fact, for the influence of Zwingli's opposition to the use of organs in church lasted longer even than that of his opposition to ecclesiastical singing. Whereas singing was reinstated, albeit with difficulty, late in the sixteenth century, up to the nineteenth century "the churches of Canton Zurich remained without organs." [13]

To be sure, the church in the little community of Ermatingen apparently possessed an organ quite late in the eighteenth century, but its use was peculiarly restricted: under no circumstances could it ever be played during the service of worship; it was to be used only for accompanying the choir during their rehearsals. Not until 1809 did a post-Reformation church in the Canton—in Winterthur—install an organ specifically for use in the service. Wädenswil followed its lead in 1829,[14] and in 1848 an organ was installed in the Fraumünster. Yet within the city of Zurich itself antipathy toward the use of the instrument was still so great that for five years it remained unused. Finally, in August 1853, it was consecrated and thereafter played.[15] There remained, then, the Great Minster. For over a quarter of a century after 1848 the church that had been the first in Zurich ever to possess an organ resolutely upheld Zwingli's opposition to it. But the demand for one evidently became too great to withstand, and an organ was at last installed in 1874.[16] It is thus a measure of the complete accord between Zwingli and Zurich with respect to instrumental music in worship that the silence the Reformer advocated in 1523 remained unbroken in the city churches for over three centuries.

THE LETTER FROM OECOLAMPADIUS: 1526

Pressures to restore music to worship were exerted on Zwingli from elsewhere, however. On April 9, 1526, a year after the liturgy without music had been established, Zwingli's good friend Oecolampadius, the great reformer

13. Gustav Weber, *Huldrych Zwingli: seine Stellung zur Musik und seine Lieder; die Entwicklung der deutschen Kirchengesangs, eine kunsthistorische Studie* (Zurich, 1884), pp. 39–40.
14. For the above see Leonhard Stierlin, "Der zürcherische Kirchengesang seit der Reformation," In *Neujahrsblatt der Allgemeine Musikgesellschaft in Zürich* (Zurich, 1855), p. 11.
15. Hermann Grossman, *Guide for Visitors to the Fraumünster in Zürich* (Zurich, 1951), p. 5.
16. Weber, *Zwingli*, p. 40.

of Basel, wrote him that "during the recent Eastertide laymen had sung psalms, but they were forbidden to do so by the magistrates. It restored the spirits of the papists, whom the large number of people who were joining my congregation had absolutely overwhelmed. But they will rejoice only for a moment" (*8, 560, 12–15*). Oecolampadius had evidently come to realize the value of congregational singing as it was spreading through Lutheran Germany, and tried therefore to introduce it into his city, but without success. As the Basel city chronicle tersely recorded it: "These same [Lutherans] tried to introduce this novelty [German psalm-singing] into the Easter celebration, but they suffered rebuff." [17] Notwithstanding, Oecolampadius had continued his efforts so stubbornly that he was finally able to write Zwingli in triumph on the twelfth of August of that same year:

Today and on St. Lawrence's day, German [i.e. Lutheran] psalms were sung in my church by the congregation. The priests realized that this would happen, as a result of my sermons, from the fact that I had cited from the psalms certain passages about the joy of the spirit and the lips [i.e. singing] bearing on this matter. Therefore they pleaded their cause before the Senate trying to stop this, and they won from the Senate the edict that singing at the mass was forbidden, but I knew nothing of it until now. But such is the nature of fighting a prohibition, so where our religious zeal excuses us, we were made still bolder. The Senate forbade it to no avail. I do not know what will come of it. Some of the evil consequences will fall upon me. But I shall take them gladly if they must be borne. Nothing has originated from me, but only God's glory is displayed. But if the Lord brings this project to an happy issue, I hope it will greatly help the evangelical cause. Pray God for me.[18]

Thus did Oecolampadius enthusiastically announce the introduction of psalm singing into Basel, adding at the end his hopes that music would assist the evangelical cause, and implying thereby that his friend and coworker might reconsider music in a similar light for Zurich.

Zwingli remained adamant. He had through much thought and study slowly come to an understanding of the form of the liturgy from which he would not be moved. "But in that, for other churches," he had written, sig-

17. Z, *8*, 560, n. 6.
18. Z, *8*, 686, 6–17; cf. the Basel city chronicle for August 10, 1526 (n. 3): "On the festival of Saint Lawrence, despite the prohibition of the Senate, the Lutherans loudly and vehemently began to sing metrical psalms congregationally, but in poor order, in the church of Saint Martin; the psalms were translated in Strasburg against the will of the magistrates."

nificantly enough, "we do not by any means reject further ceremonies—as perhaps are fitting and helpful to their service—such as song and other things; for we hope that all pastors in all places will build for the Lord and will always be busy in winning many people" (*4*, 14, 16–20). As a matter of fact, he had known since 1524 that such congregational songs had been introduced into the reformed church of Strassburg, for he wrote to Francis Lambert on the 16th of December of that year, saying: "what you write concerning the German songs and psalms is pleasing to all my colleagues" (*8*, 276, 17–18).

Furthermore, somewhat over a year after Oecolampadius had joyfully informed him of his success in Basel, congregational singing was introduced into nearby St. Gall, and in a most significant fashion. The reforming authorities there, anxious for the children of the community to learn the texts of the psalms in the vernacular, had determined that they could be memorized most effectively by means of musical settings. Thus the children were trained in psalm-singing first as a school exercise under the two principal teacher-musicians of the city, Dominick Zyli and Johannes Kessler. This experiment in evangelical pedagogy proved so successful that at length it was decided to permit the children to sing during a service as well as in the classroom. Accordingly, on September 8, 1527, both before and after the children's sermon, the little boys and girls of St. Gall sang for the first time in a church the setting of "Aus tiefer Not ich schrei zu dir," which they had learned in school.[19] Their parents, however, were not accorded the same privilege until two years later. As a result of the strenuous efforts of Zyli and Kessler, both of whom, like Oecolampadius, were enthusiastic adherents of the new Lutheran songs, the singing of the psalms in church by adults as well as by children was finally accepted, and on March 7, 1529, the first reformed service of worship with congregational singing was celebrated in St. Gall.[20] Zwingli could not have been ignorant of this situation, nor, for that matter, could he reasonably object to it in view of what he had said in the preface to his formula for the Lord's Supper. There, quite unequivocally, he permitted what was virtually a Lutheran freedom for "further ceremonies" in "other churches"; he entertained no objections to psalm-singing in Strassburg, Basel, St. Gall, or anywhere else. On the other hand, the Zurich liturgy was to be exemplary, to adhere as closely as possible to the form for Christian worship advocated by Christ and Saint Paul. In this respect, his

19. *Johannes Kesslers Sabbata,* ed. E. Götzinger (St. Gall, 1902), p. 249.
20. Ibid., p. 313.

musicianship notwithstanding, Zwingli was fully prepared to isolate Zurich from the new developments taking place elsewhere in reformed Switzerland and Lutheran Germany.[21]

THE REPLY TO FABER: 1526

While Oecolampadius labored to establish psalm-singing in Basel, spectacular objection to Zwingli's abolition of church music was raised from neighboring Constance. The vicar-general of the city, Johannes Faber (1478–1541), had formerly been a close friend of Zwingli.[22] In fact, he, Glareanus, and the Zurich Reformer had studied together at Vienna. By now, however, Faber had turned his back completely on his old friend, and on April 16, 1526, he issued a violent attack on Zwingli's reform measures entitled: *A Letter of Dr. Johann Faber to Ulrich Zwingli, Master at Zurich, with Respect to the Forthcoming Disputation Which Has Been Proposed for the Sixteenth Day of May Next at Baden and Argau Through the Assembled Citizens of the Twelve Cantons.* Though it was nominally addressed to Zwingli, it was actually an open letter to the Confederacy, and was never

21. Johann Kaspar Mörikofer, in the second volume (Leipzig, 1869), p. 93, of his *Ulrich Zwingli, nach den urkundlichen Quellen,* speculated that Zwingli might have altered his attitude toward the use of music in worship. The suggestion was made again by Theodor Goldschmid, *Das Lied unserer evangelischen Kirche* (Zurich, 1941), p. 81, by Ina Lohr in "Lieder für den Gottesdienst bei Luther, Zwingli und Calvin," *Musik und Gottesdienst, 3* (Zurich, 1949), 72, and Paul Gabriel, *Das deutsche evangelische Kirchenlied von Martin Luther bis zur Gegenwart* (Berlin, 2d ed. 1951), p. 47. Julius Schweizer, *Reformierte Abendmahlsgestaltung,* pp. 56–57, 113, has posed the question again, but in a most ambiguous and speculative fashion. The argument of Hannes Reimann, "Huldrych Zwingli—der Musiker," *Archiv für Musikwissenschaft, 17* (1960), 136–44, is unconvincing. Oskar Farner published in 1957 the following statement from Zwingli's lectures (still unpublished) on the Psalms: "Ob Lobgesang offenlich in Verstand aller Mänchen gesungen wurdend am Suntag, its guot und ze loben," *Jahrbuch für Liturgik und Hymnologie, 3* (1957), 130. On the basis of the sentence Gottfried W. Locher remarked that "the old proposition, 'Zwingli was opposed to Church Hymns,' is no longer true," *Church History, 34* (1965), 15. Locher's "old proposition," however, was proven untrue by Zwingli himself as early as 1525 in the preface to his liturgy for the Lord's Supper. Clearly he did not object to congregational singing elsewhere (*4, 14,* 16–20). But the evidence presented in the text above makes untenable any notion that Zwingli eventually would have introduced congregational singing into the Zurich liturgy. Oskar Söhngen, *Leiturgia,* is therefore quite correct in stressing the fact that Zwingli has a view of worship which cannot by its very nature include music of any sort. It is "einem gründsatzlich anderen Gottesdienstideal" (p. 20); "das hier eine neue Schau der Gottesdienstes aufbricht, bei der für Gesang und Musik kein mehr ist" (p. 22).

22. On Faber see L. Helbling, *Dr. Johann Fabri, General-Vikar von Constanz und Bischof von Wien, 1478–1541* (Münster, 1941).

sent to him personally.[23] Nonetheless, Oecolampadius hurriedly sent him a copy, and Zwingli replied to it almost at once, dividing the contents of Faber's letter into sixty-five items in order to answer them one by one. *Concerning the Unsent Letter of Faber and Zwingli's Reply* was published in Zurich on April 30, 1526.

Among several other charges, Faber had denounced Zwingli's expulsion of music from the Zurich liturgy. He knew that the organ at the Great Minster was now no longer in use, but apparently had heard, as well, that Zwingli was substituting for it an orchestra composed of all the instruments which he himself could play. Hence he wrote viciously: "And you are in no way ashamed by this bread from heaven, like the preachers of the flesh, whose way it is to erect the fleshpots of Egypt, even the golden calf for dancing, and in place of your dismembered organs, lutes, viols, and pipes." [24] Before such a tirade Zwingli remained calm, and in section ten he replied as follows:

Dear Faber, you hold flute, viol and pipe against me. I must say that I can do nothing on the flute. Without doubt you are badly informed on that point. I do not know what sort of music that is. But on the lute and viol, on other instruments also, I had some instruction which stands me now in good stead to quiet the children. You are too spiritual for cursing and haggling, however. Know, therefore, that even David was a good harper, who for a while freed Saul from the visitations of the Devil [1. Sam. 16:23]. Thus even you, if you understood the lutes of the heavenly courts, would be rid of the longing for honor, indeed even the longing for money and blood.[25] Why should you who are wise in these seven liberal arts of which you are a master, have honor and prestige, and never be reproved by goodly men? Socrates, the old man, first began to rejuvenate himself when in his old age he learned to play the harp.[26]

23. See Walter Köhler's introduction to the *Reply, Z, 5,* 34–39.
24. *Z, 5,* 53, n. 18.

25. The phrase "des gelts und blůts" is obscure, but Zwingli may mean elevation to the Cardinalate; cf. Bullinger, *1,* 51, for his account of Zwingli's description of the Roman Cardinals: "Dann schůtte man sy, so fallind dugatten und kronen herus, winde man sy, so růndt dines Suns, Brůders, vatters, und gůten frůndts blůt herus." The imagery of money and blood is in both instances virtually identical.

26. The editors suggest Sextus Empiricus as Zwingli's source (*Z 5,* 55, n. 14). A complete edition of Empiricus was not printed until 1621 at Geneva, however, and a more likely source—

Now your church considers not only music but bell-ringing as a divine service. I disturb no one with my music. May God give you something that will be different from your corrupted news of Zurich.

[5, 54, 16–19; 55, 1–12]

The entire passage illuminates Zwingli's personal attitude toward music, and his reference to David's musicianship is particularly significant. Calvin was later to comment on David's harp-playing in a sermon on the First Book of Samuel. "Saul," he explained, "had indeed been refreshed by David's harp, but it was really by the Lord's doing and inspiring that power within [David]."[27] And Luther believed even more strongly that music was a means of divine revelation. Writing in 1538, he asserted that "the Holy Spirit honours music as a tool of His work, since He testifies in the Holy Scriptures, that through the medium of music His gifts have been put into the hands of the Prophets (e.g. Elisha); again, through music the devil has been driven away, that is, he, who incites people to all vices, as was the case with Saul, the King of Israel."[28] What is instructive in both instances is that Calvin and Luther alike are agreed that it was not music per se which drove the devil from Saul, but rather the operation of God's Holy Spirit *through* music.

Zwingli was not of the same mind. More musical than either of his great contemporaries, he speaks not at all of "the Lord's doing" or of the Holy Spirit; David's harp-playing *alone* freed Saul from the visitations of the devil. Zwingli the musician knows intimately the shattering psychological power of the art in which he is himself so adept. But unlike Luther or Calvin, he is also careful to note that David's music *by itself* was powerful only "for a while." Music for Zwingli thus exists without the additional theological dimension given to it by Luther and Calvin; it is merely an art which for a little time is immensely affecting emotionally. And to music Zwingli will not accord the sanction of the Paraclete; he considered it, on the contrary, wholly secular. This is further borne out by his easy juxtaposition of a classical anecdote to the biblical one. The allusion to Socrates, while again demon-

one that Zwingli definitely knew—is Quintilian, *Institutio Oratoria*, 1. 10. 13. There is also a contemporary German source in which Zwingli may well have found the story—Rodoricus Zamorensis, *Der Spiegel des menschlichen Lebens* (1488): "Dise Kunst hat socrates in dem achtzigisten jar gelernet und hiess die iungling auch dise kunst lernen"; cf. Georg Schünemann, *Geschichte der deutschen Schulmusik* (2d ed. Leipzig, 1931–32), 2, 8.

27. Joannis Calvini, *Opera Quae supersunt Omnia*, ed. W. Baum, E. Cunitz, and E. Reuss (Brunswick, 1863–1900), *30*, 183.

28. Cited by Walter E. Buszin, "Luther on Music," *The Musical Quarterly*, *32* (1946), 81.

strating Zwingli's musical humanism—for the story was a standard one in the humanist *laus musicae* [29]—actually demonstrates that music is for him a thoroughly secular art and one, moreover, that is essentially an aspect of man's private life. It is for personal rejuvenation, for private recreation, or for quieting one's children. But no more. Yet as in his earlier letter to Heinrich Utinger, there is no hint here that Zwingli is in any wise moved to relinquish his personal musical life. Here again it is simply that the value of music is rigidly restricted to the secular realm of recreation for family and friends within the home. Hence he may truly say, "I disturb no one with my music." Possibly no other document discloses so tellingly the decision which he had reached on the role that music was to play in his own life and in that of his congregation.

Since Zwingli's private musical activity continued unabated, one may more readily understand why Bullinger reports that his opponents railed at him for being "a player of lutes and an evangelical piper," [30] or why Myconius furiously complains that "music was turned against him by his enemies as a vice as though it were a minister of pleasures rather than an aid to his studies." [31] Such barbs notwithstanding, Zwingli continued to sing and play in his home to the end of his life. Hence a pamphleteer like Thomas Murner of Strassburg was able to deride him as a "fiddler of the Holy Gospel and a lute-player of the Old and New Testament," [32] while Hans Salat, a contemporary Catholic chronicler of the Reformation, jeeringly wrote that he was "practiced in all puerilities and frivolities, taught drum-beating, piping, playing the lute, the harp and was a complete musical pedant." [33] Even his beloved friend and co-worker in the reformation of the city, Leo Jud, was subjected to similar vitriolic attacks because, among other things, as Bullinger said, "he was devoted to music." [34]

Despite such abuse, not once did Zwingli display the least animus to the art itself or toward its practitioners. His relationship with the professional organist Johannes Vogler, whom he had known for some time, is a case in

29. See, for example, James Hutton, "Some English Poems in Praise of Music," *English Miscellany,* ed. Mario Praz, 2 (Rome, 1951), esp. 8–9.

30. Bullinger, *1,* 31.

31. Myconius, *Vita Huldrici Zwinglii,* p. 4.

32. Wyss, *Chronik,* p. 5.

33. Cited in *Die Vokalmusik,* p. 44.

34. *Die Vokalmusik,* p. 51. On Jud, in addition to the older biography by Carl Pestalozzi, "Leo Judä," in *Leben und ausgewählte Schriften der Väter und Begründer der reformirten Kirche,* 9 (Elberfeld, 1961), see Leo Weisz, *Leo Jud. Ulrich Zwinglis Kampfgenosse, 1482–1542* (Zurich, 1942), and P. Schmid, *Leo Jud, Meister Leu* (Zurich, 1942).

point. Vogler had been a colleague of Fridolin Sicher, the leading organist of St. Gall, since 1523.[35] When Vogler left in 1528 for Zurich, it was certainly with Zwingli's permission and possibly even at his direct request. Once arrived, Vogler proceeded, again with Zwingli's encouragement, to establish a school of music in what formerly had been the Franciscan cloister. And that Zwingli did indeed regard him highly is indicated by his invitation to the scholarly organist to take his meals with him during his stay in the city.[36] Thus toward the close of his life the Reformer's small circle of intimate friends included at least one professional musician and teacher, as well as the ardent amateur Leo Jud. Nor in these last years did Zwingli cease to compose.

THE CAPPEL SONG: 1529

Early in 1529 the tensions between the five Forest cantons and the Reformed cantons exploded. The former, who had remained steadfastly Catholic, joined themselves in an alliance to Ferdinand of Austria, with the open intention of eradicating Zwinglianism from the Reformed cantons. Zurich, as leader of the latter body, and at Zwingli's express insistence, declared war on the Catholics on June 8, 1529. The opposing forces actually met at the town of Cappel, but battle between them was never joined, because two days later, on June 10, the Forest cantons opened negotiations for a peace to which the Reformed cantons agreed with alacrity.

Zwingli was bitterly opposed to this move. He perceived the potentially fatal inadequacies of the proposed treaty and was dismayed at the indifference shown his point of view by his allies, Bern in particular. He stood virtually alone in this critical situation, fatigue and despair adding their pressures to his terrible sense of isolation. In the midst of acute melancholy and strain, the Reformer turned again to God, with a rare intensity matched in force perhaps only by that disclosed in the Plague Song. And just as in 1520 the profundity and magnitude of his response to God could be expressed only in a union of poetry and music, so he must again use these means to formulate the great depths of his piety and his absolute reliance on God. Thus he wrote the moving poem below, imploring God's blessing for a happy outcome to the establishment everywhere of true Christianity.

---

35. On Vogler see the article in Edgar Refardt, *Historisch-biographisch Musikerlexicon der Schweiz* (Zurich, 1928), pp. 321–22.
36. *Die Vokalmusik*, p. 50.

O Lord, unless Thou take the rein,
The chariot sinks and doomed are we,
While foes make mockery of our pain,
In swaggering pride that fears not Thee.

Show forth Thy glory in our land:
Confound the vaunting troops of hell:
Renew our souls, that we may stand
Thy faithful flock who love Thee well.

O help us, till the strife be o'er;
O let all bitterness depart;
The old-time faithfulness restore,
And praise shall rise from every heart.[37]

He composed a polyphonic setting for four voices to accompany the stanzas. Of course, the Cappel Song was never intended for use *in church*. In those moments when he was wound to an almost insupportably high pitch, Zwingli expressed himself best through a union of poetry and music, essentially a personal articulation of his extraordinarily intense piety.

The Cappel Song, or Hymn, as eventually it came to be called, is a battle hymn, and as such, unlike the Plague Song, falls within a venerable extra-liturgical musical tradition. "During the Middle Ages in Europe the battle song was a spiritual song."[38] The Swiss were conspicuously famous for their singing of such hymns. Immediately before the Battle of Sempach in 1386, to cite but one example, it was reported that "the pious confederates invoked God in heaven," and so impressive was the hymn they sang that allusion was made to it almost with reverence in a polemical Catholic song as late as 1619.[39] By the sixteenth century, however, the traditional spiritual hymns apparently had given way to a new kind of song, either simply political or crudely defiant in nature, such as that hurled against the French by the Swiss mercenaries just before the Battle of Novara in 1513.[40] As a field chaplain in that memorable campaign, Zwingli must have heard the song.

37. *S*, 2², 275–76. The translation is by John Thomas McNeill in *The History and Character of Calvinism* (New York, 1954), pp. 48–49.
38. Hanns in der Gand (pseudonym for L. Krupocki), "Zum schweizerischen Kriegs- und Soldatenlied," Sonderabdruck aus der *Schweizerischen Monatschrift für Offiziere aller Waffen* (1928), p. 3.
39. Ibid., p. 2, n. 4.
40. Ibid., pp. 5, 11.

He was aware of music's power to raise spirits high in such taut circumstances; indeed, in a quite detailed campaign sketch he drew up in 1524 he was at pains to include musical directions for the trumpeters (*3, 577, 3–25*). But doubtless he was also aware that the battle songs of the Swiss had been originally spiritual. Zwingli's Cappel Song therefore not only belongs to a well-defined extraliturgical tradition; it is also, in its content, a reversion to the earlier, religious aspect of that tradition.

Bullinger records that as Zwingli "made the *modos* or the melody of his first song which he wrote on the Pestilence before this in 1519, he thus made and composed this little song in four voices. After that this song was played and sung by musicians far and wide, even at the courts of princes and in cities."[41] The hymn was therefore given wide and enthusiastic dissemination not as music designed for the church but rather as a composition for the delight of professional musicians, and suitable for performance in quite secular establishments. That Zwingli did not intend an exclusively spiritual use for it is demonstrated by the fact that even during his lifetime the melody of the hymn was put to purely secular uses. In 1530 Petrus Dasypodius used it in one of the polyphonic choruses to be sung by children between the acts of a school play performed at Frauenfeld.[42] Zwingli knew Dasypodius; the appropriation scarcely could have taken place without the former's knowledge and approval. Thus the nonliturgical Cappel Song is not even exclusively religious, a fact of great significance, as will be shown, in a final assessment not only of Zwingli's understanding of music but also of his influence on the musical history of reformed Zurich.

THE MUSIC FOR THE "PLUTOS": 1531

Zwingli had begun to learn Greek in 1513 while a pastor at Glarus, and had continued to study and read it throughout his life. He had acquired it wholly by himself, moreover, since at the beginning of the sixteenth century

41. Bullinger, 2, 182. Zwingli's original polyphonic composition is lost; cf. the most recent discussion of the problem of the music and its transmission in Markus Jenny, "Zwinglis mehrstimmige Kompositionen," *Zwingliana, 11* (1960), 165–67, and two versions of the music itself, pp. 180–82. Zwingli also set the poem to the melody of a well-known contemporary love song; cf. Söhngen, *Leiturgia,* p. 24. By 1536 it had appeared as an hymn in the Constance Hymnal, published by Froschauer in Zurich.

42. *Die Vokalmusik,* pp. 48 and 68. On Dasypodius, see G. Büeler, *Petrus Dasypodius (Peter Hasenfratz): Ein Frauenfelder Humanist des 16. Jahrhunderts* (Frauenfeld, 1920), and the article in Edgar Refardt, *Historisch-biographisch Musikerlexicon der Schweiz* (Zurich, 1928), p. 57.

Greek studies in Switzerland were barely in their infancy. Zwingli was the first to initiate the study of Greek in school at Zurich, and only after his example did other Swiss cities take up the official teaching of the language, Basel and Schaffhausen in the 1530s and Bern in 1548, through a master who had been trained in Zurich. Thus a cultural event of the first importance for Switzerland was the presentation at Zurich on January 1, 1531, of Aristophanes' "Plutos" in the original Greek.[43]

School performances in Latin of the plays of Plautus and Terence were by no means infrequent in the sixteenth century; they were an integral part of that deep-seated drive to revive the artistic experience of antiquity which, for instance, had motivated Celtis' music for the Horatian Odes.[44] Luther himself thought such classical performances pedagogically essential in order "that the boys could practice Latin speech." [45] But to present a Greek comedy, in Greek, was almost unheard of, so much so that the production that Zwingli sponsored, and may even have planned, is one of the very first recorded.

With the exception of one student, the cast was comprised wholly of older men, some of them distinguished citizens of Zurich, such as Rudolph Colin, Zwingli's ambassador to Venice in 1529, and Georg Binder, the first translator of Zwingli's Latin works into German and director of the production. The text for the play was a Florentine edition of nine comedies of Aristophanes which Colin had brought back from Venice, and it is he who records in the book in his own handwriting the fact that the "Plutos was produced on 1. January in Zurich in the reading room or stove room of the canons." The whole enterprise seems to have been undertaken partly to demonstrate the effects of the new humanistic education, and partly from sheer civic pride, a motive made patently and delightfully clear by portions of Georg Binder's Prologue:

> Athens is dumb, silent is Greece,
> Yet Zurich stands; here lingers Attica's Muse,
> All things are changed by time. Once Hellas shone

43. Arnold Hug, *Aufführung einer griechischen Komödie in Zürich am 1. Januar 1531* (Zurich, 1874), is the only monograph on the subject. For additional material on the cast see "Ein griechisches Schauspiel an Zwinglis Schule," *Zwingliana, 1* (1897), 11–13; cf. *Die Vokalmusik,* pp. 48–49.

44. Indeed, the following revealing gloss is to be found on the margin of the text of the Prologue: *"O eia, eia, mala, o eia, die zwilchinen chorherren zů Wien in Oesterrich singend ouch also";* Hannes Reimann, "Huldrych Zwingli—der Musiker," *Archiv für Musikwissenschaft, 17* (1960), 128, n. 1.

45. Hug, *Aufführung,* p. 8.

When Zurich's folk were raw, barbarous the land.
Yet now this folk has built an Attic theatre.
Therefore I present a new Greek proverb to you:
Worthless are the other cities around Zurich.[46]

What is most fascinating is that Zwingli composed the music for the production. *Modos fecit Huldrychus Zwinglius Doggius*[47] is written in his own edition of the play, possibly even in his own handwriting. The music, regrettably, is lost; the nature and extent of what Zwingli wrote is thus not known, but *"modos fecit* can mean nothing else than that he composed a musical accompaniment (probably for the chorus) and certainly an overture."[48] It is the last music on a large scale which Zwingli wrote before he died in battle on October 11, 1531.[49]

ZWINGLI THE MUSICIAN

The two problems discussed—What, first of all, was the essential nature of Zwingli's attitude toward music? and, secondly, How did he reconcile his uncompromisingly divergent attitudes toward the role of music in Christian life, and the role of music in Christian worship?—require still further comment.

J. T. McNeill has proposed that "Zwingli yet probably regarded music less seriously than did Luther who considered it a divine gift for the comfort of souls."[50] Obviously, the imputation of a lack of seriousness is not valid when one recalls Zwingli's entry into the monastery at Bern to study music. On the other hand, when one recalls Zwingli's reply to Canon Utinger in 1518 or his reply to Faber in 1526, one becomes aware that he did take music as seriously as Luther, but for reasons significantly different, if not diametrically opposite. Before 1516 Zwingli had been a humanist, and, it is true, a theologian, but the inner stress of his training and his affections lay with the humanism of the liberal arts. Thus music could rightfully be given emphasis in his thoughts and emotions. But after the dividing year 1516, the emphasis

46. Ibid., p. 23. Jenny, "Zwingli's mehrstimmige Kompositionen," p. 174, n. 31, correctly points to the fact that there is no evidence that Zwingli himself intoned the Prologue.
47. Doggius, i.e. der Toggenburger, from the name of the Duchy where Zwingli was born.
48. Hug, *Aufführung,* p. 35.
49. That he continued to compose for his friends as well as for himself is disclosed by Wolfgang Capito's request late in 1530 for some music by him: Z, *11,* 163, 7–9 and n. 12; cf. Z, *11,* 316, 13–14 and n. 17.
50. John Thomas McNeill, *The History and Character of Calvinism,* p. 21.

in Zwingli's inner life radically changed. The theologian and the new evangelist assumed an ever greater significance. The self-conscious humanist bent of Zwingli's mind was correspondingly altered and restricted. And with that alteration and restriction music was forced to the edge of the pattern not alone of Zwingli's thought but of his emotional life as well. It is now, in fact, a separate, autonomous activity, divorced from his study and experience of the Word.

In his commentary on Isaiah 5:12 Zwingli explained that "the divine prophet treats of an unrestrained and extravagant joy, in which certain people are not satisfied by becoming exhilarated with wine unless, in order to increase their madness, they abuse music itself, which was given to man to moderate and soothe savage passions, not to stimulate them more and more when aroused" (*14*, 163, 23–27). Here Zwingli reveals again that appreciation of the incalculable psychological effects of music which had so powerfully influenced his decision to eliminate music from worship. But the remainder of the passage attests eloquently to the radical difference between Luther and Calvin, on the one hand, and Zwingli, on the other, with respect to the nature of the power of music:

> The *ratio* of no other discipline is so profoundly rooted and innate in the souls of all men as that of music. For no men are so stupid that they are not captivated by it, even though they are entirely ignorant of its technique. There are none, on the other hand, who are not offended by the confusion and discord of voices, even those who cannot explain what is dissonant and what is unsuitable. So powerful is the native talent of everyone to judge what is harmonious; on the other hand, in judging *ratio* and technique, such native talent is the property of the very few.
> [*14*, 163, 27–31; 164, 1–4]

A capacity to react at once, favorably or otherwise, to sheer sound is for Zwingli an ineradicable aspect of human nature. Music alone can induce in man such an instantaneous reaction, and for that reason it is unique; but that uniqueness is interpreted wholly as a psychological or physical phenomenon. And even in so brief a passage as this it must be noted that he cannot refrain from pointedly contrasting an instinctive, uneducated reaction to sounds, pleasant or unpleasant, with an educated and disciplined perception of music as an art. Zwingli, in other words, writes, as he did to Utinger and Faber, as a musician, not as a theologian. He could not accord, even to his beloved music, the divine dimension with which Luther, and to a lesser degree, Calvin, had invested it. Music for him was a secular activity. Yet it is precisely because he persisted in his devotion to it as a secular means of relaxation, recreation, or personal expression that he may be said to have regarded music fully as seriously as Luther. Although the theologian and the musician are separated, the musician to the end clings intently to his art, and in this respect Zwingli is truly *musicae pertinax amator.*

In 1523 Zwingli wrote *Of the Education of Youth,* and toward its close he says: "I advise the young man not to despise mathematics (with which we may also reckon music), but he ought not to devote too much time to the subject. It is useful to those who know it and an obstacle to those who do not." [51] Written in the same year as the *Interpretation and Substantiation of the Conclusions,* those two sentences illustrate movingly the impact of the Word upon Zwingli's attitude toward music. Although the art can no longer be pressed into the service of either theology or the church, Zwingli cannot bring himself to exclude entirely what he so much loved from an ideal course of study. As an autonomous discipline it is useful, certainly, to those who have both its *ratio* and its technique, as did Zwingli. But precisely because its *ratio* is "so profoundly rooted and innate in the souls of all men," Zwingli feels compelled to warn them against it, because its technique is so difficult to acquire. In that it is without relationship to the Word, it is secular; its acquisition must thus forever be secondary to acquisition of the Word. To all those who must first know the Word, the longing for knowledge and control of music can be only an obstacle. The trumpets of the new song have sounded clearly above the lute; the triumph of the Word is complete.

51. The translation is that by G. W. Bromily, *Zwingli and Bullinger,* Library of Christian Classics, 24 (Philadelphia, 1953), 112.

4. HERALD OF THE WORD

Imagine how I felt, now, when I stepped
In churches into whose interiors
Music fell from heaven: whose walls and ceilings
Overflowed with multitudinous forms.
The heavenliest and the highest, actual here,
Locked in a frozen dance before my eyes.

Schiller

"There is no one who is a greater admirer of paintings, statues, and images than I," Zwingli once remarked (*3*, 906, 1–2). On another occasion he confessed: "I derive more pleasure than other men from beautiful pictures and statues" (*4*, 84, 25–26).[1] There is no other significant evidence that he loved painting and sculpture nearly so much as he did music. For this disparity of interest two reasons at least may be suggested.

First of all, after a predominantly musical early environment, the serious study of music had been an integral part of his formal education for twenty-two years. Whereas for centuries music had enjoyed a well-defined, indeed an essential role in the philosophical and educational structure of medieval thought,[2] the visual arts held no such long-established or prominent place in

1. These neutral statements can scarcely be interpreted as evidence of Zwingli's "neues, humanistisches Kulturbewusstsein," as argued by Hans Freiherr von Campenhausen, "Zwingli und Luther zur Bilderfrage," *Das Gottesbild im Abendland* (Witten and Berlin, 1959), p. 143. Cf., for example, Zwingli's contemptuous opinion of representations of Christ, Z, *4*, 121, 14–15.

2. Cf. Manfred F. Bukofzer, "Speculative Thinking in Mediaeval Music," *Speculum, 17* (1942), 165–80; and Leo Spitzer, *Classical and Christian Ideas of World Harmony: Prolegomena to an Interpretation of the Word "Stimmung"*, ed. Anna Granville Hatcher, Johns Hopkins Press, 1963, passim.

the seven liberal arts; in fact, they were not yet a part of the official curriculum of school or university. But so far as can be ascertained, Zwingli never acquired even a minimal acquaintance with them, whereas his study of music was a life-long concern. Secondly, Zwingli's lack of interest in the visual arts may be attributed in some degree to his nearsightedness, a condition to which he confessed when he was writing his last and most extensive treatise on the question of religious art. In the introduction to that work he admitted that "images are able to delight me less since I cannot see them well" (4, 84, 24–25).[3] Thus his personal experience of the visual arts differed in at least these two respects, educational and physical, from his personal experience of music.

The difference in Zwingli's attitude to the two arts is expressed also in the difference between his approach to the role of music and to that of the visual arts in worship. Whereas with the former his views were decisively set forth in the summer months of 1523, with the latter they were formulated slowly and cautiously, even with some hesitation. His decisive statement on the relationship between the visual arts and worship did not appear until April 1525. In marked contrast to the articles on the relationship between prayer and music in the *Interpretation and Substantiation of the Conclusions,* that statement was the final result of two years of grappling with a problem the awareness of which had been initially forced on him by a sequence of events within Zurich for which he was quite unprepared.

Since, for purposes of analysis, Zwingli's attitude toward painting and sculpture must be differentiated from that toward music, even though both derive from common grounds, the following chapters endeavor to trace the gradual development of his understanding of the relationship between the visual arts and Christianity and to describe the artistic and social context which compelled him to formulate that relationship systematically.

ZURICH: ART AND POLITICS, 1475–1519

At the time of Zwingli's arrival in Zurich in 1518 the city was caught up in a fever of activity in the visual arts without precedent since the thirteenth century. As a result of the Swiss defeat of the Burgundian armies at Morat in June 1476, all the cantons had been caught up in a tide of exultation and excitement from which Zurich was by no means exempted. The city was

---

3. Cf. Georg Finsler, "Zwinglis Kurzsichtigkeit," *Zwingliana, 3* (1913–20), 87–89.

singularly fortunate at this crucial juncture in its artistic history in having as its burgomaster Hans Waldmann (1435-89).[4] Indeed, with his election to office in 1483, Zurich entered upon a major phase of artistic and architectural activity which was in no small measure owing to the extraordinary personality of this great man.[5]

Hans Waldmann was ruthlessly ambitious, not only for himself but for the city of Zurich. Allusion has already been made to his interest in music and his donation in 1479 of an organ to the Fraumünster, of which he was patron. Not content merely to be the patron of an already existing church, however, he determined to build a new one on the site of a long deserted church at the foot of the hill on which the Great Minster stood. On July 12, 1479, he was given papal permission,[6] and almost at once construction was begun. Just six years later the Water Church, as it was called, was completed; the organ was installed in 1485, and the ceremonies of consecration celebrated on May 5, 1486.[7] This delicate Gothic structure was not built solely for religious purposes: it was also to function as a festival hall in which the city's war trophies and captured banners could be displayed.[8] Thus the church was designed as a monument to Waldmann and to the political and military greatness of Zurich.

As if the Water Church was still not enough, in 1487 Waldmann added to it a tiny Gothic tower with a gilded spire. Once this had been accomplished, his eyes probably traveled to the top of the hill, to the massive bulk of the Great Minster with its two squat Romanesque towers. At that time they were unequal in size, for the north tower which housed the bells was taller than

---

4. On Waldmann see Ernst Gagliardi, *Hans Waldmann und die Eidgenossenschaft des 15 Jahrhunderts*, Basel, 1912. For the history of the city under Waldmann and the ensuing years 1490-1519 consult Karl Dändliker, *Geschichte des Stadt und des Kantons Zürich*, 2 (Zurich, 1910), 159-234 aand 234-82. Cf. Farner, *3*, 1-25. For the artistic history of the same period see the detailed study by Walter Hugelshofer, "Die Zürcher Malerei bis zum Ausgang der Spätgotik," *1*, in *Mitteilugen der Antiquarischen Gesellschaft in Zürich, 30* (1928), Part IV, and the excellent survey in Richard Zürcher, *Die künstlerische Kultur im Kanton Zürich: Ein geschichtliche Überblick* (Zurich, 1943), pp. 39-76, appropriately entitled "Die Zeiten Waldmanns und Zwinglis."

5. Zürcher, *Die künstlerische Kultur*, p. 40; cf. Hugelshofer, *Die Zürcher Malerei, 1*, 22; for Waldmann "art was only a means toward the display of his power and wealth."

6. Arnold Nüscheler, *Die Gotteshäuser der Schweiz, Historisch-antiquarische Forschungen, 3* (Zurich, 1873), 421.

7. Ibid. Cf. Konrad Escher, *Die Stadt Zürich, 1*, Die Kunstdenkmäler des Kantons Zürich, 4 (Basel, 1939), 301-2.

8. Zürcher, *Die künstlerische Kultur*, p. 46.

the south. Mindful of the spires of the French cathedrals he had seen on his journey to the court of Louis XI in 1477, not to speak of those closer to home crowning the Minsters in Basel, Bern, Freiburg, and Constance, he evidently determined that Zurich, too, should have them. He therefore asked the Council to raise the south tower to a height equal to that of the north, and to erect Gothic spires on both. To begin the financing of the project, he offered 200 gulden from his personal fortune. The Council agreed with alacrity: the wood for the spires was apparently cut in that very year 1487, and the raising of the spire on the bell tower was begun in 1488. Four years later the work was entirely finished. Both towers were now equal in height, and from each rose a tapered spire, overlaid with ornate lead tracery and brilliantly painted in the Zurich colors.[9] When Zwingli came up the lake of Zurich from Einsiedeln to the city thirty years later, he would have seen before anything else the soaring blue and white spires of the Great Minster.

Waldmann was brutally and illegally executed on April 6, 1489, but despite the absence of his driving, physical presence, the artistic energies he had encouraged continued. After two hundred years of internal and external crises in which artistic activity within the city had been negligible, the last two decades of the fifteenth century and the opening ones of the sixteenth saw not only painting and sculpture but also work in wood-carving, glass-painting, and the manufacture of jewelry and plate in precious metals undertaken on a scale which was for Zurich, as far as is known, unparalleled. Money was pouring into the city, partly from its extensive new commercial activities but even more so from the huge pensions and subsidies of foreign powers to its mercenaries. Its citizens of all classes became increasingly ostentatious. They spent recklessly on clothing and jewelry, so much so that in November 1488 Waldmann felt compelled to legislate against this conspicuous consumption.[10] Considerable sums of money, however, went also toward the construction and improvement of buildings. The old Corn House, for instance, built in 1420, was replaced by an entirely new building between 1497 and 1498, and dwelling chambers for the Abbess of the Fraumünster

---

9. On the erection of the towers see Konrad Escher, *Die beiden Zürcher Münster* (Frauenfeld and Leipzig, 1928), pp. 50–52, and the exhaustively detailed account by Hans Hoffmann, "Baugeschichte bis zur Reformation," in *Das Grossmünster in Zürich, Mitteilungen der Antiquarischen Gesellschaft in Zürich, 32*, Part III (Zurich, 1941), pp. 185–93 and plates 56–61.

10. Cf. Karl Dändliker, *Geschichte des Stadt und des Kantons Zürich, 2* (Zurich, 1910), 189. For the text of the great *Sittenmandat* see W. Oechsli, *Quellenbuch zur Schweizer Geschichte, 1* (Zurich, 1893), 209–11.

were built between the Limmat and the courtyard of the church.[11] Some of the guilds within the city now undertook to erect their public houses, and many of the old wooden buildings, both public and private, were rebuilt in stone.[12] The wealthy townspeople demanded sumptuously decorated interiors for their homes as well as for their Guildhouses; walls and ceilings were richly painted and carved; the furniture and the appointments of the table were ever more lavish. For all these houses, numerous elaborately designed and painted windows were required; they gave rise in this period to the great quantity as well as the genuinely high quality of the work of the Zurich glass painters. And just as these buildings and their fittings were wholly secular in character and purpose, so too the pictorial content of their windows tended in a markedly increasing direction away from religious matter toward scenes from classical mythology and local, general, and, particularly, military history, including the frequent display within ornate settings of heraldic designs and family coats-of-arms. Even the Church succumbed to this worldly luxury, as may be seen from the ornate reception-room for the Fraumünster Abbey installed by the last Abbess, Katherina von Zimmern, in 1507.[13]

ECCLESIASTICAL ART

The outright worldliness of this secular art was paralleled by significant developments in the ecclesiastical art of the city. In terms of the monumental works of painting, architecture, and sculpture being produced in Italy, the Netherlands, and Germany—and even by comparison with what was being done in nearby Bern or Basel—Zurich was emphatically provincial, if not backward. Not until well after the middle of the fifteenth century did its artists break with the idealistic-international style of the fourteenth century, and even then that portion of the major painting from 1450 on which is preserved displays throughout a marked South-German influence.[14] Despite the fever of artistic activity, a style indigenous to Zurich did not exist; it possessed no school of its own. The creative atmosphere of the city may perhaps

11. Escher, *Die beiden Zürcher Münster*, p. 47.
12. Farner, *3, 3.*
13. Zürcher, *Die künstlerische Kultur*, p. 52.
14. Any accurate assessment of the visual arts in pre-Reformation Zurich is difficult, because so much was destroyed by Protestant iconoclasm; not a single statue has survived, for example. Nothing whatsoever is known of Zurich sculpture, and scarcely a tenth of the pre-Reformation painting has been preserved. Cf. Hugelshofer, *Die Zürcher Malerei, 1,* 20–21.

best be gauged from the suggestion that when the so-called Master of the Carnation came from Southern Germany to work in Zurich, his painting slowly lost much of its once high quality.[15]

The turn of the century brought with it new elements to ecclesiastical painting within the city, to be seen particularly in the work of the Master of the Violet. In his large panel of Saint John the Baptist and Saint Barbara, painted around 1506, a decisively new understanding of the human form is displayed. The artist's saints are no longer abstract, stylized figures but a man and a woman, two human beings of flesh and blood who clearly belong to this world. The artist has also eschewed the abstraction of the traditional gold background. The Master of the Carnation had begun to move in this realistic direction in some few of his altar panels, but the rocks and trees of his landscapes were rigidly schematized in late Gothic fashion and the whole was still set against the conventional gold ground. By comparison, the Master of the Violet endeavored in his landscape to render rocks, trees, plants, hills, and streams in completely natural fashion; and a blue sky stretches everywhere above and behind the figures and the panorama of the landscape: no trace of the gold ground survives. The artist depicted this world, and the saints became human beings in it.[16]

This obvious interest and delight in the natural world, so new to the art of Zurich, finds equally articulate expression in the panels which Hans Leu the Elder (ca. 1465–ca. 1507) [17] executed for the Chapel of the Twelve Apostles in the Great Minster. The landscapes of the Master of the Violet or the Master of the Bremgarten Altar had not been "real" in the sense that they were representations of actual sites. Their individual elements were closely drawn from nature, to be sure, but the finished scene was simply a composite of these several elements. Leu, however, commissioned to depict Christ together with the city's patron saints for the chapel, decided to paint behind them extensive panoramas of Zurich as it actually looked in the closing years of the fifteenth century. Stylistically, it is still in many respects late Gothic. On the other hand, in its insistence upon a description as exact and as detailed as possible, not of a city in general but of the churches, houses, and streets, and the natural setting of Zurich, Leu discloses a powerful impulse

15. Zürcher, *Die künstlerische Kultur,* p. 61. For a more detailed discussion of the extant work of the *Nelkenmeister* see Hugelshofer, *Die Zürcher Malerei, 1,* 30–33.

16. Cf. Zürcher, *Die künstlerische Kultur,* pp. 62–67, esp. p. 64; and Hugelshofer, *Die Zürcher Malerei 1,* 35.

17. On the elder Leu see Paul Ganz, "Die Familie des Malers Hans Leu von Zürich," *Zürcher Taschenbuch* (Zurich, 1901), pp. 156–61.

toward the new empirical spirit of the Northern Renaissance. The topographic interest of his work admittedly outweighs its artistic merit, but therein lies its significance. The panoramas of the city are statements of fact. Against them Leu placed the figures of Christ and the saints, but with no attempt at an artistic or spiritual integration of the two: the image of the city is one thing; the religious images are another. The discontinuity between the two goes to the heart of a growing tendency in the ecclesiastical art of the city after 1500. The official intent of much painting was still sacred. Artists were still commissioned to depict scenes from the life of Christ and the saints. Yet increasingly their interest lay in what might be called the non-sacred aspects of their work—that is to say, in the background where the sacred figures were to appear. Nature, the world of fact with its variegated and endlessly intriguing phenomena, lured their attention more and more; it was to be studied for its own sake. The landscape was to be realized first; afterward the religious figures could be set against it.[18] Just as south of the Alps the great Christian themes were being used by artists like Mantegna "as fitting occasions for the reproduction of the Antique world," [19] north of the Alps, in Zurich, they were being used by anonymous masters as vehicles for the reproduction of the natural world.

Side by side with the art demanded by the townspeople, which was openly secular, there was emerging within the art commissioned for the Church an ever stronger impulse toward a realism and an absorption in nature that was potentially secular. The corporate patronage of the Church, too, had found a competitor in the patronage of individual laymen, so that there were now two sources for commissions. As a result, the city housed masters from Colmar, Augsburg, Ulm, Nuremberg, Würzburg, and Heidelberg. From 1475 to 1523 no fewer than fifty such masters are known to have been active in Zurich.[20] On the other hand, little creative originality can be attributed to the city's native masters.[21] They were evidently not so much artists as

18. Cf. W. Wartmann, "Tafelbilder des XV. und XVI. Jahrhunderts," *Zürcher Kunstgesellschaft Neujahrsblatt* (Zurich, 1922), p. 38.

19. Bernard Berenson, *Italian Painters of the Renaissance* (New York, 1952), p. 148.

20. Hugelshofer, *Die Zürcher Malerei, 1,* 20.

21. The *Nelkenmeister,* for example, definitely came from South Germany; one of the finest surviving pre-Reformation wall paintings, the Votive Tablet that Waldmann commissioned for the Fraumünster, was the work of a foreign artist; the "most significant master in Old Zürich," the painter of the fresco cycles in the crypt of the Great Minster, came probably from the art circle of Constance; it is doubtful even that the *Veilchenmeister* was a native artist, although he was active for many years in Zurich; and South German masters such as Henry of Erfurt and Hans of Heidelberg were responsible for much of the renovation of the interior

artisans, producing works "without the impulse to greatness, without high intentions." Zwingli had come to a city which, in artistic respects, was fundamentally "without its own will to expression." [22]

ART AND THE CHURCH, 1475-1519

The impetus for much of the art produced, far from being one of "high intentions," was ostentation and a craving for personal luxury on the part of wealthy citizens. An impetus fully as powerful and fully as productive for the visual arts was the extraordinary complex of religious emotions which swept over Northern Europe at the turn of the century.

A fear of the end of the world and of the Last Judgment, never absent from the emotional life of the Middle Ages, suddenly and inexplicably became more personal and more awesome than ever before.[23] This pervasive dread was further aggravated by rumors of portents of all sorts which spelled the coming either of Anti-Christ or the End. Northern Europe seethed with tales of sudden appearances of miraculous signs, especially of ones relating to Christ's Passion. Nature herself seemed to threaten that the last days had come. A huge meteor, reported to have fallen at Ensisheim in Alsace in 1492, for example, was the subject of a terrifying broadsheet by Sebastian Brant, who concluded it by addressing the Emperor Maximilian with the minatory words: "Notice the stone was sent to thee; God warns thee in thine own country." [24]

Encompassed by such admonitions, natural and supernatural, the salvation of his soul became the goal of every individual. Under these apocalyptic pressures what had been a routine concern for the average Christian was transformed into a mounting fear of eternal damnation. Guarantees of salvation were sought on all sides, in all ways. Nevertheless, the Church could not extend to the people the comfort of complete assurance. Penance, obedience, and at best a relative certainty could be its only answer. As a result, the sac-

---

of the Fraumünster (1469-70) as well as much of the work on the towers of the Great Minster; cf. Hugelshofer, *Die Zürcher Malerei, 1*, 23, 28-29, 35, and Escher, *Die beiden Zürcher Münster* p. 46.

22. Both quotations from Hugelshofer, *Die Zürcher Malerei, 1*, 22.

23. Cf. Willy Andreas, *Deutschland vor der Reformation: Eine Zeitenwende* (Stuttgart-Berlin, 1932), p. 189; cf. pp. 146-83 and 189-98 for a survey of significant aspects of popular piety during the period.

24. Cited by Fritz Saxl, "Illustrated Pamphlets of the Reformation," *Lectures* (London, 1957), *1*, 258; *2*, plate 177. Cf. esp. Brant's despondent letter of 1504 to Peutinger, *Konrad Peutingers Briefwechsel*, ed. Erich Konig (Munich, 1923), No. 18, pp. 34-35.

rament of penance assumed even greater importance, together with indulgences and good works. But no one could be certain that he had done enough
in terms of any one of the three, for each was in itself relative. Every act of
penance accomplished, every indulgence obtained, every good work performed clearly could be excelled by another. The people's recourse to these
visible, tangible acts which might contribute in some way, no matter how
small, to their ultimate salvation led them to the execution of good works of
every conceivable variety. It induced them to search out and venerate relics
as never before. It drove them on pilgrimages everywhere in larger and
larger numbers: 142,000 faithful, to cite one instance, made the journey to
Aachen in the year 1496 to see the four "Great Relics" in the Cathedral.[25]
And the Church, far from trying to calm this frenzy of ceremonial piety,
encouraged it, allowing free rein to the common people's desire to increase
the number of saints and the fiercely competitive acquisition of relics by
princes and cities, while attaching to the saints, their relics, and the shrines to
which such pilgrimages were made more numerous and more extravagant
indulgences. The institution and the people were locked in a desperate tension which apparently could wind itself only to higher and yet higher pitch.

Zurich was caught up completely in the visible manifestations of this
tension. Even the city itself had become a goal for pilgrims. In the Middle
Ages the most rewarding pilgrimage the faithful could undertake was the
one to Rome, for there, owing to the indulgences attached to the seven great
churches of the city, they could obtain more spiritual benefits than in any
other single place in Christendom. But in 1480, by a special dispensation
from Sixtus IV, Zurich acquired privileges identical with those of Rome. If
the pilgrim attended the city's seven churches, namely the two Minsters,
Saint Peter's, the Water Church, and the cloister churches of the three
orders, he would derive from the journey to Zurich as much spiritual profit
as from traveling to Rome.[26]

The Zurichers, too, went on processions and pilgrimages. Annually within

25. The cathedral at Aachen had been the goal of pilgrimages as early as 950, pilgrimages
that increased greatly after the canonization of Charlemagne in 1165. The four "Great Relics"
(the swaddling clothes of the infant Jesus, the winding sheet of John the Baptist, a cloak
belonging to the Virgin Mary, and the loincloth worn by Christ on the Cross, on which His
blood was still visible) were housed in a magnificent reliquary and exhibited to pilgrims every
seven years, a practice dating from 1354 at least, if not earlier. See the comprehensive article
"Aix-la-Chapelle" by L. Boiteux in the *Dictionnaire d'histoire et de géographie Ecclésiastiques*
(Paris, 1912 ff.), esp. cols. 1258–62, and the extensive bibliography cited.

26. Farner, *3*, 20.

the city, on Palm Sunday and Whitsunday, the relics of Saints Felix and Regula were carried in state from the Great Minster across the Limmat to the Lindenhof and back again. There were frequent pilgrimages to the shrine of Saint Lioba on the Zurichberg or to Küsnacht on the lake of Zurich.[27] Once every year a huge pilgrimage was undertaken to the shrine of the Virgin Mary at Einsiedeln,[28] an event of such importance that every house in the city was required to send at least one person. And in ever-increasing numbers the faithful went to the new shrine of Saint Anne at Ober-Stammheim.

The fantastically rapid spread of the cult of Saint Anne after 1485 illustrates admirably the furor of piety that had gripped Northern Europe.[29] To venerate not only the mother but the grandmother of Jesus quickly became so popular that the humanist Jacob Wimpheling once wryly observed that "the blessed Anne seems almost to obscure the fame and glory of her daughter." [30] Statues, paintings, and chapels dedicated to her appeared everywhere. For some time a statue of Saint Anne had stood in the open air at Ober-Stammheim. In 1507 miracles were suddenly attributed to it. At once pilgrimages to the statue began, and either in 1508 or 1509 a chapel was built to house it, to which the Zurich city council presented a painted window. After 1510 the importance of the shrine grew with incredible rapidity; [31] in-

27. Farner, *3* 19-20; cf. Emil Egli, "Zürich am Vorabend der Reformation," *Zürcher Taschenbuch* (1896), pp. 158-59.

28. Einsiedeln is a monastery some few miles south of Zurich where since 948 there had been a chapel sacred to the Virgin Mary. According to legend it had been dedicated by the Angel of the Covenant (Christ Himself). Owing to this *Engelweihe*, to the statue of the Virgin in the chapel which was purported to be of miraculous origin, and to the fact that plenary indulgence had been granted to all those who journeyed there, Einsiedeln rapidly became the goal for an ever-increasing number of pilgrimages, until by the sixteenth century it was the principal shrine of South Germany and Switzerland; for a detailed history of the shrine see Odilo Ringholz, *Wallfahrtsgeschichte unserer Lieben Frau von Einsiedeln* (Freiburg im Breisgau, 1896), cf. also Z, *7, 120,* 1-2.

29. On the cult of Saint Anne see esp. the comprehensive monograph by Beda Kleinschmidt, *Die Heilige Anna, ihre Verehrung in Geschichte, Kunst und Volkstum* (Düsseldorf, 1930), and, most recently, Louis Reau, *Iconographie de l'art Chrétien* (Paris, 1958), *3,* 90-96. For the cult during the late Middle Ages cf. the brief survey in Willy Andreas, *Deutschland vor der Reformation: Eine Zeitenwende* (Stuttgart-Berlin, 1932), pp. 161-64, and the detailed monograph by Ernst Schaumkell, *Der Kultus der Heiligen Anna am Ausgange des Mittelalters: Ein Beitrag zur Geschichte des Religiösen Lebens am Vorabend der Reformation* (Leipzig, 1893).

30. Quoted in Beda Kleinschmidt, p. 138, n. 1.

31. See Alfred Farner, *Geschichte der Kirchgemeinde Stammheim und Umgebung* (Zurich, 1911), pp. 108-11, 135; cf. Z, *3,* 178, 9-16; Z, *4,* 102, 21-24.

deed, within a decade its fame had become such that a certain Hans Stockar of Schaffhausen, who had journeyed to the Holy Land and Compostela in 1519, did not disdain to make a special pilgrimage to the shrine of Saint Anne at Ober-Stammheim in 1520.

In addition to going on pilgrimages with almost hysterical zeal, the citizens of Zurich devoted themselves strenuously to the performance of good works, and it is precisely at this point that the Church exerted such enormous influence on the quantitative productivity of the artist. To create a work of art for the Church, whether it was a monumental painting or an altar vessel, a statue or a Mass garment, was one way, and obviously a distinctive way, of working toward one's salvation. This was true of both the artist personally and the layman who subsidized him. "The doctrine of good works had been one of the most powerful factors in the development of art," [32] in fact, and at no time more powerfully than in Northern Europe on the verge of the Reformation. Again Zurich was no exception. Waldmann's construction of the Water Church, for example, had provided the people with inspiration for the building of small churches in the communities immediately around the city, in such quantity that the phenomenon has aptly been described as "uncanny." [33] Beginning in 1487 with the new church at Pfäffkon, Zollikon and Veltheim each built one in 1498, Mettmenstetten in 1499, and Russikon and Wiesendangen in 1500. Between 1505 and 1516 eight more such village churches were erected, and another was begun at Dürnten in 1517. [34] Thus within a span of only three decades, in the Zurich area alone, fifteen new churches had been completed and one was under construction. Each required at least one altar, and each altar required works of art of all sorts. Before Waldmann built the Water Church, the city had seventy-three altars. In 1518 the total number in the Zurich area had risen to at least one hundred, so that in thirty-two years twenty-seven new altars had been dedicated. [35] A small number, to be sure, in comparison with the twenty-three erected in Nuremberg in 1490–91, [36] yet for a city the size of

32. Johannes Janssen, *History of the German People at the Close of the Middle Ages,* trans. A. M. Christie (London, 1907), *11,* 40; cf. Hartmann Grisar, *Luther* (London, 1916), *5,* 222; and Emil Egli, "Zürich am Vorabend der Reformation," *Zürcher Taschenbuch* (1896), pp 154–56.

33. Farner, *3,* 19.

34. Zürcher, *Die künstlerische Kultur,* pp. 48–51.

35. See Arnold Nüscheler, *Die Gotteshäuser der Schweiz, Historisch-antiquarische Forschungen, 3* (Zurich, 1873), 347–59, 368–71, 377–79, 399, 418–21, 455, and 460.

36. Hans Preuss, *Die deutsche Frömmigkeit im Spiegel der Bildenden Kunst: van ihren Anfängen bis zur Gegenwart dargestellt* (Berlin, 1926), p. 122.

Zurich it was considerable. But the desperate intensity of the need for salvation, served by commissioning works of art for the Church, may best be grasped by the fact that not a hundredth part of the paintings and statues that Zwingli would have seen in 1518 had been made in 1500.[37]

THE GREAT MINSTER

What Zwingli actually did see cannot be ascertained with any certainty except for the Great Minster, his parish church from 1518 until his death in 1531. He must have been familiar with its every detail.[38]

The initial construction of the building had been undertaken almost immediately after fire razed the old church in 1078, but only after 1230 were the massive Romanesque walls gradually raised to their present height. The high altar was dedicated in 1278, and two years later work on the early Gothic vaulting was begun. In five years it had been completed, so that with the exception of the towers, the austere exterior of Zwingli's church stood then in 1285 virtually as he was to see it over two centuries later. Its principal entrance lay through the Romanesque portal on the northern side, a low but wide doorway flanked by six slender columns and partially hidden by a double staircase leading to the choir loft, which had been built against the northern wall in the fifteenth century. On this side of the building also stood the chapter house, on the western wall of which had been either painted or carved a huge image of Saint Christopher, covered over with a roof.

Although no contemporary description of the interior exists, the extant building-records provide some idea of what must have confronted Zwingli once he had entered the Minster. The main portion was divided into a nave and a choir; the latter was subdivided in turn by a tall arch known as the "Passion Arch." The two pillars supporting it were decorated with paintings, and from its center depended a huge wooden cross. Behind the arch, at the easternmost end of the choir, stood the high or "Passion" altar, dedicated to Saints Felix and Regula, on which were placed two elevated reliquaries con-

37. Farner, *3*, 19; cf. Z, *4*, 123, 10–12; 126, 20–24.
38. The following reconstruction of the interior of the Great Minster is based on Escher, *Die beiden Zürcher Münster*, pp. 49–58; the extensively detailed and technical description by Hans Hoffmann, "Baugeschichte bis zur Reformation," in "Das Grossmünster in Zürich," *Mitteilungen der Antiquarischen Gesellschaft in Zürich, 32*, Part III (Zurich, 1941), 196–217; and Escher, "Das Zürcher Grossmünster am Vorabend der Reformation," *Zwingliana, 4* (1921–28), 477–85.

taining the remains of the martyred saints. Ordinarily, these remained covered with purple Burgundian cloths, but for the annual procession to the Lindenhof they were uncovered, taken down, and carried with much ceremony through the city. In addition, silver gilt and jewel-encrusted busts of the two saints were displayed on the altar on great feast days. The Passion Arch was flanked on both sides in the fore choir by smaller altars—one for Saint Gallus, the other for the Virgin Mary; among the decorations on the latter was a gilded statue of the Mother of God which was especially venerated by the people. Two more altars, dedicated to Saint Mary Magdalene and Charlemagne respectively, stood on either side of the flight of steps leading down from the entrance to the choir into the nave, and several more were placed in the nave, although in no regular arrangement. On the gallery, which extended across the west end of the Minster over the row of confessional booths installed in 1515, there were three more altars, two of which, owing to the indulgences attached to them, were particularly esteemed as places of worship by townspeople and pilgrims alike. The ancient crypt beneath the choir contained the altar of Saint Mauritius, and in the Chapel of the Twelve Apostles, set against the southern wall of the nave and the choir, there were at least five more altars. Thus in 1518 the Great Minster, though it was by no means a large building, boasted no fewer than seventeen altars.

The interior was richly decorated throughout. The walls of the choir, broken up into twelve blind arcades, were brilliantly painted. Each arcade contained a scene from Scripture, such as the Last Supper or the Adoration of the Magi (to which probably five arcades were devoted), or saints' figures. Among these Saints Felix and Regula were represented as being greeted by Christ, and in the first arcade on the northern side there was a Saint Veronica holding the sudarium. Opposite her on the south wall was a Last Judgment. Both of them, significantly enough, had been painted just around the turn of the century. Paintings covered not only the walls of the nave but even some of the heavy pillars which supported the vaults, and yet another representation of the Last Judgment could be seen in the middle of the west gallery. To the left of that, in the southwest corner of the gallery, was the organ, newly installed in 1507, whose carved wooden case was painted bright red and blue. On the walls of the crypt was a monumental cycle of frescoes executed in the last decade of the fifteenth century, depicting the legend of the Theban legion and the martyrdom of the city saints.

Most elaborate of all, however, was the Chapel of the Twelve Apostles. Here, on the side of what once must have been an ancient place of worship, were the graves of Saints Felix and Regula. All that was left of their bones was contained in the reliquaries over the high altar, but there were nevertheless two ornate sepulchers in the chapel, surrounded by costly railings and covered with precious gilded panels and silken cloths, provided by the donations of countless pilgrims to the shrine. The graves themselves, as well as specific instructions for visiting them, are recorded as early as 1260. In order to keep alive the memory of their martyrdom in boiling oil, the perpetual light before the altar of the Twelve Apostles was cast in the form of a cauldron, and candles burned constantly on the four other altars, illuminating walls that were covered with brightly colored murals depicting scenes of Christ with His disciples. Here, too, were the great panels of Zurich, with Christ and the city saints, which had been painted in 1497 by Hans Leu the Elder.

The chapel also contained a so-called "Easter Grave" for Christ. For this sight the pilgrim was prepared symbolically on entering the chapel, since over the portal leading down into it was a wall painting of Christ standing in the tomb with the instruments of His Passion on either side. Once the pilgrim had descended, he would have seen a wooden sepulcher under a canopy supported by pillars, likewise of brilliantly painted wood. Surrounding the sepulcher were large wooden statues of Mary, Mary Magdalene, and Saint John, while in it, wrapped in a white coverlet with silken tassels, was laid a wooden replica of the body of Christ, which was removed from the grave on Easter Sunday. The painting over the entrance was done at the turn of the century; the extraordinarily elaborate Easter Grave was not installed until 1515, only three years before Zwingli's arrival in Zurich.

The whole interior of the church faithfully mirrored the two major aspects of popular piety immediately prior to the Reformation: the cult of Mary and the saints,[39] and the insistence of the people on experiencing religion visually. They looked up to saints' images on the walls of the nave, the choir, and countless chapels; they knelt before their altars and kissed their statues; they venerated their relics; they delighted in telling and retelling the stories of their lives and miracles. Above all, they prayed to them. The Mother of God alone stood higher in their devotion. Saint Valentin guarded them against epilepsy; Saint Sebastian protected them from the plague; Saint Barbara stood between them and unexpected death. For as long as they carried with them an image of Saint Jerome, they would be immune from

39. See Hermann Siebert, *Beiträge zur vorreformatorischen Heiligen-und Reliquienverehrung* (Freiburg im Breisgau, 1907).

all temptations; should they see an image of Saint Christopher in the morning, they were assured a joyful evening that day. Hence the image of Saint
Christopher on the west wall of the Great Minster was so placed that anyone
entering the church could not fail to see it and be protected by it. The popular, vernacular religious literature of the time was devoted almost exclusively
to Mary and the saints. Scarcely a preacher of significance failed to publish at
least one collection of his "Sermons on the Saints." [40] Of such sermons by
the great Dominican preacher Johannes Herolt, for example, forty-six edi-
tions were published in Germany alone between 1468 and 1500.[41] And the
little books of instruction for the pastoral clergy, the so-called *Summa
Rudium* or *Summa Praeceptorium,* underscored the doctrine that veneration
of the saints was ultimately one with adoration of God, and consistently
stressed the importance of their intercessory activity.

The existence of all these statues and images to which the people had become so perfervidly attached was defended at length in these same *Summae,*
although the arguments advanced for their propriety were by no means new.
Western theologians had long upheld the value of visual experience in the
religious life of the faithful, particularly of the illiterate. During the pontificate of Gregory the Great, Serenus, Bishop of Marseilles, destroyed some
images in his church when he discovered that certain members of his congregation were worshiping them. Upon receipt of the news of his iconoclasm, the Pope wrote to Serenus:

> We commend you for your zeal against anything made by hand being
> an object of adoration, but we declare that you should not have de-
> stroyed these images. For pictures are used in churches for this reason:
> that those who are ignorant of letters may at least read what they cannot
> read in books by looking at the walls. Therefore, my brother, you should
> have preserved the images and at the same time have prohibited the peo-
> ple from worshiping them.[42]

It is not too much to say that with that brief paragraph the propriety of
ecclesiastical art in the West was assured, for Gregory's decision became
normative for the Latin Church. The visual arts not only could be but
should be employed for the religious education of those of the faithful who
could not read.

40. Siebert, p. 2.
41. Ibid., p. 8.
42. Migne, *Patrologia Latina,* 77, Epistola CV, cols. 1027–28; cf. 77, Epistola XIII, cols.
1128–29.

Such visual experience was defended also as an aid either to inducing or to intensifying piety, a later argument compactly formulated by Saint Bernard of Clairveaux, who maintained in his *Apologia* that "since the devotion of the carnal populace cannot be incited with spiritual ornaments it is necessary to employ material ones." [43] His decision became as normative for the West as Gregory's had become, and the two lines of defense, the one didactic, the other hortatory, soon were inseparable. Indeed, the argument for the necessity of images advanced by Saint Bonaventura, which is typical of the High Middle Ages, is in effect nothing other than a more extensive restatement of the combined ideas of Gregory and Saint Bernard. Images, he wrote, were introduced and maintained in churches for three reasons:

(1) They were made for the simplicity of the ignorant, so that the uneducated who are unable to read Scripture can, through statues and paintings of this kind, read about the sacraments of our faith in, as it were, more open Scriptures.

(2) They were introduced because of the sluggishness of the affections, so that men who are not aroused to devotion when they hear with the ear about those things which Christ has done for us will at the least be inspired when they see the same things in figures and pictures, present, as it were, to their bodily eyes. For our emotion is aroused more by what is seen than by what is heard.

(3) They were introduced on account of the transitory nature of memory, because those things which are only heard fall into oblivion more easily than those things which are seen.[44]

Thus, Bonaventura concludes, images are indispensable, by implication even for those who can read; the memory of the literate is not infallible. Such an idea was, in fact, openly asserted two centuries later, for a religious manual from Augsburg expressly states that "in order that matter should be fruitful to all, it is exposed to the eyes of all, as much through letters serving the educated only, as through images, serving the educated and uneducated simultaneously." [45]

43. Cited by Otto von Simpson, *The Gothic Cathedral* (New York, 1956), p. 43, n. 56.

44. Liber III, Sententiarum: Dist. IX, Art. I, Quaestio II, *Opera Theologica Selecta* (Florence, 1941), p. 194.

45. Cited by Immanual Schairer, "Das religiöse Volksleben am Ausgang des Mittelalters nach Augsburger Quellen," *Beiträge zur Kulturgeschichte des Mittelalters und der Renaissance,* ed. W. W. Goetz (Leipzig-Berlin, 1914), *13,* 64; see p. 63 for the significant comment by Sebastian Brant: "imperitis pro lectione pictura est."

As a result of such teaching, the Church relied increasingly on visual aids to devotion, so much so that by the late fifteenth century the Augustinian Eremite Gottschalk Hollen actually insisted that one could be led to piety more effectively "through a picture than through a sermon." [46] As famous a preacher himself as Johannes Herolt, he had come nonetheless to believe more in the power of the visual image than that of the spoken word, so that in his *Summa Praeceptorium* he developed for the faithful the following fourfold doctrine of images. They are essential to the religious life:

(1) In order that we may embrace a knowledge of things unknown.

(2) In order that we may be animated toward doing the same thing.

(3) In order that through the image we may remember.

(4) In order that we may venerate him whose image it is.[47]

As thoroughly characteristic of the late Middle Ages as it was enormously influential, Hollen's defense of images constitutes an epitome of medieval thought on the subject.

Through the universal application of such ideas, popular piety had naturally come to be predominantly sensuous. The people were accustomed to expressing their religious ideas and emotions in sensuously perceptible forms—above all, in visible forms. To secure the intercession of the saints it was necessary for them to see, if possible even to touch, their relics. Merely to pray to Mary and the saints was insufficient; their devotions and prayers had to be performed before paintings and statues. The reality of their religious experience was to be measured almost entirely in terms of its immediate palpability, a religio-psychological condition disclosed most strikingly, perhaps, in their insistence upon grasping the various aspects of Christ's Passion in as visually realistic a fashion as possible. From such a deeply felt demand arose the practice on Palm Sunday, in Zurich as elsewhere, of drawing down the nave of the Great Minster a wooden donkey bearing a statue of Christ. Just as His entry into Jerusalem had to be enacted before their eyes to be fully comprehended, so, too, His agony in the Garden. Hence outside the Great Minster, against either the north or west wall, there stood under a canopy a group of statues representing Christ with His disciples on the Mount of Olives.[48] His effigy in the Easter-Grave enabled them to meditate

46. Siebert, p. 22.

47. Ibid., p. 21. For a brief but comprehensive survey of the history of image doctrine in the Middle Ages see Johannes Kollwitz, "Bild und Bildertheologie im Mittelalter," *Das Gottesbild im Abendland* (Witten and Berlin, 1959), pp. 109–31.

48. Escher, *Die beiden Zürcher Münster,* p. 53.

on His dead body wrapped in the linen shroud. Even the miracle of the Ascension had to be presented to them visually, so that on Ascension Thursday a huge image of Christ was slowly raised up from the floor of the choir until it disappeared from the people's sight through a hole in the vaulting contrived especially for the purpose.[49] Doctrine was thus mediated in every conceivable way through sense experience, primarily that of the eye, to such a degree that for the majority of the people "the mere presence of a visible image of things holy sufficed to establish their truth." [50] The faithful, in short, had fallen completely captive to the senses. Consequently, when Zwingli walked through the Great Minster in December 1518, seeing for the first time the saints' images, the Gethsemane group, the Easter-Grave, the reliquaries, the eternal lights, all these combined to form for him a visual epitome of the "corporeal things" and "corporeal ceremonies" against which he had come to preach.

ZWINGLI'S ATTACK ON THE DOCTRINE OF THE SAINTS

The impulse guiding Zwingli's opposition to this sensuous, ceremonial piety was, as has been shown, fundamentally a humanistic one. Just as his early absorption of the humanist ideal of *Christianismus renascens* had provided him with the necessary precondition for his decision to eliminate all music from worship, so did humanism initiate Zwingli's opposition to the cult of the saints. Such opposition derived, in fact, directly from Erasmus himself. The great humanist on many occasions had mercilessly satirized institutions such as pilgrimages, the veneration of relics, the proliferation of the saints, and the wildly exaggerated popular belief in their intercessory powers. But in 1514 he published a Latin poem entitled *The Complaint of Jesus,* in which he disclosed both the depth and the seriousness of his distress at the fact that within the structure of popular piety it was invariably to the saints rather than to Christ that the people turned in their prayers.[51] The one true mediator had become lost in a welter of substitutes. While at Glarus, Zwingli had read the poem; so indelible was the impression it left on his mind that he could still recall its impact vividly in 1523. Toward the close

49. Escher, "Das Zürcher Grossmünster am Vorabend der Reformation," *Zwingliana,* 4 (1921–28), p. 482.

50. Jan Huizinga, *The Waning of the Middle Ages* (London, 1949), pp. 136–59, esp. p. 148; cf. Preuss, *Die deutsche Frömmigkeit,* pp. 119–25, on the *Sinnenverhaftung* of late medieval piety.

51. Cornelis Reedijk, *The Poems of Desiderius Erasmus* (Leiden, 1956), pp. 291–94.

of his massive assault on the cult of the saints in the *Interpretation and Substantiation of the Conclusions,* he said:

> Beloved brothers in Christ Jesus, I shall not conceal from you how I arrived at the opinion and the lasting belief that we need no mediator other than Christ, moreover that no one other than Christ alone can mediate between God and us. I read eight or nine years ago a comforting poem on the Lord Jesus, written by the most learned Erasmus of Rotterdam, in which in many beautiful words Jesus laments that men did not seek all good in Him in order that He might be a fountain of all good for them, a Saviour, solacer, and treasure of the soul. Here I thought, if that is indeed true, why then should we seek help from any other creature? And although I discovered other hymns or songs to St. Anne, St. Michael, and others by this same Eramus,[52] in which he addresses those to whom he is writing as intercessors, still these could not deprive me of the knowledge that for our poor souls Christ was the sole treasure. I began, nevertheless, to look through Scripture and the Fathers in order to find in them evidence for the intercession of the saints. In short, I have found in the Bible none at all; among some of the Fathers I have found it; among others I have not.   [2, 217, 5–23]

This public confession is of the greatest significance for the history of Zwingli's intellectual development. At precisely the same time he was beginning to immerse himself in the Erasmian critique of ceremonial piety, he appropriated Erasmus' conviction that Christ alone is mediator between God and man. Furthermore, he had discovered that the intercessory activity of the saints was wholly without scriptural warrant. Within the general antinomy that Erasmus had formulated between corporeal and spiritual worship, the awareness of a particular antinomy between the worship of Christ and the veneration of the saints had thus been maturing in Zwingli's thought at least since 1515. It is scarcely surprising, then, that in his strenuous effort to return Christ to Christianity as the sole object of faith and worship, the cult of the saints would sooner or later be called into question.

His preaching against that cult began soon after his arrival in Zurich. On June 7, 1519, in reply to a letter from Beatus Rhenanus in Basel concerning Luther's Exposition of the Lord's Prayer, he wrote:

> I have no fear that Luther's Exposition of the Lord's Prayer will displease me. . . . I shall buy a great number of copies, particularly if in

52. Ibid., pp. 202–05; 229–36.

his Exposition he deals somewhat with the adoration of the saints, for this I have forbidden. . . . The invocation of the saints I have permitted somewhat more, but I have restricted this to that on behalf of the living. . . .   [7, 181, 3-4; 6-10]

The evidence, although indirect, is nonetheless telling. Only six months after beginning his monumental sermon cycle on the New Testament, Zwingli had preached against the cult of the saints. Moreover, within that short time he had already explicitly forbidden their adoration by the people. Such adoration, to be sure, had always been forbidden, from Gregory's letter to Serenus to the *Summa Rudium* and the *Summa Praeceptorium;* the latter, in particular, were replete with warnings to the faithful not to accord to the saints that adoration which was due solely to God. Thus Zwingli was not so much saying something new as attempting to restore to the consciousness of the people of Zurich a forgotten distinction between adoration and veneration. On the other hand, by forbidding prayers to the saints on behalf of the dead, he was taking a considerably more radical step. Indeed, he confessed to Rhenanus that with regard to the people's opinion in this matter he would not be averse to the additional support of Luther's ideas. The remark points to strong popular reaction. Evidently Zwingli had discovered that preaching against the cult of the saints involved an assault upon the nerve center of the people's faith.

Nonetheless, he persevered in his opposition. Two years later, on December 29, 1521, he apologized to Berchtold Haller in Bern for being as yet unable to send him his "Sermons on faith and the cult of the saints" (7, 486, 21–24), because he was still preparing them for publication. Zwingli must thus have preached on the subject more than once during the intervening years. By 1522, however, his critique of the doctrine apparently had become a full-scale attack. The caution displayed in 1519 in merely forbidding prayers for the dead was completely abandoned. According to Bernhard Wyss, he now

rejected Mary and all the saints who are in heaven as well as their intercession and prayers addressed to them; in many writings he explained that one must pray only to God and to no other creature. But if one wanted to honor one of the saints, then one should imitate their good works. That above all would please them, since they desire no honor, but only that God be honored. It was for this reason that all the martyrs had suffered death, and in their suffering they called out only to God; no saint in his need would ever have called upon anyone else.

And Wyss concluded his account with the pointed remark: "The entire city was informed of this." [53]

Much publicized also was the debate in this same year between the Reformer and Francis Lambert of Avignon.[54] The latter, a distinguished Franciscan who had come to Zurich on Haller's recommendation, defended the intercession of Mary and the saints in the fourth of a series of sermons which he had been invited to deliver in the Fraumünster. Zwingli challenged him to debate the doctrine, and he accepted. On July 16, 1522, they met in the chapter house of the Great Minster. Zwingli argued solely from Scripture, and eventually "brought the monk to the point where he lifted both hands together, thanked God, and said that in all his needs he wanted to call only on God and to relinquish all crown-prayers and rosaries." [55] It was a signal victory for the Reformer.

Two months later, before the nuns of the Oetenbach cloister, Zwingli delivered a sermon on the Virgin Mary, in which he pursued his theme relentlessly. "The babbling of a given number of words of the Ave Maria" (*1, 425, 22*) was no honor to the Mother of God. On the contrary, he insisted, she was made happy and honored only by those prayers which were addressed to Christ. Consequently, he said,

> Everyone should know that the highest honor one can accord Mary is properly to recognize and honor the beneficent act of her son done for us sinners . . . if her greatest honor is her son, it is also her greatest honor that one properly recognize Him . . . then the more the honor and love of Jesus Christ grows among men, the more the worth and honor of Mary grows . . .   [*1*, 426, 5–7; 16–27; 19–20]

But the intensity of Zwingli's attack was not fully disclosed until the First Zurich Disputation. Held on January 29, 1523, the discussion was presumably to focus on the sixty-seven Conclusions which Zwingli had published for the purpose ten days earlier. It became instead a discussion of the problem of ultimate authority, in which the unconditional primacy of Scripture

53. Both quotations from Wyss, *Chronik*, pp. 11–12.
54. See Andres Moser, "Franz Lamberts Reise durch die Schweiz im Jahre 1522," *Zwingliana*. *10* (1954–59), 467–71.
55. Wyss, *Chronik*, pp. 16–17.

was steadfastly asserted by Zwingli against the primacy of the Church. The latter position was upheld by his former friend Johann Faber, the vicar-general of Constance, who by now had definitely rejected the Erasmianism of his youth. Within the overall context of the debate on authority, Zwingli's profound concern for the forms of worship emerged precisely with regard to the question of the intercession of the saints. Urban Weiss, the pastor of Fislisbach, had been arrested in November 1522 for announcing publicly that he would no longer invoke either the Virgin Mary or the saints. Inasmuch as he had been examined in Constance, Zwingli questioned the vicar-general about him. Faber admitted that he had discussed with him the question of the intercession of the saints, and then continued by asserting that "the Scriptures prove that even before the birth of Christ the dear saints were prayed to and called upon for others" (*1*, 504 4–6). Zwingli at once replied: "Show me the place and the text, also the words of Scripture, where it is written that one should call upon the saints as intercessors, so that if I have erred, and am in error now, I may be better taught" (*1*, 507, 14–17). Faber, unable to do this, had recourse to tradition, suggesting that such matters be referred to a General Council or to the universities. Hardly satisfied with this reply, Zwingli pointed out that the decrees of councils were often ignored. Referring further to Faber's assertion that the invocation of the saints had been customary in the Church since the pontificate of Gregory the Great, he insisted that "we are not questioning here when something began in the Church . . . we wish to hear from Scripture only how my lord vicar is certain that we should call upon the saints. For if such a custom began during the time of Gregory, it did not exist before then" (*1*, 515, 10–11; 14–15).

Eventually it became clear to Faber that the issue was by no means simply one of the cult of the saints. Although he himself was appalled even that the doctrine of their intercession was under debate, he was aware now that the matter did not stop there. He realized that Zwingli was ultimately concerned as much with the forms of faith as with its content, that, in fact, Zwingli considered them inseparable because they both derived solely from Scripture. "Very well, Master Ulrich," he asked toward the close of the debate, "do you say that one should keep only what is written in the Gospel, and nothing else" (*1*, 552, 6–7)? Had Faber read the *Archeteles* in which Zwingli had made clear his intention to try "all things by the touchstone of the Gospel," the question need not have been put. Such obviously was Zwingli's intent, of which the liturgy without music of the following year was the initial result. The centrality of Christ and the denial of any validity to "invented, external worship" (*1*, 487, 9) are the two great themes of Zwingli's four years of preaching in Zurich. Although he no longer understood the doctrine of "Christ alone" in terms of the Erasmian philosophy of Christ from which he had initially appropriated it, the Christocentric position from which he argued either explicitly or implicitly throughout the debate was ultimately based on the concept formulated by Erasmus, as was his attack on the intercession of the saints. What Zwingli said in 1523 cannot, in fact, be understood fully without reference to his reading of Erasmus' *The Complaint of Jesus* in 1514–15.

The course of the debate breaks sharply with the thought-world of humanism not simply in Zwingli's evangelical understanding of Christ but also in his insistence upon Scripture as the sole norm for Christian life and worship. Christ's true service must derive, not from the traditions of the Church, as Faber would maintain, but from Christ's true words in Holy Scripture. The law of Christ that conditioned Zwingli's arguments against the use of music in worship was now to operate just as forcefully in his opposition to the veneration of the saints. But inasmuch as it was a matter of Zwingli preaching, and then putting into practice, what had only been implied by Erasmus, the Disputation contains a humanistic dimension which hitherto has not been sufficiently appreciated. Moreover, just as Zwingli's attack on the cult of the saints eventually led to his elimination of the visual experience from worship, his attitude toward the role of both music and the visual arts eventually derives from his humanism.

THE PROBLEM OF ICONOCLASM

The propriety of the intercession of Mary and the saints was, of course, inextricably bound up with that of their visual representation in statues and paintings. It is difficult to determine, however, whether in attacking the former Zwingli had attacked the latter as well. It is striking that in contradistinction to music, images are barely mentioned in the sixty-seven *Conclusions* of 1523; it is the more so since Numbers 19, 20, and 21 fall under the rubric "On the Intercession of the Saints" (*1*, 460, 11–17). Furthermore, Zwingli's lengthy substantiation of the twentieth *Conclusion* is a rigorously sustained indictment of the cult of the saints—both an amplification and an intensification of everything Erasmus had compressed into *The Complaint of Jesus;* indeed Zwingli's critique concludes with his confession that in this matter particularly he was the willing pupil of Erasmus. But in all the fifty-seven pages devoted to the subject, the longest *Substantiation* appended to any one of the *Conclusions,* Zwingli mentions images once and then only in passing (2, 218, 16–30; cf. 192, 10–23). It would seem, then, from the evidence available, that as late as the summer of 1523 he had not as yet come to consider the existence of ecclesiastical art per se as worthy of engaging his best attention. Nor does he seem to have considered the problems raised by the physical destruction of images, despite the fact that as early as June 1520 at least one iconoclastic incident had taken place, ironically enough in his native Duchy of the Toggenburg. While in a tavern a certain Uli Kennelbach, a farmer, had mutilated a painting of the Crucifixion, saying that "images are useless there and of no help." Zwingli would have approved the thought. The deed, in brazen defiance of authority, could not be countenanced, and by order of the Council Kennelbach was promptly executed.[56]

On December 19, 1522, over two years later, Oswald Myconius wrote Zwingli from Lucerne urgently requesting his advice. At some earlier and unspecified time a woman by the name of Frau Göldli had fallen seriously ill while in the house of her husband in Zurich. To assist in the cure of the disease, she had ordered a statue of Saint Apollinaris to be made and erected in a Beguine church in Lucerne. She was eventually healed. During her convalescence, however, she became so troubled by her conscience—because she had not only made an idol, but also put her trust in its healing powers—that she herself finally took the statue from the Beguine church and burned it. The Beguines were furious and protested vehemently to the civil authorities. The Council of Lucerne subsequently summoned her, and, declaring that such an act was "contrary to the faith, contrary to the Catholic Church, contrary to the Gospel of Christ, contrary to everything sacred and profane" (7, 640, 8–9; 641, 1), fined her forty gold pieces and demanded the immediate restitution of the statue as well.

Frau Göldli paid the money willingly. On the other hand, she obstinately refused to have another statue of Saint Apollinaris made. As Myconius wrote, "she sees that her conscience is weighted down in two ways; for there will have been the ancient scruple, and a new one is added if she will obey men against God" (7, 641, 7–8). Myconius obviously sympathized deeply with her point of view as well as her predicament. Like Zwingli, he too had rejected the doctrine of the intercession of the saints, and regarded the practice of erecting images of them as a reversion to pagan idolatry. "We have

56. Egli, doc. 126

considered the matter and we have weighed it on every side, nor can we find a way in which she can replace the idol with a clear conscience; for it is an idol, nothing else" (7, 641, 9–11). Apparently he had tried without success to persuade the Lucerne Council of the validity of Frau Göldli's position. The letter to Zwingli was thus his last desperate measure. "We consult you, therefore, as to what course you think we should follow in this matter which may be for the good of her soul. We shall depend upon you entirely" (7, 641, 11–12). He concluded by asking for Zwingli's reply by the same messenger.

In his immediate answer Zwingli began with a rhetorical flourish in which the soldiers of Christ overturning the idols and their cults in the sixteenth century are compared with those who had done likewise in the early days of Christianity. Then he continued: "you must prepare a gentle and timely speech by which the Council must be quietly taught what doubtless it does not know" (7, 644, 9–10). He thereafter proceeded to write what he considered a proper and effective speech for Frau Göldli to deliver before the Council. She should confess humbly to its members that she had ordered the statue to be made not at all from reasons of piety but from hypocrisy and worldly pride, even feminine instability. She should say further that her action had afterward caused her so much inner anguish that at length, overwhelmed by the enormity of her crime against God, she had destroyed the statue in order to relieve her conscience before God and man. The speech as it stands thus far is by implication simply a plea for both freedom of religious conscience and freedom to act according to the dictates of that conscience. Zwingli no doubt was carried away from the precise case at point while composing it, since it was written in such haste that he had no time to revise it. But it is as impractical as it is eloquent. If, as Myconius reported, he had indeed said everything that he could think of, then surely he had said much the same thing to the Council on Frau Göldli's behalf, although not perhaps with such formidable rhetoric. The same must be true also for Frau Göldli herself. The point at issue, however, was not so much the theoretical one of freedom of conscience but an intensely practical one involving civil authority: Should Frau Göldli respect the orders of the Lucerne Council? Should she erect another statue of Saint Apollinaris against her conscience? Should she, in a word, obey God or man?

To that aspect of the problem Zwingli put the following words in her mouth:

What pertains to the restoration of the statue I beg of you, fathers, that you favor me, namely to the extent that you should not force an unhappy woman against her conscience to build up again what surely she had begun in wickedness in the first place . . . for I am not concerned about the expenditure of money; I have, however, an abhorrence of what is dangerous to the soul. And so that this will be the more evident, I am prepared to pay to the Beguines as much money as the image cost, and leave it entirely to them as to how the money is to be used.

[7, 645, 11–13, 14–18]

The one practical suggestion made by Zwingli, that Frau Göldli present the Beguines with a sum of money equivalent to the cost of the original statue, is an obvious one which Myconius had probably considered also. But it barely solved the problem of Frau Göldli's conscience, and, more important, it does not at all solve the problem of idolatry over which Zwingli had been so concerned in the opening of his letter. With the money thus proffered, the Beguines themselves could, and would, promptly erect another statue. Consequently, the idolatry against which Zwingli had been preaching would continue, and Frau Göldli's sensitive conscience would be wracked anew by the fact that she had made such idolatry possible.

"Thus far I was speaking as the woman, and I urge that she speak for herself. Nor should she be afraid, because He who has ordered us to be without fear in what we speak, and so forth, will be present" (7, 645, 19–21). But, continues Zwingli, if the Council refuses to accept this compromise, "then I am unable to give advice other than that of the apostles when they said: 'it is better to obey God than man.' Therefore I would urge her rather to suffer death than to yield. All other things are nevertheless to be tried first" (7, 645, 26–29). A financial concession to authority or death without compromise—such were the solutions Zwingli offered Myconius in his dilemma.

The letter is a peculiarly significant document, in that it shows Zwingli almost entirely unprepared to deal with the *practical consequences* of iconoclasm. Although he could express himself freely in the letter, he had in fact little to suggest other than the two quite obvious solutions above, together with the vague phrase "all other things are nevertheless to be tried first." He may not yet have preached specifically against the visual representation of saints, but he had certainly preached against the doctrine of their worship and intercession, and despite the example of Kennelbach's execution had evidently failed since then to consider seriously what would happen or should be done if the images themselves were attacked or destroyed by individuals or even whole groups. It was, after all, not a very considerable step from denying the validity of the doctrine of the intercession of the saints to denying the propriety of their images. And their images were everywhere to be seen, creating a potentially explosive problem involving private property, ecclesiastical property and authority, and lay authority as well.

Yet there is some evidence to suggest that he had finally begun to preach against the images themselves, probably after the arrival in Zurich, late in 1522, of his intimate friend Leo Jud, who had come from Einsiedeln to be people's priest at St. Peter's Church. According to a statement made in October 1523, both men had "for a long time now" preached "in sermons based on the Holy, Divine Scriptures that idols and images should not exist" (2, 731, 3; 5–6). The precise time unfortunately is not specified, but "a long time" must at the very least have been within a year of the statement.

Thus as midsummer of 1523 drew to a close in Zurich, the city rang with denunciations of the images. From the pulpits of the Great Minster and St. Peter's, the Deuteronomic injunction was invoked against the statues and paintings beneath and around them. The Word of God was clear; there could be no doubt; the people had heard it, and often. God had commanded those who believe in Him not to make images. As a result of such preaching, the city early earned a reputation for heresy. Thomas Platter, for example, recounts in his *Autobiography* how he was once accosted by a priest who asked him whence he had come. Upon hearing that the youth was returning to Zurich, he bitterly accused the city of heresy, "because they have abolished the mass and images from the churches," to which Platter replied: "That is not true." [57] And Platter was right: the images in fact continued to stand; despite repeated proclamation of the Word, nothing was being done to obey it. Those who heard Zwingli and Jud attack ecclesiastical art could, even during the delivery of their sermons, look around and see, perhaps even reach out and touch, these evidences of idolatry. Everywhere in the city churches, plaster and stone and wood ranged themselves in voiceless defiance of the Word. When would these images be cast down? How long before

57. *Thomas Platter, Geisshirt, Seiler, Professor, Buchdrucker, Rektor, Ein Lebensbild aus dem Jahrhundert der Reformation,* ed. Horst Kohl (Leipzig, n.d.), p. 41; cf. Erasmus' imaginary letter from the Virgin Mary to Zwingli thanking him "for busily persuading people that the invocation of the saints is useless," complaining at the same time, however, that now she has "more peace, but less honor and wealth," *A Pilgrimage for Religion's Sake* in *Ten Colloquies of Erasmus,* trans. Craig R. Thompson (New York, 1957), pp. 60–62.

idolatry would be swept aside? When would God's Word be obeyed? Such an obvious disparity between preaching and practice in a community newly filled with religious zeal could not maintain itself forever. There had been no iconoclasm in Zurich; [58] order had thus far been preserved. But how much longer could it continue?

58. At some time late in 1522 or early 1523 Melchior Küfer was imprisoned for six days and admonished by the Council for uttering obscene remarks about images: Egli, doc. 317 (undated).

5. DEMONSTRATIONS IN SEPTEMBER

What can I make of church history? I can see nothing but clergymen. As to the Christians, the common people, nothing can be learned.

Goethe

LEO JUD'S SERMON

At last the long calm ended. On Tuesday, September 1, 1523, Leo Jud, the people's priest, delivered a sermon in St. Peter's denouncing the use of ecclesiastical images, statues, or paintings. The sermon was explicit and was preached "with especial candor and severity."[1] Not only did Jud condemn works of art in the churches; he maintained, possibly for the first time in public, that they be removed as well. Simon Weber, a member of his congregation, reported that "Herr Löw [Jud] preached on St. Verena's day that it could be proved from the Holy Scripture that it was right for idols to be taken out from the churches."[2] The explosive content of the sermon to-

1. Farner, *3,* 438. Emil Egli, *Schweizerische Reformationsgeschichte* (Zurich, 1910), p. 96. Rudolph Staehelin, *Huldreich Zwingli: Sein Leben und Wirken nach den Quellen dargestellt, 1* (Basel, 1895), 330. No detailed study of iconoclasm in Zurich has thus far been undertaken. For brief comment see Johann Kaspar Mörikofer, *Ulrich Zwingli nach den urkundlichen Quellen, 1* (Leipzig, 1867), 191–92, and Staehelin, pp. 330–31. A somewhat more extensive account is given in Farner, *3,* 428–32. The following reconstruction of the events of September 1523 is based almost exclusively on the contemporary documents in Egli; unless otherwise indicated, quotations in the text are taken from the same document in Egli until reference is made to a different one; so, for example, until Egli, doc. 414, is cited, all quotations are drawn from Egli, doc. 416.

2. Egli, doc. 416.

gether with Jud's eloquence combined at once to produce violent and conflicting reactions within the city. Because some few trial records have been
preserved, it is possible even now partially to reconstruct what the average
citizen of Zurich felt and thought when confronted with such radical reforming zeal.

The conservative reaction was immediate. On the very day on which the
sermon was delivered, a devout Catholic, a certain Thomas Kleinbrötli, was
overheard exclaiming sourly that "God should give the preachers and their
followers both a plague in body and soul." Later the same day Kleinbrötli,
Simon Weber, and two other men, Rudolph Bitziner and Peter Effinger,
gathered together at the Corn House to talk further about Jud's sermon. As
their discussion advanced, Kleinbrötli became more and more incensed. He
believed that if Jud himself had put statues or paintings in St. Peter's, he
could quite legitimately do with them as he pleased, an idea which was later
to become one of the guiding principles for the official removal of images
from the Zurich churches.[3] But he had no right whatsoever to remove or
destroy any work of art that had been placed in the church by others. "If
another had paid something and had it made, he [Jud] should allow it to
stand or go back from whence he came. God should give the plague to those
to whom this is pleasing and those who are followers of such preachings."[4]
Finally, he turned to Rudolph Bitziner and concluded with acerbity: "Löw
wanted to knock the idols from all the altars with an axe. He had given
nothing for them and therefore should not knock them off. He should go to
Strassburg in the name of all devils and smash up images there."[5]

The next day, Wednesday, September 2, Kleinbrötli's fury embraced
Zwingli as well: "both priests had preached lies from the pulpit." Furiously,
he spoke again to Bitziner: "If the priest should knock down the idols from
the pulpit with an axe, then he for his part would put them up again and
place the images in their [the priests'] laps and send them thus to Strassburg." Though Kleinbrötli's outbursts alone are recorded, they may serve as
a revealing index to the feelings of the average Catholic layman, who with
increasing anxiety saw the visual forms of the old order threatened.

Equally illuminating are Kleinbrötli's remarks a few days later to a certain

3. Cf. Egli, docs. 422, 458, 543, and 546, section 3; Z, 2, 814, 11–15; Z, 3, 115, 16–18; Z, 4,
150, 6–9; and Z, 8, 130, 11–12; see below, n. 44.

4. Egli, doc. 416.

5. Kleinbrötli's allusion to Strassburg is owing probably to the tolerance of religious differences
for which the city was renowned; see Philippe Dollinger, "La Tolérance à Strasbourg au
XVI⁰ siècle," *Hommage à Lucien Febvre* (Paris, 1953), 2, 241–49.

Nicholas Spreng. In a more reflective mood now, he declared that "Zwingli has sown unrest in this city and the people previously had been more of one mind than now after their [Zwingli's and Jud's] preachings. And those who had placed images in the churches had been more pious than those who wanted to take them out." Nothing else is known about Kleinbrötli, but here, briefly, he speaks for all those citizens of Zurich who did not want a Reformation, who were perfectly content to live out their lives under the old dispensation. Unwittingly he defines their traditional piety and devotional conservatism as he contrasts those who for centuries had reverently placed statues and paintings in the city churches with those who would now in one day drag them out. His abhorrence of the new ideas is testimony that Zwingli faced opposition not only from the learned in Constance and the chaplains and canons of the Great Minster but also from the burghers of his own city.

THE FIRST INCIDENT: ST. PETER'S CHURCH

The great Feast of the Nativity of the Virgin on September 8 passed quietly. Early in the morning of Wednesday, the ninth, however, what Jud had preached the previous Tuesday was put into practice in his own church. A certain Hans Kolb went to St. Peter's for the celebration of early Mass, and was appalled upon entering the dimly lit church to see a "wild rumpus"[6] in the distance: according to his later testimony before the Council, paintings, inscriptions, and statues of the saints were being torn down. By the time he reached the choir the iconoclasts had disappeared. No one was there except the Mass-helpers, who at that time "said nothing and reported these acts to no one." Kolb, likewise, for the moment remained silent.

On a later morning, perhaps even the same day, he went to the house of another devout Catholic, Herman Merzhuser, to talk about what he had seen, for the latter had also been present at that tumultuous early Mass. While they were talking together, Laurenz Meyer,[7] one of the Mass-helpers

6. Egli, doc. 414; cf. Farner, *3*, 428–29, and Vögelin, *Das alte Zürich*, p. 578.

7. Laurenz Meyer's entire career (1497–1564) was evidently a hectic one. Before coming to Zurich (the precise date of his appointment to St. Peter's is unknown), he served as a canon at Heiligenberg. As a result of his iconoclastic activity, he left Zurich sometime after September 19, 1523. By December of the same year he had been appointed a deacon at Winterthur. During 1524 he left that post to go as a pastor to Stammheim, which he represented at the great Bern Disputation of 1528. His crude behavior occasioned more and more complaints, until finally, on a charge of adultery, he was dismissed from his pastorate in 1543.

who had "said nothing," came by and casually asked what they were discussing so intently. They replied that "they were talking about the paintings and saints' statues which were torn off and torn up" at St. Peter's. "Thereupon the said helper grew pale, saying that they did not need to make such a bother, for it was to be expected that he who had done such a thing would come forth and confess it." The fact that he had not reported the episode was ill received. Felix Steinbrückel, another of those present at the conversation, retorted curtly that "whoever did this was a church thief and not as good as he." Obviously they felt that Laurenz Meyer had been won over, at least in part, by Jud's preaching, and was now in sympathy with the evangelical iconoclasts: his failure to report the incident at once to the authorities suggested this; so did his nervousness before the conservative group at Merzhuser's house.

As a matter of fact, Meyer was a wholehearted adherent of the new teaching. Indeed, his position in St. Peter's brings sharply into focus the two attitudes currently at issue in Zurich. Leo Jud was one of the leaders of Zwingli's movement for the reform of the liturgy. The chaplain, Herr Jörg, was attached with equal firmness to the old faith. Meyer, one of Jörg's assistants, had been converted to the evangelical cause. Tension between the old and new in the one church was inevitable. As early as July 1523, for example, Laurenz Meyer had actually gone up to Chaplain Jörg while he was "decorating the altar" and confessed quite frankly that "he would like it very much if he [the chaplain] did away with the idols hanging over the altar."

By September Meyer could endure no longer the sight of paintings and statues in the sanctuary. So he and his assistant Hans Pfifer, "had gone to the church, waiting until the bells had stopped ringing. And when they went up to the high altar an old painting stood there on which was painted the Descent of Our Saviour from the Cross as Our Lady holds Him in her lap." Meyer admitted that he could not help asking Pfifer ironically "what the picture was doing there and who had brought it there." "I will put it elsewhere," he said, and pulled it down. It fell, and the frame "which was very old" broke into pieces, whereupon he contemptuously pushed the wooden panel under the altar platform. Just then Chaplain Jörg entered the church, thereby bringing any further destruction to an abrupt halt. Resolutely, the

---

Although pardoned and reinstated two years later, he left Stammheim in 1547, and from then until he succumbed to the plague in 1564 he served as preacher successively to three more small communities in Cantons Glarus and Zurich; see Egli, docs. 345, 414, 1414; and Wyss, *Chronik*, p. 29, n. 3.

chaplain began to decorate the high altar "with gold, silver, and other costly things," and as he was thus engaged, Laurenz Meyer pled with him:

> It would please him [Meyer] very much if the chaplain would knock the idols off the altar with the candlesticks, because there were so many poor people who sat in front of the churches and in other places and had very little, but had to suffer great hunger and wretchedness, who could easily be helped with such decorations; for one can easily find in Ambrose that such decorations are food for the poor.[8]

The two men at the altar symbolize the ineluctable collision which the Reformation forced at all levels of society. Here is no Luther confronting his Emperor at Worms. Here instead are two humble men, a chaplain and his assistant, known now only by chance. And just as Kleinbrötli gave expression to the feelings of the old order, so now does Meyer with similar stubbornness and eloquence formulate the ideas of the new. The money which had for centuries been poured into church art to mirror and secure the glory of the world hereafter must go instead to provide for the poor in this world here and now. Zwingli, to be sure, had devoted an entire *Conclusion* to advancing just such a proposition;[9] but he meant that doctrine to be implemented slowly. While he would not discontinue his preaching for the restoration of the forms as well as the substance of true Christianity, yet only gradually and above all, legally could the new order replace the old. But as happens so often, the disciple was not controlled by the master's vision. If Zwingli had written that the money should go to the poor, and Jud had preached that images should be removed from the churches, why then should these things not be done now? This was what Zwingli most feared; it savored too much of Karlstadt's Wittenberg. Yet his continual preaching, as well as Jud's, was certain to create the kind of tension that resulted in

8. Egli, doc. 414. For the views of St. Ambrose on the problem of poverty and excessive wealth in a Christian community, consult esp. Martin R. P. McGuire, *S. Ambrosii De Nabuthae: A Commentary, with an Introduction and Translation*, and Lois Miles Zucker, *S. Ambrosii De Tobia: A Commentary, with an Introduction and Translation*, Vols. *15* (1927) and *35* (1933) respectively, in the Catholic University of America Patristic Studies. See also A. O. Lovejoy, "The Communism of St. Ambrose," *Essays in the History of Ideas* (Baltimore, 1948), pp. 296–307. For the sources of Ambrose's ideas see the bibliography in Gerhart B. Ladner, *The Idea of Reform: Its Impact on Christian Thought and Action in the Age of the Fathers* (Cambridge, 1959), p. 130, n. 63.

9. "Property unjustly acquired shall not be given to temples, monasteries, ministers, priests or nuns, but to the poor, unless it can be returned to its lawful owner" (*Z, 1,* 462, 11–13; cf. *Z, 2,* 295–98).

Meyer's outburst. Nor was the city unaware of the situation. When Thomas Kleinbrötli heard about this first iconoclasm, he said at once that "such came from their sweet teaching." [10] Then turning to Simon Zimmerman, a convert to the new faith, he told him bitterly that "he should believe in the Scripture and his idol, that Zwingli," to which Zimmerman replied that "he held Zwingli neither for an idol nor for a god, but as another man."

To Laurenz Meyer's impassioned plea Chaplain Jörg "did not give answer," [11] and sometime shortly after September 9, Meyer was put in prison by order of the Council. Yet when all the evidence had been sifted, there seem to have been neither statues broken nor images shattered in St. Peter's. The sole destruction officially reported was the broken picture frame and the damaged panel of the Pietà. Therefore, on Saturday, September 19, according to the official records, "since nothing more than the foregoing has been found against Herr Laurenz, he was freed from jail without further fine on an oath to keep the peace."

LUDWIG HÄTZER'S PAMPHLET

At some time during this period—the exact date is not now known—further encouragement to iconoclasm was provided by Christopher Froschauer's publication of a small pamphlet by Ludwig Hätzer entitled *The Judgment of God Our Spouse as to How One Should Hold Oneself toward All Idols and Images, According to the Holy Scriptures.*[12]

A native of Canton Thurgau, Hätzer had been born in Bischofzell around the turn of the century, and educated there, possibly for the priesthood, at the collegiate school of St. Pelagius until 1517, when he matriculated at the University of Basel.[13] The humanism for which Basel was now famous was definitely the most important aspect, indeed the core, of his university education. His Latin style is markedly humanistic, and there can be little doubt

10. Egli, doc. 416.
11. Egli, doc. 414.
12. "Ein urteil gottes un- / sers eegemahels / wie / man sich mit allen götzen und / Bildnussen halte soll / uss der / heiligen gschrifft gezo- / ge durch Ludwig Hätzer"; cf. Charles Garside, Jr., "Ludwig Hätzer's Pamphlet against Images: A Critical Study," *Mennonite Quarterly Review, 34* (1960), 21, n. 6.
13. For Hätzer's early career see the detailed discussion in J. F. Gerhard Goeters, *Ludwig Hätzer (ca. 1500 bis 1529), Spiritualist und Antitrinitarier: Eine Randfigur der frühen Täuferbewegung,* Quellen und Forschungen zur Reformationsgeschichte, 25 (Gütersloh, 1957), 9–17, and the briefer account in Goeters' article "Haetzer," *ME,* 2 (1956), 621.

that during these years he had also acquired both Greek and Hebrew. However, he did not take a degree, for reasons which remain unknown.

In 1520 he was ordained a priest and assumed his first post as chaplain of the community in Wädenswil. It may or may not be significant that an incident of iconoclasm occurred in the year of his arrival there; in any event, his name is not associated with it.[14] Nothing is known of his life and work for the next two years, save that at some time in the late summer or early fall of 1522 he left Wädenswil and moved to Zurich. Not until the appearance of the polemic against images a year later does he emerge from obscurity. It is impossible even to determine whether he wrote it at Wädenswil or after his arrival in Zurich.

The little pamphlet, only eighteen pages in all, excluding the title page, was divided unevenly into two parts.[15] The first and longer one was subdivided into three unequal sections in strict conformity with the formal structure of an academic disputation, each section consisting of a thesis followed by a catena of scriptural texts, in direct quotation, paraphrase, or compact summary. The initial thesis, "God our Father and Spouse forbids us to make images," was supported by nine passages.[16] To the second thesis, "God intends to destroy images as well as those who possess them and honor them," nineteen such passages were appended.[17] The concluding thesis, "The deed of those who have done away with images and idols will be praised and glorified," was defended with five passages.[18] There were no explanatory notes, no connecting passages of any kind, nothing at all save

14. Goeters, *Ludwig Hätzer,* p. 14.

15. There is no evidence to support Goeters' suggestion (*Ludwig Hätzer,* p. 23) that the pamphlet was "perhaps" an apology for the iconoclasts, or his unqualified assertion ("Haetzer," *ME,* 2, 621) that "this booklet was intended to defend the repeated acts of iconoclasm which had taken place in Zürich."

16. Exod. 20:3, 4, 5 (incomplete); Exod. 20:22, 23; Exod. 34:17; Lev. 19:4; Lev. 26:1; Deut. 4:15 (incomplete), 16–19; Deut. 4:23, 24; Deut. 5:6–8, 9 (incomplete); I Sam. 7:3 (incomplete).

17. Num. 25:4 (with a summary of 25:1–3); Deut. 4:25–28; Deut. 7:5, 6 (incomplete); Deut. 12:1–13 (Hätzer incorrectly cites chapter 2 in his text); Deut. 13:1–4, 5 (incomplete); Deut. 27:15; Jos. 24:19, 20 (Hätzer incorrectly cites chapter 27); Jgs. 10:15, 16; Ps. 69 (clearly another error; Ps. 69 has no relevance to the iconoclastic theme; probably it is meant to be Ps. 96:5); Ps. 115; Wisdom 14:11–13 (a paraphrase), 14 (incomplete), 27 (a paraphrase); Is. 42:17, 8 (incomplete); Is. 44:6, 9–20; Jer. 10:14, 15; Jer. 13:9, 10 (incomplete); Ezek. 14:2–6, 7, 8 (a paraphrase); Ezek. 6:3 (incomplete; Hätzer incorrectly cites chapter 16), 4, 5, 6 (incomplete), 7 (incomplete); Mic. 1:7; Heb. 2:18, 19.

18. II Kgs. 18:4 (almost complete); II Kgs. 23:14, 15, 4 (paraphrased in part); II Chron. 33:15 (a paraphrase); II Kgs. 17 (a brief summary); Bar. 6 (a brief summary).

texts from the Old Testament dealing with God's commandment against images, the punishment meted out to those who worshiped them, and the happier fate of those who destroyed them. The result is a massive indictment of images from the Word of God alone. Why the pamphlet should have been such an immediate success is apparent: to search laboriously for texts against images was no longer necessary. Hätzer had collected thirty-three of the most radical ones, translated them into the vernacular, and made them easily accessible to the learned and unlearned alike.

The second part of the pamphlet, only six pages long, was written by Hätzer himself. There he proposes what he considers the four principal Arguments in defense of images, and then subjoins to each a brief but vigorous Answer, as follows: [19]

The First Argument

All these [scriptural passages] are only citations from the Old Testament which no longer binds us or has reference to us Christians.

Answer

Everything pertaining to morals and reverence for God which is ordained in the Old Testament applies to us as well. If that were not so, we could also cast aside the Ten Commandments. Therefore just as God's First Commandment applies to us, you shall not have strange gods, so also does that pertaining to images apply to us, for they stand beside one another in the same commandment. Moreover, just as you are enjoined by the commandment of God to kill no one, and to honor your father and mother, just so are you enjoined neither to have nor to revere images.

But that you may also have authority from the New Testament, hear then what that chosen vessel Paul says in the First Epistle to the Corinthians at the fifth chapter [9]: I wrote to you before in a letter that you should have no dealings at all or association with fornicators. By this I take it that Paul does not mean the fornicators of this world, but rather those who pretend that they are Christians. Indeed, moreover not with the greedy, nor with robbers, nor with the harlots who revere im-

---

19. The translation above has been made directly from the text of the first edition in the Goshen College Library; cf. Nelson P. Springer, "The Mennonite Historical Library at Goshen College," *Mennonite Quarterly Review*, 25 (1951), 313. For portions of the German text see Walter Köhler, *Das Buch der Reformation Huldrych Zwinglis* (Munich, 1926), No. 164, pp. 126–28.

ages. Here Paul, the Apostle of Jesus our Saviour, speaks not with respect to the heathen, but with respect to Christians.

Item. In I Cor. At the eighth chapter [4] he also says: we know (as if he were to say there can be no dispute) that they are not gods, and that there is no more than one God. He also says in I Cor. at the tenth chapter [7; 14]: you [Christians] should not offer reverence to images as some of you have done. Paul also accounts and understands reverence for images among the works of the flesh the which whoever does them will nevermore come into the inheritance of the Kingdom of God; in Galatians at the fifth chapter [20–21].

Peter, the Apostle of Jesus Christ, in his First Epistle at the fourth chapter [1–4] likewise accounts reverence for images as among the most abominable sins, saying: Since Christ now has suffered for us in the flesh, arm yourselves then with the same mind, for whoever has suffered in the flesh has ceased from sin. So that during the time in which he still has left to live, he shall live not according to the desires of men, but to the will of God. It should be sufficient for us that in time past we have done the wantonness of the heathen when we have lived in lasciviousness, in lusts, in drunkenness, in gluttony, in carousing, and in shameful reverence for images. Hear then clearly that we shall not reverence images. All that which is said to the Israelites is said to us as well, for now we are the chosen people according to belief in Christ, as Paul signifies in many places in his epistles.

Hätzer's Answer to the first Argument is two-fold. He first of all asserts that inasmuch as the prohibition of images is inextricably bound up with the First Commandment, a denial of the obligation and force of one is therefore inevitably a denial of the obligation and force of the other. Secondly, he introduces evidence for the first time from the New Testament to demonstrate that concern for idolatry was just as intense after the coming of Christ as it was before. That done, he proceeds to the second Argument, in which he undertakes to refute the long-established idea that such honor as is rendered to representations of the saints is given not to the visible image itself, but to the saint represented by it.

The Second Argument

But we do not honor images nor pray to them, but rather the saints whom they portray to us.

Answer

Say what you will, godless ones, even though you do not revere them, Christians shall have no images. Thus speaks God. If, then, you say that you revere the saints, you do that without the commandment and the Word of God, for to no other will He allow the reverence due to Him. He is a jealous one who will not permit the soul to rely on the creature or to seek help, health, solace, or anything else from the creature. He [Christ] wishes us to look for these as much in Him as in Our Father; Matthew, at the eleventh chapter [28]. Come to me, all those who labor and are burdened; I, I will give you peace.

Item. The saints did not want to tolerate such reverence from men, as you have in Acts at the third chapter [12–16] in which Peter and John did not want to be regarded as if they had helped the forty-year-old cripple, but cast all reverence before Jesus. For in no other is there salvation, health, or blessedness save in Him alone, and there is no other name under heaven in which there is salvation except in the one name Jesus. Acts 4 [12]. But that we do seek such things from the dead saints and not from God is clear enough. We sacrifice to them and burn oil candles before them. For each particular sickness we have a particular saint, and if we get well, we then ascribe all honor to them by hanging waxen ears, hands, feet, and eyes on their soot-blackened images.

Item. We run to them to Stammheim, Rome, Einsiedeln, Aachen. All this they [the saints] did not want to tolerate during their lifetime. Acts 14 [14–18]. God alone wants to be adored, called upon, and reverenced. By your own deeds I shall prove that you have honored images which are made of wood and stone. Is not the fact that you put them on the altar which should have been erected for God alone a great honor? If a baptized Christian were to stand up, you would then practically tell him who is a member of Christ to get down, and you would put in his place a soot-blackened oil-idol.

Item. You put them in the church, which is a house of God, where only God should be reverenced and called upon, and thus you make of it a murderers' pit. Are not images and oil-idols murderers when they kill souls and lead them away from God their Spouse? Away with them to the fire; that is where the wood belongs.

Item. One says that these are saints; that this is Our Lady, that that is St. Anne, and so forth. If they are saints, then any sculptor can make a saint; indeed, the Pope and the sculptor can do exactly the same thing.

Then shall we not have a crucifix? We shall apprehend Christ no longer according to the flesh, but according to the spirit. I Cor. 5 [3–5]. For we are a new creature. Our prayers shall no longer be made before images, but in Spirit and in Truth. John 4 [23–24].

Item. It is known that one honors them. Why does one gild the idols? Why then does one dress them up frequently in silk? Why does one seek compassion from them? Why does one bow down before them? In sum: say what you will, to these shabby idols one still accords honor which is due to God alone. From whence comes the familiar verse: *Christophore sancte, virtutes sunt tibi tantes,*[20] and so forth.

In this Answer, the longest of the four, Hätzer clearly wishes to prove beyond doubt that popular veneration of the saints has in fact became veneration of their images instead. Having set forth his evidence on that score, he turns to an attack on the Gregorian doctrine which had been so influential for the retention of images in churches in the West.

The Third Argument

They are books for laymen.

Answer

That is human folly. Gregory says such things, but God does not. Indeed, God says completely otherwise. God repudiates images, and you want to teach from that book which God has repudiated. O Antichrist, you love what God hates and is a bane to God. Do you want to learn to know God? Then read the Scripture which gives witness of Him in John 5 [37–40]. Read His word, not that of men. He speaks in John 10 [27]: My sheep hear my voice, and so forth.

Finally Hätzer rebuts the notion that the sight of religious images will encourage men to lead better lives.

The Fourth Answer

They induce men to reverence and improvement.

20. The complete text of the verse is as follows: "Christophore sancte, virtutes sunt tibi tantae: Qui te mane videt, nocturno tempore ridet." Cf. Joannes Molanus, *De Historia SS. Imaginum et Picturarum pro vero earum usu contra abusus,* in Migne, *Theologiae Cursus Completus* (Paris, 1843), 27, col. 242. See also Luther's condemnation of the veneration of St. Christopher in his sermon of 1516, *De Decem Praeceptis:* "Tantum habet honoris, ut nullus apostolorum sit ei conferendus; virtutes sunt tibi tantae; qui te mane videt, nocturno tempore ridet, nec satanas caedat nec mors subitanea laedat," cited by Hermann Siebert, *Beiträge zur vorreformatorischen Heiligen-und Reliquienverehrung* (Freiburg im Breisgau, 1907), p. 34.

Answer

O hypocrite! All the images on earth carried to one pile cannot by a hair make you more pious or more reverent or draw you toward God. For Christ speaks in John 6 [44]: No one comes to me unless God my heavenly Father draws him. Why do you attribute to the wood that which Christ ascribes only to his heavenly Father? *Item.* John 14 [6]. No one comes to the Father except by me. He is the way; He is the door. Why then, you lubberhead, do you come to God through these idols?

Therefore let all Christians strive diligently to do away with idols without hesitation before God visits them with that punishment which he is accustomed to send to all those who do not follow His word. If anyone here still wishes to decorate a temple, let him give diligently to the poor who are a living temple. Thus we will have eternal joy. Amen.

Since January 1523 Zwingli had had power of censorship over all books published in Zurich,[21] so that there can be little doubt that the pamphlet was issued at least with his knowledge and probably with his approval. In an atmosphere just recently disturbed by the open iconoclasm of Meyer, however, the appearance of such an inflammatory tract was potentially dangerous, and a somewhat more serious iconoclastic demonstration did indeed occur in the Saint Nicholas Chapel of the Fraumünster.

THE SECOND INCIDENT: THE FRAUMÜNSTER

On Sunday, September 13,[22] Uoli Richiner of Sulz was standing before the Fraumünster at dinner time when he saw three men coming toward him. Two of them he could identify as Lorenz Hochrütiner, a weaver,[23] and the carpenter Wolfgang Ininger; the third he did not know. They crossed the wooden bridge over the Limmat leading into the small square before the church, and paused there to "read a little book," [24] in all likelihood that by Ludwig Hätzer. When they had finished reading, the three men ran behind the Fraumünster and entered it by way of the St. Nicholas

21. Egli, doc. 319.
22. The date may be determined exactly inasmuch as the event occurred "on the Sunday after Sts. Felix and Regula" (Egli, doc. 415); the latter day, in 1523, fell on Friday, September 11.
23. Egli, doc. 442.
24. Egli, doc. 415; cf. Farner, *3*, 429–30.

Chapel.[25] Richiner followed them cautiously at a distance, and when he at last entered the church, he saw that "Hochrütiner and Wolfgang the carpenter were taking down the lamps which hung before the preacher's chair in the church of Our Lady, and that the same Hochrütiner threw such lamps behind an old painting beneath the preacher's chair so that the oil was shaken out and the lamps soiled." By the time Richiner had walked up to the two men, they were throwing holy water on each other, cheerfully saying that "they would exorcise one another." In a burst of enthusiasm they offered to do likewise for Richiner. He demurred, however, "in a friendly manner; he could do it himself," he replied.

Richiner's want of sympathy may have dampened their exuberance, for at that they left the church. But once outside, Hochrütiner turned defiantly to Richiner. He and Wolfgang "did not fear him," he said, "since it had taken place openly and not secretly." He went on to explain why they had destroyed the lamps. The new teaching had so deeply affected them that they "would not and could not stand such idolatry any more." Richiner, who was a conservative Catholic like Thomas Kleinbrötli, stubbornly answered that "they should not have done this (since it had been an eternal light) and should allow other people to follow their own bent in their own way, unchanged." Richiner's objection provoked a more emphatic rebuttal from Hochrütiner. Had Richiner "gone to school for such a long time and still did not know what it was?" To those who had heard and understood the Word, the answer could not be more clear; such an oil lamp purporting to be an eternal light "was nothing else than idolatry." Hochrütiner's statement illustrates vividly how profoundly the evangelical teaching and preaching had affected those in Zurich who had heard it and willingly taken it to their hearts. Unlike the educated Laurenz Meyer, Hochrütiner was a common man, a weaver, and Ininger was a carpenter. Yet both were so filled with the newly discovered Word that no delay in fulfilling any of its demands could be tolerated. Zwingli and Jud, however, were not solely responsible for such enthusiasm.

"The thirst for a greater knowledge of the Gospel was so great, and there were so many who either could not read or could not readily interpret, that many of the common people gathered around 'readers' to whom they listened for exposition of the Scripture."[26] These groups, known as "Bible

25. On the St. Nicholas Chapel see Vögelin, *Das alte Zürich,* pp. 534–35.

26. Harold Scott Bender, *Conrad Grebel c. 1498–1526, the Founder of the Swiss Brethren Sometimes Called Anabaptists,* Studies in Anabaptist and Mennonite History, 6 (Goshen, Indiana, 1950), 90.

schools," had sprung up in many places in Switzerland, and one of the most notable was that in Zurich, which was begun sometime in 1522 by the lame bookseller Andreas Castelberger.[27] He was evidently an inspiring teacher, and since Hochrütiner knew him, there can be little doubt that he attended Castelberger's classes. Castelberger lacked Zwingli's patience and foresight, so that Hochrütiner's impetuosity may in no small part be due to his inflammatory influence.

The day after the destruction of the lamps, Monday, September 14, Richiner once again met Hochrütiner, who was talking with Castelberger in the Street of the Printing Press. "Look," exclaimed Hochrütiner to Castelberger, "there goes the one who has given us away and spread these things abroad." [28] Richiner admitted that he had reported their iconoclasm. Furthermore, he could not understand "why they were not conscience-stricken." Hochrütiner replied that "as far as he was concerned he had done it only because he wanted to have light eternally; this [the lamps], however, was nothing but idolatry." Castelberger reassured Hochrütiner that "they did not need to fear him because of this, for they had done it in broad daylight," and thus the conversation ended.

Castelberger's lack of concern is peculiarly significant. On what grounds could the authorities possibly take action against Hochrütiner and Ininger? They had done only what the Bible commanded, and what Jud and Zwingli had preached; furthermore, they had done it openly, in the light of day as well as in the light of the Word. Such overwhelming single-mindedness illustrates one way by which the Reformation was able to seize a city such as Zurich so quickly.[29]

While the leaders debated for weeks, even months, in castles and palaces, the very movement they were debating rushed ahead of them in the market squares. Richiner could not understand Hochrütiner's sudden "blasphemy." Hochrütiner, on the other hand, was amazed at Richiner's continuing idolatry. The Bible does not countenance, does not even mention, such "eternal lights"; prostration and prayer before them is no way to "light eternally"; such idols must therefore be destroyed. How, then, could he be conscience-stricken? Before such uncompromising conviction, Catholics like Richiner could only retreat in bewilderment.

27. On Castelberger see the articles by Christian Neff in *ML, 1,* 91, and *ME, 1,* 523–24. Cf. Farner, *3,* 381–84, and *Z, 8,* 342, n. 8.
28. Egli, doc. 415.
29. Cf. Lacy Baldwin Smith, "The Reformation and the Decay of Mediaeval Ideals," *Church History,* 24 (1955), 213.

Not so the Zurich Council. On Saturday, September 19, the day it released Laurenz Meyer from prison, it decreed that "Lorenz Hochrütiner and Wolfgang the carpenter are, because of the above-mentioned crimes, consigned to the tower for three days." [30] The Council added that it would be impossible for the two men to commit such crimes again and not have it known. Further "if it happened again they would add the one offense to the other and punish them more severely." What the third of the three men did is not exactly known. But since "on the same evening [Sunday, September 13] two lamps in the Chapel of St. Nicholas which were still whole at vespers time were, at the time above, broken and thrown through the screen into the choir," this may have been his work. Certainly Richiner saw only Wolfgang and Hochrütiner in the Fraumünster, and while they were "exorcising" each other, the third man could have been smashing the lamps within the chapel. The trial records do not indicate whether or not he was accused and sentenced.

The extent of the actual damage in the city churches was still very small: one painting and possibly some other objects in St. Peter's, two votive lamps in the St. Nicholas Chapel of the Fraumünster, and an undisclosed number of the same within the Fraumünster itself. Thus far in Zwingli's own church there had been no destruction at all. He would doubtless continue to ensure that his own congregation would restrain themselves from open demonstrations. Moreover, he could, in his capacity as Jud's intimate friend as well as his senior colleague, persuade him to modify or even discontinue his radical preaching for the actual removal of images. Although "teachers" like Castelberger would continue to expound the Bible in ways that might incite further iconoclasm, Castelberger's classes could if necessary be suspended by the Council.[31] Hochrütiner and Ininger had been thrown into prison with a severe, public reprimand, an example which would hopefully prevent any further out-breaks. In brief, even though vehement discussion would probably continue in the city, the problem of active iconoclasm seemed, by the weekend of September 20, to be for the moment under official control.

30. Egli, doc. 415.
31. Castelberger was expelled from Zurich by the mandate of January 18, 1525 (Egli, doc. 624).

STADELHOFEN

But the equilibrium was soon upset again. Near the lower gate of the city of Zurich, in the little community of Stadelhofen, there stood an "especially large and beautifully carved crucifix" known as the "Lord God of Stadelhofen," which had been erected by a wealthy and pious shipbuilder named Anthony Stadler.[32] Some time after Wednesday, September 23,[33] the shoemaker Klaus Hottinger, a thorough convert to the evangelical cause and later one of its first martyrs,[34] removed the great crucifix from the column on which it had been mounted.[35] He was assisted by Hans Ockenfuoss, the village tailor, and the same Lorenz Hochrütiner who by now had been released from prison.[36] Their intent, as Hottinger himself expressed it, was "that they should sell the wood and would give the money got from it to the poor people who could best use it."[37] According to Bullinger, Hottinger was "an upright man, well read and well informed in religion."[38] Like Laurenz Meyer, he had been deeply affected by Zwingli's preaching and writing against the church's misuse of money, and would wait no longer to see this injustice officially righted. He would do it himself. "He wanted to present my lords [of the Council] or the people in the poor house with a pail of wine so that he would be permitted to take an axe to the paintings in the Water-church and split them up and thus he should do a good day's

---

32. Bullinger, *1*, 127; cf. Farner, *3*, 432.

33. Bullinger, *1*, 127, simply gives "in the fall of the year before St. Michael's day (September 29)." The date of the incident may be established somewhat more exactly, however, because Lorenz Hochrütiner was involved (Egli, doc. 421). On September 19 he had been sentenced to jail for three days (Egli, doc. 415). The first day on which he could possibly have assisted Hottinger was therefore Wednesday, September 23.

34. On November 4, 1523, by order of the Council, Hottinger was banished from Zurich for two years. Shortly thereafter, on March 26, 1524, he was burned at the stake in Lucerne; cf. the articles in *ML*, 2, 351, and *ME*, 2, 820–21, as well as Egli, *Schweizerische Reformationsgeschichte*, pp. 254–56.

35. There is no evidence available for any *direct* connection between the publication of Hätzer's pamphlet and the Stadelhofen episode, as is argued by Frederick Lewis Weis, *The Life and Teachings of Ludwig Hetzer: A Leader and Martyr of the Anabaptists 1500–1529* (Dorchester, Mass., 1930), p. 31.

36. Writing at a much later date, Bullinger (*1*, 127) reports "a company of angry citizens, of whom the angriest was Klaus Hottinger"; he mentions neither Ockenfuoss nor Hochrütiner. Egli, doc. 421, to the contrary reports only the three men, with no reference to "a company." Inasmuch as it is both a contemporary document and the official record of Hottinger's trial, the latter account has been preferred.

37. Egli, doc. 421.

38. Bullinger, *1*, 127.

work and leave peacefully." [39] The Council, needless to say, had refused his request, so he turned instead to the crucifix at Stadelhofen, and from that "had sold some wood-work and from this had given the money to the poor people." Hottinger had talked much about images with Heini Hirt, the miller of Stadelhofen, but Hirt was more cautiously evangelical. If images were not permissible, "then he would like to see that the crucifix at Stadelhofen was also taken away." On the other hand, when goaded by the impatient Hottinger—"Come on, Hirt, when are you going to get rid of your idols?"—he carefully replied that the idols "would not lead him astray there; he did not have to ask anything of them and would let my lords act in this case; for he was not learned and did not understand these things."

Hirt's answer expresses exactly an attitude that Zwingli would have approved entirely. The miller was now fully educated to the fact that religious images were condemned in the Bible. Protected by this knowledge, he would at least no longer be moved by such images as the crucifix; they would not lead him astray; he would pray to them no more. But not by himself would he destroy the images; that must be left to the judgment and the legal action of the City Council. Such an understanding combined with moderation and respect for authority was precisely what Zwingli intended to inculcate in his followers, whereas the impetuosity exhibited by Hottinger was what he most dreaded. Hottinger had been educated by the Word, but immoderately so. He was convinced that if Hirt truly "were a good Christian man then he would get rid of them [the images], since he had been taught from the divine Word that such idols should not be." And so unwilling and unable to wait longer for the Council or Zwingli, he took down the crucifix with the aid of his friends Hochrütiner and Ockenfuoss, and then came to Hirt and exclaimed triumphantly: "Hirt! I have got rid of the idols."

There is some reason to believe that a few members of the Council itself were in open sympathy with Hottinger's impatience. When speaking to the miller he had said "that he had not done this without the advice of some of my lords, that namely he had gone to Master Claus Setzstab and had received advice from him. The latter had advised him to do this and said that he might well get rid of them." Before the members of the Council themselves Hottinger said the same thing and named more names. He had not removed the crucifix

---

39. Egli, doc. 421; on the paintings in the Water Church, later destroyed, see the brief allusion in Bullinger, *1*, 175, Vögelin, *Das alte Zürich*, p. 227, and Arnold Nüscheler, *Die Gotteshäuser der Schweiz, historisch-antiquarische Forschungen* (Zurich, 1873), *3*, 422.

without the knowledge and consent of some of my lords of the Great and Small Councils, and Master C. Setzstab, M. Thoma Sprüngli, and Heinrich Trüben had allowed this. They did not prevent him from doing this, but said that they considered it, in their opinion, to be a good deed and thought that such images should be taken away . . . and . . . if all of the above-mentioned people together, or any one of them, had prevented his doing so with one word, then he would not have taken this up, and would have remained inactive.

Hottinger's testimony is so self-contradictory and so much at variance with that of Hirt that it is by no means wholly reliable. Nevertheless, he would surely not have uttered only lies before the Council, nor actually cited councilors by name, unless there were some truth in what he implied.

Particularly noteworthy is Hottinger's tremendous conviction, in all ways comparable to that of Castelberger, that what he did was absolutely right. Zwingli had not only been proclaiming the Gospel but condemning abuses in the Church as well, among which he explicitly included images. Jud, going one step farther, had preached publicly that the Scriptures demanded the *removal* of images. And Hätzer's pamphlet had expatiated on God's promise of punishment for those who did not destroy them immediately. Hans Ockenfuoss' remark could thus have been no very great exaggeration when he told the Council that "one hears daily that such crucifixes and all other images of God our Redeemer are forbidden." For Hottinger to have taken down the crucifix was therefore not entirely unwarranted; according to what was being proclaimed from the pulpit and circulated in print, he was absolutely right. His error consisted actually in his inability or unwillingness to wait until the Council acted.[40] And, like Meyer and Ininger, what he had done, he had done in broad daylight.

His companions shared his deep convictions. Hochrütiner declared that "since other people had taken images of the saints and crucifixes from the churches and no one had stopped them, he thought that he would do no wrong," and Ockenfuoss sincerely believed "that he had neither acted unlawfully nor done wrong." These statements, particularly that of Hochrütiner, suggest that the obvious contradiction between theory and practice was becoming strained for others as well as for Hottinger. After September 19, no further incidents of destruction in the churches of the city proper were reported. But that some furtive, nondestructive iconoclasm was now taking

40. Zwingli, in fact, described him as an able man who had been too severely punished; see Z, *8*, 30, 19–20.

place is confirmed by Hottinger's friend Master Uolrich Trinkler, who "showed him some images that he had in his house under the staircase and said that he had a great deal of expense concerning them, and still had carried them from the church so that no one would do reverence to them."[41] Undoubtedly a few people in the city were secretly removing paintings and statues from the churches, perhaps those which they had donated in the first place, and possibly with the knowledge or even the unofficial approval of some members of the Council. The number of works of art removed was so negligible that no losses were publicly noted, but any iconoclasm whatsoever, together with an incident such as that at Stadelhofen, presented a problem to the authorities considerably graver than either of those created by Meyer and Hochrütiner.

HÖNGG

Hottinger and his two collaborators were quickly sentenced to jail, but the real issue of the Stadelhofen episode was unresolved. What actually was the response of the people to iconoclasm? Did they really favor the removal or destruction of images? The question was vividly clarified in nearby Höngg.

Simon Stumpf, who assumed the pastorate in the little village in 1520, had always been radically inclined.[42] In September of this year, Langhansi Buri, a member of his congregation, reported that Stumpf "had spoken publicly from the pulpit to the effect that a congregation should see to it that images came out of the churches,"[43] and by the end of September the congregation

---

41. Egli, doc. 421. For a revealing contemporary account of such occasional secret iconoclasm in Zurich see *Thomas Platter: Lebensbeschreibung*, ed. Alfred Hartmann (Basel, 1944), pp. 61–62. Nevertheless, contemporary evidence thus far available will not substantiate the statement of Egli, *Schweizerische Reformationsgeschichte*, p. 97, that at this time "many citizens . . . began to carry their property home."

42. Before assuming the pastorate at Höngg, Stumpf had been a monk in his native Franken; almost nothing else of his life before 1519 is known. In July of that year he was in correspondence with Zwingli; three years later when he was in difficulty with the Bishop of Constance he sought the Reformer's protection. As a result of his iconoclastic agitation he was dismissed by the Council from the pastorate at Höngg on November 3, 1523, and on December 23 of the same year compelled to swear an oath never again to enter Canton Zurich. He must have violated the ban, however, for in April 1527 he was imprisoned in the city. Of his career during the intervening years nothing is known. On April 25, 1527, he was released from prison and once more banished from the Canton, this time to suffer death should he return. Thereafter he disappears from sight. Cf. Egli, docs. 300, 323, 326, 441, 446, 463, 692, 1167; Wyss, *Chronik*, p. 28, n. 2; and *ME*, *4*, 648.

43. Egli, doc. 422.

seems to have been largely won over to his point of view. There were even some ardent spirits like Felix Grossman and Uoli Nötzli who "had publicly cried out in church that images and idols must come out of the churches." And so they did.

Shortly before Sunday, September 27, there was taken "from the church in such a manner that no one knew where such an image had gone to a portrait of Our Lord on the Mount of Olives." That was apparently the first instance of actual iconoclasm at Höngg, for when the congregation gathered for the morning service on Sunday, a near-riot promptly ensued in the church. First of all Stumpf "preached publicly from the pulpit that he who took such a portrait of Our Lord from the church had not done wrong." Then Felix Grossman, speaking from his seat, reinforced Stumpf's remark saying that "the saints [i.e. statues] or their portraits must all be taken from the church." Clewi Buri, a conservative member of the parish, protested violently: "neither he nor any other should take such portraits away, other than with the permission of the law." Grossman obstinately repeated: "they must come out. And here Heini Nötzli entered into the discussion saying: he thought one who took such portraits out of the church not the more evil for it." Then Uoli Nötzli rose to say that "the idols belonged outside and he wanted to have them outside. Thereupon Heini Nötzli got up beside Uoli: he said that for his part he wanted to have them outside and that they must go outside." Felix Grossman reported that "he had been in Zurich and had seen how people carried out the saints [i.e. statues, etc.] just like manure. Further he said that he wanted to . . . take all the idols from the church at Höngg." At that point, according to the subgovernor Hans Himmler, "there was such an uproar and dissension in the church that he . . . had to ask them to hold their peace under the oath which they had sworn to my lords, and the whole situation was slowly quieted down." A sullen peace having been restored, Stumpf concluded the morning service. Then, however, he returned to his pulpit "and said for the last time that he wished to proclaim the Word of God that evening." Clewi Buri at once complained again "that he should not preach so much; for no images would be left in the church," thus leaving no doubt that Stumpf's current preaching was directed in large measure against church art.

Stumpf's evening sermon evidently heaped more fuel on the fire, for after the service, in Hans Grossman's words, "Jakob Nötzli had sat before his house and said: the idols must go. Thereupon three images were lost and disappeared away; but he did not know who did it." Actually Nötzli did know and had, in fact, destroyed more than three. He admitted later to stripping completely two altars of all their furnishings and throwing them, together with a ceremonial banner, into the Lake of Zurich. He also took five paintings from the church and burned them. Uoli Wyss, on hearsay only, said "that Kaspar Liechte had taken two angels from the church and had excused himself by saying that they had been put there by him and his forebears." [44] Liechte's open removal of the two angels because they had been donated by his family is the first example officially recorded in Canton Zurich of the principle which was soon to become a major policy for the removal of works of religious art from the Zurich churches. Even the conservative Catholic Kleinbrötli thought that if such action was necessary at all, then only in this way could it be accomplished.

But the larger significance of the events of September 27 does not lie in the damage done, despite the fact that it was considerable. In addition to Nötzli's iconoclasm, three pictures had been torn down and thrust behind the altar, and a crucifix and one other picture had simply been thrown out into the courtyard of the church. [45] The real importance of the episode lies in the fact that the removal of images from churches had become a matter of public debate for the whole congregation. In Zurich iconoclasm had thus far been perpetrated by individuals in the largely impersonal context of the city. But in the small villages the problem of church art could be discussed and acted upon by the whole community. Stumpf, beyond doubt aware that Zwingli and Jud were preaching against images in the city, resolved that his congregation should decide whether or not the images should remain in the church at Höngg. The congregation responded, and although the iconoclasm proper was secretly committed by individuals, with the exception of Kaspar Liechte, the context of their action differs fundamentally from that of Zurich. Excepting some few conservatives like Clewi Buri, the congregation as a body apparently approved their deeds in public and before their pastor.

WIPKINGEN

Another illustration of rural response to iconoclastic doctrine occurred in the episode at Wipkingen. Late in September three men from that village

44. Egli, doc. 422; cf. above, n. 3.
45. Cf. Heinrich Weber, *Die Kirchgemeinde Höngg urkundlich geschildert* (2d ed. Zurich, 1899), pp. 167–71.

attended a wedding in Höngg, where they met Thomas Grossman. Since Grossman, together with Hans Appenzeller, had recently thrown a painting out of the church in broad daylight, the conversation turned inevitably to what was obviously a favorite topic in the community—the propriety of religious art. After a while, the three guests decided "to take the idols from the church at Wipkingen. Thus they climbed into the church at night, carried the idols out of it, broke them up, and threw them into the lake." [46] Again the iconoclasts believed they were doing no wrong. They simply could not wait for the authorities to practice what was everywhere being preached. As they themselves said, "they did not behave unpeacefully, not wishing to get anyone angered; but, as they hoped, to do it in good opinion." Nor were they alone in their beliefs. The entire congregation of Wipkingen officially requested pardon for them, "because had there been a meeting previously, the images might perhaps have been carried out." As a matter of fact, the removal of the statues and paintings would in all probability have gone entirely unreported had it not been for a conservative Catholic member of the congregation. His fellow worshipers all wished "that Felix Burkhart had not complained about such things, because they approve of this [the removal] insofar as it is not counter to the wishes of my lords." The implications of this attitude are of crucial importance. The response to iconoclasm at Höngg had been vociferous, and generally favorable. Now at Wipkingen a whole congregation had almost unanimously, and voluntarily, assented to the removal of works of religious art from their church. Popular response to the Stadelhofen incident was becoming more and more clear: the people at large seemed to favor the removal of the images.

INTERVENTION BY COUNCIL

On Tuesday, September 29, the agitation at Höngg was reported in Zurich.[47] When the news reached the Council, it came as a final blow. Within less than a fortnight there had been iconoclastic demonstrations at Stadelhofen, Höngg, and Wipkingen, not to speak of the open, as well as furtive, iconoclasm in the city about which some members of the Council were probably informed. It was apparent that unless official action were

---

46. Egli, doc. 423; cf. further C. Escher and R. Machter, *Chronik der Gemeinde Wipkingen* (Zurich, 1917), pp. 35–36.

47. Egli, doc. 422.

taken immediately, such incidents of destruction would not only continue in Zurich but increase. The demonstrations of the preceding weeks constituted a growing threat to general peace and order in the city and its environs. More important, such action was critically endangering Zwingli's centrally planned and unified program of reform, with which the Great Council in particular was sympathetic.

On that very day, therefore, September 29, the city authorities acted. Electing four men from the Small as well as the Great Council, they issued the following decree: "J. Jakob Grebel, Master Setzstab, Master Binder, Master Berger, Master Wegman, Konrad Escher, Hans Usteri, and Heinrich Werdmüller, with the three people's priests [Zwingli, Jud, Engelhart], shall be responsible for the regulations concerning images and other things." [48] The eleven-man committee investigated the problem of images for two weeks, during which time no further iconoclasm was reported either in the city or in the countryside surrounding it. Its deliberations, however, were attended by heated, indeed "angry" discussion, for according to Bullinger, Hottinger's action had many defenders as well as opponents among the Council members.[49] On Monday, October 12, its decision was finally handed to the Council: a public disputation should be held on the propriety of religious art and the Mass. The Council accepted the recommendation and a disputation was accordingly planned for the last week in October:

> Upon the investigation of the three people's priests concerning "the Mass and images," it was decided to permit invitations for a Disputation on Monday after the Sunday before Simon and Jude [October 26] to be sent to the Bishops of Constance and Chur, to the Confederacy, and to all prelates and governors in the territory of Zurich in order that they may hold conversation and help to make a decision, based on the Holy Scriptures of the Old and New Testament, with respect to images and the Mass; how this matter is to be resolved so that it may be done in the way most pleasing to God the Almighty and in the way most satisfactory for all Christian, believing men; and in order that we shall live according to the will of God and His Holy Scriptures of both Testaments, since up to now there have been many misusages. Moreover, the prisoners shall remain lying in their jail until then.[50]

48. Egli, doc. 424.
49. Bullinger, *1*, 127.
50. Egli, doc. 430; the prisoners were Hottinger, Hochrütiner, and Ockenfuoss.

THE CHARACTER OF THE DEMONSTRATIONS

As a problem of public disorder or disturbance of the peace, iconoclasm had come to an end, for the September demonstrations were almost the only ones of any importance in the entire history of the Reformation in Zurich. Since these few scenes were so comparatively unspectacular, the historian is then compelled to ask why there should have been such scenes in the first place? What constituted the inner nature of iconoclasm in Zurich? True, the demonstrations were on a small scale: there were no spontaneous mass movements involving literally thousands of people as at Basel in 1529,[51] nor were there riots openly organized by one man, such as those under the leadership of Gabriel Zwilling at Wittenberg in 1521.[52] But some organization there must have been, for with the exception of Laurenz Meyer, the iconoclasts were openly associated with a radical reforming group which had emerged in Zurich in the spring of 1522.[53] Its existence posed a problem for Zwingli from the day in Lent, 1522, when its members surprised him by eating meat at Froschauer's house. Hochrütiner, Ininger, Hottinger, and Ockenfuoss were present at that meal. So, too, was Andreas Castelberger. By the end of the year Conrad Grebel had assumed leadership of the group, and by midsummer of 1523 Simon Stumpf was deeply involved as well. These men sought a fundamental reform of the Church, particularly its forms of worship, culminating in the abolition of the Mass. Some of their aims were thus not inconsistent with those of Zwingli. Their radicalism lay rather in

51. For vivid contemporary accounts of the iconoclastic riots in Basel see: (1) the detailed report of Councilman Fridolin Ryff, ed. Friedrich Fischer, "Der Bildersturm in der Schweiz und in Basel insbesonders," *Basler Taschenbuch, 1* (Basel, 1850), 17–37; (2) the considerably briefer description by the Dominican Johann Stolz, "Zur Geschichte des Bildersturms von 1529," *Basler Taschenbuch, 5* and *6* (Basel, 1855), 194–96; (3) the melancholy letter of Erasmus to Willibald Pirckheimer, *Opus Epistolarum Des. Erasmi Roterodami,* ed. P. S. Allen (Oxford, 1906–58), *8,* No. 2158, p. 162; and Oecolampadius' long letter to Wolfgang Capito, *Briefe und Akten zum Leben Oekolampads,* ed. Ernst Staehelin, Quellen und Forschungen zur Reformationsgeschichte, 19 (Basel, 1934), Vol. 2, No. 636, pp. 280–82. The letter was translated and appeared in 1529 as a pamphlet entitled *Was sich zuo Basel uff den achten tag des Hornungs/ der Mess und goetzen halb zuo tragen hat.—Item das die Mess der Bepstler zuo Strassburg abgethon Anno MDXXIX.*
52. On the iconoclastic riots in Wittenberg see Hermann Barge, *Andreas Bodenstein von Karlstadt* (Leipzig, 1905), *1,* 311–460.
53. Cf. Goeters, *Ludwig Hätzer,* pp. 31–32. For an extensive, closely documented study of this radical party I am greatly indebted to the doctoral dissertation of Robert Cutler Walton, "Zwingli's Theocracy" (Yale University, 1963).

the rapidity with which they wished to initiate and implement cultic reform. After four years of Zwingli's preaching, however, there had been in fact only one major change in the liturgy, the introduction at St. Peter's Church on August 10, 1523, of a simplified baptismal service in the vernacular.[54]

Not until July and August of this very summer of 1523 had the Reformer declared his intention to eliminate music from the liturgy because it was an unscriptural abuse. Less than a year passed before the Council took positive action on his decision. Ever since 1519, on the other hand, he had been criticizing the cult of the saints as one of the principal abuses of the Church. Yet after almost five years of such preaching, the images of these same saints remained as before. The majority of the citizens of Zurich evidently were content to abide by the decisions of the Council. But Hochrütiner, Hottinger, Ininger, and Ockenfuoss lacked Zwingli's foresight and had none of their fellow citizens' docility. The ever-widening disparity between proclamation of the Word and fulfillment of the Word had become for them literally unendurable. They would wait for Zwingli no longer. They could not by themselves eliminate the celebration of the Mass, or attack a church choir physically, even had they wanted to. On the other hand, they could, on their own initiative, remove paintings and saints' statues from the churches and destroy them. Ecclesiastical art had become the only possible, indeed the only remaining, focus for all their pent-up frustration. The contradiction between theory and practice was thus sharpened by the iconoclastic demonstrations of these radicals, and unspectacular though they were, they were nonetheless sufficient to compel Zwingli and the Council at last to official action. The September demonstrations were simultaneously a measure and a result of the gap between intention and action in Zurich. The decision to hold a formal disputation on the question of images represents the first stage in the closing of that gap.

54. Schmidt-Clausing, *Zwingli als Liturgiker*, p. 49.

6. THE WORD DEBATED

*Thou shalt not make unto thee any graven image, or any
likeness of any thing that is in heaven above, or that is in
the earth beneath, or that is in the water under the earth.*
Exodus 20:4

The public debate on images and the Mass was set for Monday, October 26,
1523. A sense of urgency must have attended all the plans, for on Monday,
October 12, the very day on which the eleven-man committee had recommended that a disputation be held, the Great Council issued a formal invitation to all the clergy in Canton Zurich,[1] as well as to the Bishops of Constance, Basel, and Chur, the University of Basel, and all the cantons in the
Confederacy. The response must have been disheartening. The Bishop of
Constance replied on Saturday that he would be guilty of insubordination—
not to the Pope only but to the Emperor as well—were he to take part in
such a discussion. He urged instead that Zurich relinquish the plan and wait
for the summoning of a General Council. Five days later the Bishop of Basel
returned much the same excuse, in addition pleading old age and poor
health. The Bishop of Chur and the University of Basel ignored the invitation entirely. Of the cantons, St. Gall and Schaffhausen alone agreed to send
representatives; the others either failed to answer or refused to participate.
The brusque, bitterly-worded reply from Obwalden received by the Council
on Sunday, October 25, the day before the disputation was to begin, best
reveals the strength of the opposition to such a debate from the Catholic
cantons of the Confederacy:

1. Bullinger, *1*, 128.

We reply as follows: we are happy at all times to be at your service; nevertheless we do not have particularly well-educated people, but rather pious and reverent priests who interpret the Holy Gospels and other Holy Scriptures for us, as were interpreted also for our forefathers, and as the Holy Popes and Council [sic] have commanded us. This we will maintain and in this we will believe until the end of our lives, and for this suffer even death, until a Pope or a Council command otherwise, for we do not intend, in so far as it is within our power, to alter what has been determined so regularly of old by the whole of Christendom, both spiritual and secular. Furthermore we do not believe that our Lord God has given so much more grace to Zwingli than to the dear saints and doctors, all of whom endured death and martyrdom for the sake of the faith, for we have no special information that he leads, as a result, a more spiritual life than others, but instead that he is disposed to agitation more than to peace and quiet. Therefore we shall send no one to him, nor to anyone like him, for we do not believe in him.[2]

Such thinly veiled indifference and open hostility notwithstanding, the Council realized that only a debate could ease the disturbing tensions within the city, and so it went forward stubbornly with its plans. On Monday morning, October 26, between eight and nine hundred priests and laymen of all sorts crowded into the Town Hall for the Second Zurich Disputation.[3] Since the iconoclastic demonstrations in the preceding month had been the principal reason for the calling of the debate, the problem of iconoclasm was given priority over that of the Mass. Doubtless because he was the author of the notable pamphlet approved by both Zwingli and Jud, Ludwig Hätzer was made recording secretary of the proceedings.[4]

The morning session of the first day began with the customary formalities of organization. Burgomaster Roist at once tactfully appointed the two delegates from St. Gall, Doctor Joachim Vadianus and Doctor Stoffel Schappeler, and the delegate from Schaffhausen, Doctor Sebastian Hofmeister, to preside over the several sessions of the debate. Kaspar Frey, the city clerk, read the text of the official invitation which had been sent out two weeks

2. For the text of the invitation see Z, 2, 678, 18 to 680, 4; cf. the abbreviated version in *Die Eidgenössischen Abschiede aus dem Zeitraume von 1521 bis 1528,* ed. Johannes Strickler, 4.*1*.a (Brugg, 1873), pp. 342–43. For the replies see, respectively pp. 343–44, 344–45, 345.

3. The exact number is a problem; see the discussion in Farner, *3,* 435.

4. The text of the Disputation was published on December 8, 1523; cf. Hätzer's account of its preparation, Z, 2, 673, 11–29.

previously. After these preliminaries, Zwingli spoke about the nature of the disputation to be undertaken, carefully emphasizing, as he concluded his brief remarks, that any practical action taken as a consequence of the debate would be determined later by the civil authorities of Zurich.[5] The sole responsibility of the present assembly was one of principle, namely to hear the Word of God on the matter of images and the Mass. Because Scripture alone was to be admissible evidence, the validity of the entire procedure was instantly called into question by Conrad Hoffman (683, 35; 689, 28), one of Zwingli's most determined and articulate opponents in the chapter of the Great Minster, but after much fruitless wrangling he was silenced by President Hofmeister. Only after that was actual debate on images opened, with a bluntly worded speech by Leo Jud, who, by inciting the September demonstrations with his sermon in St. Peter's Church, had in effect made such a debate necessary.

THE INITIAL DEBATE: JUD AND LÜTI

Jud began by recommending Hätzer's work to the assembly. "There exists," he said, "a small book printed here a few days before this in which images are sufficiently condemned by clear Holy Scripture" (690, 12–14). The allusion was to the first, and much the longer, section of Hätzer's pamphlet. By maintaining that these thirty-three biblical passages so adequately supported the iconoclast position that it was unnecessary to cite them or rehearse their contents, Jud immediately made it clear that the fundamental direction of his argument was to be shaped exclusively by evidence from Scripture. With regard to images, he stated that he would "accept only the spring and source from which all subsequent writings and prohibitions flow, namely the text of Exodus 20" (690, 17–18).

Jud did not, however, rest his argument solely on that text. He pressed the attack on images further by introducing evidence from the New Testament, in order, as he said, that "no one might say that these passages are only from the Old Testament, which has to do solely with the Jews and not with Christians" (291, 1–3). His principal text at this point was Paul's First Epistle to the Corinthians, 5:11: "But now I have written unto you not to keep company, if any man that is called a brother be a fornicator, or covetous, or an idolator, or a railer, or a drunkard, or an extortioner; with

---

5. Unless indicated to the contrary, all references in the text are to Vol. 2 of Zwingli's works.

such an one do not to eat." The passage was especially important for Jud, because in it the Apostle discriminated between Christian and non-Christian with respect to the practice of idolatry. It would be humanly impossible, Paul maintains, to shun all genuine pagans who worship images. The responsibility of the genuine Christian, therefore, is to avoid his brothers who persist in idolatry while yet styling themselves Christians. Jud is at great pains to stress the difference. "Here," he says, citing the preceding verse of the same chapter, "St. Paul definitely speaks of Christians, for he also indicates that he does not mean the heathen" (691, 8–9). The parallel that Jud saw between ancient Corinth and sixteenth-century Zurich, although implicit, is clear. The iconophiles in Zurich, in terms of the Pauline distinction, are Christians in name only, and in consequence must be shunned by those who would be genuine Christians. In this fashion Jud concluded his initial remarks, challenging anyone present to rebut his position, provided that scriptural evidence only was employed to that end.

The speech evidences to a remarkable degree his familiarity with the work of Hätzer. The major scriptural texts are substantially the same in both, they follow one another in the same sequence, and the arguments adduced from them are identical. The delivery of Jud's speech was doubtless, as President Hofmeister remarked, "powerful and clear" (691, 34), but with respect to content it was, in effect, little more than a spoken version of Ludwig Hätzer's first Answer.

It is not surprising, then, that after Jud sat down, Hätzer himself spoke out, saying, "Doctor! Secret images also are forbidden. For this we have a clear passage in Scripture in Deuteronomy 27" (692, 11–12). Inasmuch as Jud had complimented his pamphlet with paraphrase as well as public praise, Hätzer evidently felt that neither Jud nor he had made it sufficiently explicit that *all* images were forbidden *everywhere,* and not simply in places of public worship. To this radical extension of the image ban, no objection was voiced. Indeed Conrad Grebel affirmed it, remarking that "if images should not exist among Christians, then they should also not be kept in secret" (692, 21–22).

Silence followed. President Hofmeister asked if there was anyone who wished to object. After a pause, Heinrich Lüti, who as recently as June of 1523 had left Zurich to assume new pastoral duties at the town of Winterthur, rose from his seat to answer Jud.[6] The ensuing dialogue between the two men was not, however, a debate in the usual sense of the word. Lüti

6. On Lüti see the biographical note and further references in Z, 2, 693, n. 1.

attacked Jud's position only, as he said, "in order that we may have something to argue about" (693, 13); he would do so from Scripture "insofar as it was possible" (693, 16). And when at last he had finished, Hätzer recorded that "he did not raise such objections because he was of that opinion, but only that they might be spoken of" (699, 7–8). Lüti, in other words, was simply going to play devil's advocate before the assembly.

"Master Leo!" he began, "It appears to me that all places and passages in the Scripture which you have brought forward to prove that images should not exist have to do only with the images of the idols of the heathen and not with the likenesses of Christ and the dear saints" (693, 23–26). Jud insisted that he prove his allegation from Scripture. Lüti replied first by referring to the Golden Calf of Aaron, perhaps the most notorious instance in which the Israelites had outraged the Lord by making and worshiping an image, and then by reiterating his contention that God's prohibition of such images did not extend to likenesses of Christ and the saints. "That does not, however, prove that one should therefore have images" (694, 17–18), Jud retorted. Undaunted, Lüti pointed out that God had commanded Moses to erect a brass serpent for the Israelites. Furthermore, at His instruction, two golden cherubim were affixed to the Ark of the Covenant. "Thence," Lüti concluded, "it is clearly seen that He has no horror of images" (694, 28–29).

The introduction of these two precedents for the propriety of images, precedents not only sanctioned but commanded by God Himself, constituted a major attack on the extreme iconoclastic position which Jud had adopted. Against this evidence he now advanced a long, closely reasoned speech which suggests that he was thoroughly prepared for just such arguments: "The commandment of God in Exodus 20 remains throughout eternity firm and unbroken, although God has ordered certain persons to act against the commandment at various times. That He ordered the serpent to be made, I admit. From that it is not proper, however, for anyone to act contrary to the commandment and to make images and idols" (694, 32–34; 695, 1–3).

The permanent validity of the Second Commandment on which Jud had insisted earlier still constituted the nerve center of his argument. But having thus reiterated his fundamental position, Jud spoke directly to Lüti's objections. Any violation of the commandments recorded in Scripture is divinely ordained. So, he admitted, "God has ordered us not to kill and yet directs Abraham to kill his son" (695, 7–8). Furthermore, "God has forbidden us to steal and yet directs the children of Israel to take from the Egyptians their silver and gold finery" (695, 16–18). There are, then, such exceptional instances, but they are particular exceptions which do not invalidate the commandments generally. Those who have broken them have done so under a special dispensation given only by God Himself.

Relentlessly pursuing his argument, Jud proceeded to combine the idea of a special dispensation with the conventional typological analysis of the serpent as a prefiguration of the Cross. The erection of the serpent "is a figure and shadow of the Old Testament which symbolizes the lifting up of our Redeemer Jesus Christ on to the Cross, as the Lord Himself has declared and shown [John 3:14]" (695, 27–29). This allusion to the Gospel of John permits him then to incorporate into his argument the Johannine doctrine of worshiping in spirit and in truth, but applied now in unconventional fashion to the serpent-Cross typology. Christ is the living serpent without poison who has banished the deadly brass one; immortality has thus banished mortality, and consequently internal, invisible, and intangible reverence has replaced any necessity for external, visible, and tangible representations, either in the Old Testament form of the brass serpent or in the New Testament form of the Cross. The true Christian requires no such aids to devotion, for he worships in spirit and in truth. "Palpable and external images are," in fact, "a hindrance to the spirit" (696, 13–14). Moreover, that assertion obtains without qualification, even with regard to the physical presence of Christ Himself, because it was for that very reason, Jud maintained, that Christ had said, "unless I go from you, the spirit, the comforter will not come [John 16:7]" (696, 11–12). Wherever the spirit is, all images are unnecessary, even that of a crucifix. Thus Jud epitomizes the intensity of both his Johannine spirituality and his aversion to any visual representation of the content of Scripture.

His defense of iconoclasm against Lüti had been thus far scriptural. He was concerned, as was his opponent, exclusively with the interpretation and exegesis of biblical texts. But his real opponent, after all, was the widespread and extreme, if not idolatrous, reverence of the common people for relics and such cult statues and images as that of St. Anne at Ober-Stammheim. Thus as he moved toward his conclusion, Jud spoke for the first time to the practical problem of the people's excessive veneration or adoration of visible representations. They "accord such images great honour, and entreat them with ornaments, silver, gold, precious stones, with sacrifices and with reverence, that is by taking off their hats, bowing, and kneeling before them, all of which, however, God has forbidden" (696, 17–20). Such behavior, so clearly verging on idolatry, was more than sufficient reason for the total prohibition of images. And Jud did not fail to demonstrate that to the scriptural evidence for their prohibition could be added scriptural warrant as well for their destruction, for King Hezekiah had torn down the brass serpent because the Israelites burned incense before it (696, 26–28).

Having countered Lüti's allusion to the serpent, Jud spoke now to the problem of the two cherubim. Returning to his initial argument, he maintained that these were to be understood as special and restricted dispensations from the Second Commandment, ordained by God. Indeed, the cherubim could not even be classified, strictly speaking, as images. They were rather an "ornamentation and decoration on the cornice of the Ark" (697, 5–6), which in turn was "a ceremonial thing" (697, 1–2). This being so, the two cherubim could therefore be dismissed as visual aspects of Jewish ceremonial law which, in contrast to the moral law, had been abrogated and was no longer binding on Christians.

To Jud's interpretation of Scripture, Lüti could not reply. He drew instead on what had constituted for Hätzer the third major iconophile Argument: "Everything which the Pope regulates, ordains, and does is right and cannot be in error. Pope Gregory directed pictures to be made as books for laymen. Thus to have images is not wrong" (698, 4–9). Gregory's decision had indeed become normative in the West, but it was nevertheless a papal decision, grounded not in Scripture but on Gregory's reaction to the immediate exigencies of a given situation. Thus Lüti's citation of Gregory was, in effect, the tacit admission of his inability to rebut Jud further in accordance with the terms of the disputation, and the exchange between the two thereafter was brief and inconsequential. The devil's advocate had played out his part; the first phase of the disputation was finished.

A PROPOSAL FOR COMPROMISE: KONRAD SCHMID

At this juncture Konrad Schmid rose to address the assembly. Born probably in 1476, the son of a wealthy peasant from Küsnacht in Canton Zurich, he had studied at the University of Basel, where he had earned both a bachelor's degree in theology and a master's in philosophy. After his return to Zurich, he was appointed Commander of the Knights Hospitalers of St. John at Küsnacht on March 10, 1519, Zwingli's first year as people's priest at the Great Minster. Despite the fact that he was some eight years Zwingli's senior, he and the Reformer soon became fast personal friends. By 1522, for example, Schmid, who was also a pastor at Küsnacht, had delivered a sermon for Zwingli at Lucerne; and seven years later, while Zwingli was away at Marburg, he preached at the Great Minster in the latter's stead. He had accompanied Zwingli in 1522 to Einsiedeln for the ceremonies of the Angelic Dedication; in 1528 he would travel with him again, on this occasion to the famous disputation at Bern, where he was one of the four presidents as well as a preacher; and on October 11, 1531, at the second battle of Cappel, both he and his great friend perished, still fighting together for the evangelical cause.[7] In his own right the Commander was a figure of influence and importance in the canton. That he was on such intimate terms with Zwingli enhanced his already considerable prestige, so that his opinion on any subject would not be lightly regarded by the gathering. His speech represents the moderate point of view at its best, and what he advocated with such eloquence is of major significance for the course of the debate.

He hastened to make known his wholehearted agreement with Jud that the Word of God in Scripture must be the exclusive norm of judgment for the Christian answer to the problem of images. That done, he moved toward the center of his argument, namely that Jesus Christ constitutes man's only means of access to God: "There is no way to eternal life other than Christ [John 14:6]. There is no mediator between us and God other than Christ. There is no intercessor or advocate other than Christ Jesus [1.Tim. 2:5]. There is no sacrifice for sins other than He [Heb. 9:26]. There is no solace or succor other than in Him." (702, 25–30). Schmid further stressed his conviction that in all possible divine-human encounters, the Son alone mediates between God the Father and man: "He is lord and master over all pious Christians, and furthermore over everything which they require: over remission of sins and grace, over succor and solace, intercession and propitiation, righteousness and godliness, health and sickness, over hell and heaven, death and life, over joy and salvation in heaven and on earth" (702, 34–36; 703, 1–2).

The full significance of his argument is disclosed only when Schmid added: "And that is His true sovereignty, *which He may give to no one*" (703, 2–3; italics mine). The Lordship of Christ is so unconditional that even He is powerless to delegate any one of His manifold functions to another, even though He Himself might wish to do so. No other creature may rightfully lay claim to possession of any one of those functions or any part of any one of them. Accordingly, anyone who believes that creatures participating in Christ's sovereignty do exist cannot, for that very reason, regard

7. Cf. Z, 2, 699, n. 5.

himself as a true Christian. But, Schmid continued, such is the present condition of Christianity that men in fact do believe in such creatures and in the power of their images (703, 8-9). With that pointed allusion to the saints *and* their images, Schmid cut through to the heart of the problem.

Jud and Lüti both had discussed the propriety of the existence of images, citing and counterciting biblical proof texts, for the most part in academic fashion. Neither had squarely confronted the fact that the real issue was not so much the propriety of images in general as the nature, power, and function of the saints who were represented by them. Of this issue Zwingli had been fully aware, to be sure, since his reading of Erasmus' poem *The Complaint of Jesus,* and much of his preaching after his arrival in Zurich had been a sustained critique of the saints. But such concern as he might have had with respect to their representation in painting and sculpture had definitely been subordinated, as has been shown, to his attack on the people's belief in their intercessory powers. Now Schmid was to force that crucial question to the center of the debate. For him, as for Zwingli, fruitful discussion would have to direct itself first to the cult of the saints, then to their images.

The denial of Christ as exclusive mediator in all divine-human encounters had issued in what is for Schmid "the greatest and worst idolatry of all" (703, 13)—the general belief that the saints may intercede with God on man's behalf. This initial theological error had been compounded further by the attribution of particular intercessory powers to particular saints. Paintings and statues of them served only to exacerbate this false piety, inasmuch as the images themselves were increasingly invoked and invested with power instead of those whom they represented. In such fashion "an endless number of idols has sprung" (703, 13-14) from that initial error of belief, all of which ultimately are tangible and visible expressions of either the qualifications or of the outright rejection of the unconditional Lordship of Christ (703, 36-37; 704, 1-5). Since through external and material forms they not only express but also perpetuate an inner and spiritual belief which is false, images of the saints cannot be tolerated. This idea, intrinsically important, is especially significant, for it is possibly the first public expression of an iconoclastic argument that Zwingli was to develop at considerable length two years later in his *Answer to Valentin Compar.*

The saints themselves, Schmid continued, wish neither to be venerated nor to be worshiped. They desire neither to be intercessors nor to be regarded as such. Precisely that argument had been advanced by Hätzer, citing Acts

3:12–16 in the second Answer of his pamphlet. Schmid cites the same passage and draws from it an identical, if somewhat more strongly worded, conclusion. "If, then, the saints, during that time and while they were alive on earth . . . did not wish accorded to them the praise or honor which one should give only to Christ, how much the less do they want this when they are in heaven and have escaped from all evil desires for praise and glory" (704, 16–20). Scriptural evidence clearly invalidates any belief in the intercession of the saints. To invoke a saint in heaven, even without the aid of an image, is utterly wrong. Accordingly, images of the saints are as much an offense to the saints themselves as they are to Christ (704, 5–7).

Schmid's concluding argument, directed now to the question of the representation of Christ, continued to focus on the problem of correct belief: "For it is a great idolatry if men picture Christ Jesus differently in their hearts, and create an image [*gestalt*] of Him other than that which the Divine Word paints for us. . . . Now the Divine Word paints and depicts him to us as the only mediator and redeemer, as the only sacrifice for sins" (703, 14–16; 20–22.) In other words, Schmid declared, all representations of Christ, whether mental or physical, must conform to a single, exclusively scriptural type. Such extreme legalism, however, clearly enjoins what is beyond attainment: no two Christians can ever have in their minds identical images of Christ "as the only sacrifice for sins." Luther, for example, once confessed that "whether I will or not, when I hear of Christ, an image of a man hanging on a cross takes form in my heart, just as the reflection of my face naturally appears in the water when I look into it." [8] That is perhaps the most obvious image of Christ as "sacrifice for sins," but it is certainly not the only one, as Luther would have been the first to admit, nor is it the only possible image of Christ as mediator. At this point the difficulties of combining uniformity of vision with theological exactitude require no further comment. And even if the picture of "a man hanging on a cross" were the theologically correct one, no artist, professional or amateur, could translate that mental picture into a sensible form, because he could never determine exactly the shape or the colors of "the man" in accordance with the "Divine Word," since the physical appearance of Christ is never described in the Scriptures. Given the terms of Schmid's radical restriction to Scripture, there is no possibility whatsoever for the activity of the creative imagination. Accordingly, no objective, visual representation of Christ is possible. Thus,

8. *Luther's Works,* ed. Jaroslav Pelikan and Helmut T. Lehmann, *40* (Philadelphia, 1958), 99–100.

although the course of his argument had been notably different, Commander Schmid had reached at last a conclusion identical with that of Jud.

Schmid's disagreement with Jud lay on grounds of procedure, not of principle. He was evidently far more sensitive than Jud to the enormous strains which the traditional piety of the average Christian would experience by the immediate abolition of images to which he had been so long attached. Nothing would in fact be accomplished except God's command. He urged instead that the Council allow them to remain where they were, untouched, but that the people be instructed rigorously and continuously that "there is neither life, holiness, nor grace in them" (705, 1–2), so that in time images would simply be ignored:

> One should not take from the hand of a weak man the staff on which he leans; one should give him another, lest he fall to the ground. But if a weak man clings to a reed that wavers with him, one should leave that in his hand, and at the same time show him a stronger staff, so that he will then of his own accord let the reed fall, and grasp the stronger staff.   [704, 30–36]

Such a compromise was not without precedent, for the course of action he proposed had already been realized earlier at Stadelhofen. Precisely because it would no longer "lead him astray," Heini Hirt had refused to aid Claus Hottinger in destroying the great crucifix at the city gate. Through education in the Word, the miller had voluntarily dispensed with a reed and was in possession of a stronger staff, so that actual removal of the image was unnecessary. Schmid may have heard Hirt's testimony. Whether he had or not, he was now arguing that all the people of Zurich were to be taught in similar fashion that images are in themselves useless.

But the Commander's program for the education of the city was twofold. It was to consist not merely in a verbal assault on visible images but also in a total reorientation of the internal structure of popular piety, in an attack on what he had earlier termed "the greatest and worst idolatry of all," the people's belief in the intercessory powers of the saints. A concerted attempt to obliterate belief and trust in the saints was far more necessary and far more urgent than the obliteration of their images. "Thus," he said, "I would wish one to do away with the inner images through vigorous preaching of God's Word" (705, 32–33), and in their stead gradually place the single figure of Jesus Christ, for if "through right knowledge Christ were in the hearts of men, then all images would be put aside without offense" (705, 6–8). Any physical removal or destruction of images was therefore unnecessary. Indeed, no other course of action was possible, he warned, for "if some one does not have in his heart the rightly created image of Christ, and then destroys every image on earth, he is nevertheless a devilish man and an Anti-Christ" (706, 23–26).

Then what did Schmid intend when he referred to the "rightly created image of Christ"? Such a statement would at first appear to stand in open contradiction to everything that he had said before. Actually, however, the phrase leads into the heart of all his arguments. Through ever more intensive instruction in Scripture, the people would come to realize that images of Christ cannot be understood in any way as material objects of painted stone or wood. There is, in fact, only one possible image of Christ, a purely spiritual one—namely, man's attempt to live the Christian life. Therein lies the final goal of what is, in its essence, a thoroughly Erasmian ethical program: "Whoever has the true picture [*war bild*] of Christ in his heart, that is *whoever lives as Christ lived* . . . that is His genuine image [*rechtes bild*]" (706, 3–8; italics mine). *The image of Christ is thus the imitation of Christ.* Creating that image is a response to the challenge of the Gospels which can be undertaken by any individual who acknowledges Christ and bends every effort to live as He did. Thus the Christian becomes in his person a living image of Christ to the degree in which his imitation is achieved.[9] And only in this way can the ideal of a uniformity of the Christ image, which Schmid had earlier advocated, be attained. Schmid developed this idea no further, however, for at this point, while still formulating the compromise, he was cut short. President Hofmeister interrupted his speech to remind him that he was not permitted to make specific recommendations to the assembly (707, 7–13). Schmid started to protest when Zwingli himself rose to speak.

THE COMPROMISE REJECTED: HULDRYCH ZWINGLI

The Reformer had chosen his moment well. Jud's radical position on the image question had been well known in Zurich, at the very least since the

9. In all likelihood under the influence of the published text of the Disputation, Oecolampadius employed a similar argument against images in his commentary on Isaiah 44:6–20; cf. *Das theologische Lebenswerk Johannes Oekolampads,* ed. Ernst Staehelin, Quellen und Forschungen zur Reformationsgeschichte, 21 (1939), 208; cf. pp. 344–45, 559–60, where the arguments adduced in his commentary on Daniel 3:1 are clearly influenced by those of Zwingli in the *Answer to Valentin Compar.*

first of September. Lüti had merely been acting as devil's advocate, and the exchange between the two had largely been an exercise in biblical citation. Schmid, on the other hand, by focusing attention on the popular belief in the saints, had approached the problem from a point of view with which Zwingli was in complete accord. In addition, he had submitted a realistic as well as reasonable solution to the practical question of what was to be done with the images—a solution which, in its Erasmian moderation and its marked emphasis on instruction in God's Word, would likewise seem to have Zwingli's approval. And so, at first, it did. After warmly seconding Jud's insistence that images should not be made, worshiped, or venerated (707, 23-26), he confessed "that my lord and brother the Commander here advises that one should first educate the world with the Word of God and preach the same firmly pleases me very much indeed, and I am of exactly the same opinion" (707, 26-29).

Agreement between the two friends ceased there. Against Schmid, Zwingli argued that images ought to be removed as soon as possible, in all likelihood because he had interpreted the iconoclasm of September as an indication that the people of Zurich were in fact ready for their abolition: "Had the useless priests and bishops earnestly preached the Word of God as they were ordered . . . it would never have come to the point where the poor layman who is unknowing of Scripture has had to learn about Christ from walls and illustrated pages" (708, 18-22). After more than four years of his preaching, however, the people were fully aware that "images are not to be tolerated. For anything which God has forbidden is not an indifferent thing" (708, 22-24).

During the course of his plea for a compromise, Commander Schmid had cited scriptural evidence in support of the procedure he was advocating. Daniel, Shadrach, Meshach, and Abednego all had worshiped God steadfastly amid a welter of Babylonian idols. That they were surrounded by these idols had in no way undermined their faith, as proved by the spectacular ordeals of the den of lions and the fiery furnace (706, 10-17). "Moreover, Paul allowed images to exist among the Athenians and let them remain; but he taught that there was neither divinity nor grace in the carved images" (706, 18-20). From these examples Schmid had argued that the existence of images as an aid to the weak in faith could be prolonged without danger to the strong in faith.

Zwingli replied with a radically different interpretation of the same evidence:

That Shadrach, Meshach, and Abednego allowed idols or images to remain is true. But who compelled them to do so? Their king, who was
not a Christian. Otherwise they would not have tolerated that. Thus if
we lived among heathen, then we would have to endure that also. I
hope, however, that we are living among Christians. If an unbelieving
prince were to erect an image, then I must let the same stand;—but no
Christian should do that. The same is true likewise of Daniel; the king
also was not a believer. That Paul allowed the Athenians to keep their
idols is right, moreover, for they were not yet Christians. Had they been
Christians, then he would not have allowed it.   [709, 16–26]

To be sure, all examples adduced by Commander Schmid had a pattern in
common, that of an individual or a group professing one religion set over
against an authority or a community professing another. Under similar circumstances Zwingli admits that he himself would tolerate the erection of an
image by non-Christian authorities. Why, he asks, would I want to overturn
the images of the Turks (709, 26–27)?

But, he continues, the situation in Zurich does not conform to the pattern
of this conflict between two antithetical religions. The entire city is at least
nominally Christian, so that the conflict is one wholly *within* Christianity, an
opposition between true belief and false belief, true practice and false practice. Between the historical situations in the Near East or Athens and the
present situation in Zurich, Zwingli carefully draws the following pointed
distinction: "There are two kinds of offense. Some are an offense not because
they are sick and weak in belief, but because they are completely godless.
That is not *infirmitas;* indeed, that is a genuine, true *malignitas,* for they do
not believe at all. Some, however, are weak in right belief, and are to be
treated with particular consideration." (709, 29–33.) All the examples on
which Schmid had drawn were instances of believers, either in the God of
Israel or Christ, confronting pagan *malignitas.* Zurich faced an entirely
different and less simple problem. Here Christians were confronted by
Christian *infirmitas*—that is to say, men and women who were still weak in
Christian belief. God's prohibition of images means that they cannot be employed to aid the weak under any circumstances, for Zurich is a Christian
community; all its members live under God's Word. Therefore, to continue
to rely on images, even for a short time more, would be not only to prolong
one of the worst abuses of the Roman Church but to prolong idolatry itself.
Indeed, man is always subject to "sinful temptations [*Anfechtungen*]"

(710, 9), equated here by Zwingli with "inward idols" (710, 7). Inasmuch as no Christian ever could be strong enough in his faith wholly to withstand temptation, and inasmuch as images were an ever-present temptation to the sin of idolatry, the least that could be done was to remove them as quickly as possible. For "if one were to wait with the idols until no one was offended by them any more . . . then the commandment of God to do away with the idols would never be fulfilled" (710, 3-6). A compromise would thus be intolerable. In banning images God actually "has foreseen such idolatry. He would not otherwise have forbidden it with such express words in both testaments" (709, 2-4). On these grounds Commander Schmid's plea for an indefinite postponement of the removal of images was completely rejected. There was no further debate at this point between Zwingli and Schmid. Indeed, according to Hätzer's report, the latter expressed not only satisfaction but also pleasure with the Reformer's arguments (710, 31-32).

THE DISPUTATION CONCLUDED

Others, however, did raise objections to Zwingli's attack on the cult of the saints. One of his stubborn opponents in the chapter of the Great Minster, Jakob Edlibach, returned to the controversial fourth chapter in Exodus 20 and sincerely reaffirmed Lüti's contention that it did not prohibit images of the saints, "for Saint Martin has done charitable work. May one not then paint him in doing so, in order that he may encourage the giving of alms?" (711, 27-29). Zwingli had already made clear his point of view toward the passage in Exodus. To the idea of pictorial representation of the saints as a source of inspiration for Christians, he retorted that "no one should exhort you except the one God and His Word" (711, 35; 712, 1). Johannes Widmer, a chaplain at the Great Minster, protested, saying that "one should honor the saints as members of Christ" (713, 24), to which Zwingli replied that "Christ alone was given us as a model for living, and not the saints; for the head must lead us, and not the members" (714, 5-7).

After an adjournment for lunch, the assembly reconvened. President Hofmeister urged that any one present who objected to the conclusions reached that morning speak out, but there was no one in the hall who would seriously defend in public either the use of images or the cult of the saints. The only distinguished guest to speak was Dr. Balthasar Hubmaier of Waldshut, who supported the iconoclastic position at length and with enthusiasm (716, 17-33; 718, 1-2), although he contributed nothing new or of note to the several arguments already brought forward. Over four years previously, in 1519, he had been appointed the first chaplain of a chapel in Regensberg dedicated to the Virgin Mary. The chapel had rapidly become famous as a miraculous shrine, and Hubmaier evidently believed completely in the miracles wrought there.[10] Although his thinking had begun to change in the spring and summer of 1523 while he was pastor at Waldshut, his unqualified opposition to images in October is significant, for it discloses the impact of such a disputation on a sensitive mind in a state of transition between the traditional form-life of the Church and a radically new faith.

On the morning of the second day he attacked the use of images again, even more strongly (760, 33-35; 762, 1-22), and upon his return to Waldshut he quickly drew up eighteen theses for debate, the seventh of which read: "Images are good for nothing; wherefore such expense should be no longer wasted on images of wood and stone, but bestowed upon the living, needy images of God."[11] Although there is some doubt whether a debate was ever held, there is no doubt that what Hubmaier proposed was put into practice: by June 1524 all pictures and statues had been removed from the town church.[12] That such decisive action was taken—a month before the removal of the images in Zurich—is a not inconsiderable practical result of the disputation.

Hubmaier's speech excepted, the remainder of the afternoon discussion proved to be of little consequence, and President Hofmeister, realizing that nothing of value was being accomplished, decided to conclude the session. Speaking for the entire assembly he thanked God that the first day had been a profitable one in that it had been decisively demonstrated from the Word of God, as well as approved, that images should not be tolerated among Christians. He closed by entering an eloquent plea for Klaus Hottinger and his two companions who had been imprisoned ever since the Stadelhofen episode, pointing to the fact that they had simply put into practice what Zwingli and Jud had been preaching, and what in fact had now been approved by the assembly (730, 27-35; 731, 1-13). In response to his appeal for clemency Burgomaster Roist courteously assured Hofmeister that the Coun-

---

10. Henry C. Vedder, *Balthasar Hübmaier, The Leader of the Anabaptists* (New York, 1905), pp. 44-46.

11. Ibid., p. 70.

12. Strassburg followed Zurich some three months later. On October 18, after the customary St. Luke's Day procession, the citizens began to remove images and altars from several of the city churches; cf. *La Chronique Strasbourgeoise de Jacques Trausch et Jean Wenker*, Fragments des Anciennes Chroniques d'Alsace, 3 (Strasbourg, 1892), p. 153.

cil would consider the matter when the disputation was finished (731, 16–17). Thus the first day ended.

On Tuesday and Wednesday the question of the Mass was debated, and although there was sporadic discussion of images on both days, it was significant only in disclosing agreement with the decision reached on the first day. Benedikt Burgauer of St. Gall (758, 31–33), Jos Haas, the Prior of Embrach (769, 6–10), and Konrad Irmensee of Schaffhausen (770, 12–19) all expressed their approval. So likewise did Zwingli's supporters in the chapter of the Great Minster (763, 10–21; 764, 2–3), and even the Prior of the Augustinian monastery in Zurich confessed, albeit reluctantly, to his acceptance of the decision (776, 4–5).

Of all those who had come to agree with Zwingli the most influential was Commander Schmid. In a lengthy address given toward the close of the third day, he proposed that the Council prepare a memorandum on preaching the Gospel which would be normative for the whole canton (795, 4–38; 796, 1–14). He made no plea either for the retention of images or for any postponement of their removal from the churches. His silence on that point is eloquent testimony to the extent of Zwingli's victory: the most significant advocate of compromise had been won over completely to his point of view. Thus the Second Zurich Disputation ended in success for the Reformer: the necessity for the abolition of images had been approved in principle. Now it was the responsibility of the Council to reduce that principle to practice.

7. WAR AGAINST THE IDOLS

The Church
In which I had grown up, abominated
The pleasures of the senses, abhorred pictures,
Honouring but the incorporeal word.

Schiller

The Council decided immediately to act on Commander Schmid's proposal, and Zwingli was requested to prepare an introduction. He wrote this hastily between October 28 and November 9, 1523; on the latter day, after having read it to the Council, he saw it approved, and the manuscript was at once given over to Froschauer. On November 17 it appeared in print bearing the title *A Brief Christian Introduction*.[1] In addition to the two questions which had just been debated, Zwingli discussed simply and compactly the topics of sin, the Law, the Gospel, and the relationship between the two. The content of the brief section on images[2] is inseparable from that of the Second Disputation to a degree not hitherto fully appreciated, for it is singularly important as an epitome of what Zwingli considered the most substantial iconoclastic arguments proposed during the course of the debate. At the same time it indicates that he himself had initiated an approach to the problem of images independent of the debate. Thus the document reaches not only back to the disputation but forward as well to the extensive treatise against images in the *Answer to Valentin Compar*.

1. Z, 2, 630–63.
2. Z, 2, 654, 10–658, 23.

A BRIEF CHRISTIAN INTRODUCTION

First, with respect to educating pastors in the textual authority of Scripture, Zwingli referred to Hätzer's pamphlet with approval, much as Jud had done: "The little book concerning the abolition of images which appeared a short time ago may serve this purpose well; for it contains many citations from Scripture" (654, 14-16; cf. 690, 12-14). For those who did not own or could not obtain a copy of the pamphlet, Zwingli himself provided an extensive list of biblical passages which, with few exceptions, were based directly on those given by Hätzer. Second, with respect to the Gregorian dictum that images are of use in providing religious instruction, as Lüti had suggested, he insisted again that "we should be taught only by the Word of God; but the indolent priests, who should have been teaching us without respite, have painted doctrines on the walls, and we, poor, simple ones have been robbed of teaching thereby, and have fallen back upon images and have worshiped them" (656, 15-19; cf. 708, 18-22). As for the controversial chapters in Exodus (20:3-4) with which the disputation had begun, Zwingli provided now an interpretation which, despite its brevity, discloses a more penetrating approach to the problem than had hitherto been made.

When God commanded that man should have no other gods before Him, Zwingli declared, He intended the prohibition to be understood unconditionally, not only with respect to external, visible representations—that is to say, idols or images conventionally understood—but also with respect to *internal* images—ideas or patterns of human thought which are *invisible*. God alone was to be invoked for aid of any sort, for "whoever has sought in a creature the succor and solace for which the believer should seek only in God has made a strange god [*frombden got*] for himself; for it is always true that one's god is the one from whom he seeks help. That, therefore, is one thing which may draw us away from God: strange gods" (655, 21-25). In other words, by reliance on "strange gods" Zwingli, unlike Commander Schmid, does not mean simply belief in the intercessory powers of the saints or visible images of the saints, but rather all means of recourse, invisible or visible, which man may employ in times of trouble, anxiety, fear, or despair. In the religious life of the mind any idea, any movement of thought, which is directed not instinctively and immediately toward God but toward someone or something else is just such a "strange god," precisely because "one's god is the one from whom he seeks help." Thus, he argued, the two crucial sentences " 'you shall have no strange gods [Exod. 20:4]' and 'you shall have neither pictures nor likenesses [Exod. 20:4]' are, as it were, a protection and clarification of the First Commandment: you shall *trust* in one God" (655, 12–15; italics mine).

The most significant aspect of this brief commentary is that Zwingli carefully and explicitly draws a distinction between these "strange gods" of the mind, on the one hand, and visible images, such as those of the saints, on the other. The former may draw us away from God; the "other things which may draw us away are images" (655, 25–26). The existence of the former is clearly the more challenging problem for him, but he had neither the time nor the space to discriminate further between the two. What he has begun, however, is an initial exploration of the manifold implications of the phrase "inward idols of temptation [*inneren götzen der anfechtungen*]," which he had employed once in his debate with Schmid (710, 7–8). Since he would develop them at considerable length in the *Answer to Valentin Compar,* the passage here marks a distinctive and substantial step forward in the development of his thinking on the problem of ecclesiastical art.

Turning to a discussion of the visible images of the saints, Zwingli was at pains to refute the idea proposed by Jakob Edlibach in the debate that pictorial representation of good deeds and martyrdoms would inspire Christians to better lives. "For what reason have the saints done such things?" (657, 13–14), he asks, and to that question he replies, "from true belief" (657, 14–15). Consequently, "should one show us where their belief has been painted or pictured, we could only point out that it is in their hearts" (657, 15–16). Just as he had explicated the text of the Second Commandment in psychological fashion, so now Zwingli treats the examples of the lives of the saints. Rather than their great works themselves, the interior motivation which led the saints to perform them constitutes for him the more important aspect of their lives, and this motivation was nothing other than an exceptional belief and trust in God. He reiterates here what, according to Wyss, he had preached in 1522 with respect to their martyrdoms. The saints were saints because they had neither material images nor spiritual "strange gods" to whom they turned instead of God. Their belief and trust in God cannot be represented in form and color or in wood and stone, precisely because it is an exclusively spiritual phenomenon, a continuing state of mind, wholly beyond the reach of the artist's brush and the sculptor's chisel. "We cannot learn it from walls, but must learn it only from the merciful direction of God, from his own Word. We find here that images lead us only to outward stupidity and cannot make the heart believing. Thus we see indeed outwardly what the saints have done; but the belief from which all things must happen cannot be conveyed to us by images" (657, 18-24). Zwingli's ideal for all Christians is thus an intensity and a constancy of faith in God which at least approximates that which motivated and sustained the saints. Toward the attainment of that spiritual ideal, pictorial representation of their outward lives cannot possibly assist; it leads, on the contrary, to idolatry: "We call pieces of wood by the names of saints. One piece of wood we call Our Lady and the Mother of God, another we call Saint Nicholas, and so forth. And those who do this cry out that people want to destroy the honor due to the saints, while actually they are destroying the saints when they call the idols by their names" (656, 9-14). Commander Schmid had maintained that representation of the saints actually constituted an affront to them, because they would not want to be venerated, as people now venerated them, through their images. Zwingli pushes Schmid's objection to its limit by asserting that such spiritual value as the lives of the saints might have for the faithful is, in fact, completely obliterated by material images, because they are not even venerated through them but rather worshiped *in* them.

How, then, is the Second Commandment to be understood? Just as Lüti had done, Zwingli cited the cherubim as an example, referring in addition to the sumptuous appointments of Solomon's Temple (657, 31-33; 658, 1-4). Such purely ornamental objects are by no means forbidden, he maintained, echoing Jud's argument, for they do not conduce to idolatry (658, 8-14). But there is a radical difference between the decorative representation of palm trees or flowers in the Temple, and the pictures and statues of the saints crowding the churches of Zurich, because the latter "have clearly given birth to the danger of idolatry. Accordingly one should not let them remain there, nor in private rooms, nor in the market place, nor anywhere else where one does them honor. Above all they are not to be tolerated in churches, for everything which we have therein is sanctified" (658, 14-19).

Zwingli's decision is unequivocal. No work of art can be displayed, because it could induce a feeling of reverence on the part of the beholder which would, as Zwingli understood the problem, be ipso facto misdirected reverence. His prohibition, not merely for churches but for all public places and even private homes, recalls Hätzer's insistence that "secret images also are forbidden" (692, 11). But on the other hand, "if someone places representations of historic events [*geschichteswyss*] outside the churches, this may be allowed so long as they do not give rise to reverence" (658, 19–20). Zwingli hastened to add, however, that "when one begins to bow before them and to reverence them, then even these are not to be tolerated anywhere on earth" (658, 21–22). The artist's activity is to be limited henceforth to the representation of historic events.

What Zwingli intended by the word *geschichteswyss* is not precisely clear from its immediate context, but its implications may in great part be explained by a significant passage from the later *Answer to Valentin Compar.* Within the Great Minster there stood an altar panel on which was painted a kneeling Charlemagne, together with a replica of the Minster. Outside the Great Minster there had been set in a niche high up on the so-called Charles Tower a statue of Charlemagne seated on his throne.[3] Of these works of art Zwingli wrote to Compar: "We have had two great Charleses: the one in the Great Minster, which was venerated like other idols, and for that reason was taken out; the other, in one of the church towers, which no one venerates, and that one was left standing, and has caused no annoyance at all" *4, 95,* 18–21; 96, 1). The painting, merely because it stood within the Minster, was potentially capable of a religious interpretation, whereas the statue outside was not. The former, moreover, represented Charlemagne in a religious role, as legendary founder of a church; the latter represented him in a secular role, as legendary founder of a city. Consequently, the altar painting belonged to that category of images which for Zwingli "have clearly given birth to the danger of idolatry," whereas the statue was a pertinent example of the purely secular representational art to which he had no objection. Yet almost as if reiterating his earlier statement in *A Brief Christian Introduction,* Zwingli pointedly warned that with regard even to the statue of Charlemagne on the tower "as soon as anyone goes astray also with idolatry, then that, too, will be taken away" (*4,* 96, 1–2).

Thus by November 9, 1523, the Reformer seemed to have annihilated, in theory at least, any opportunity for the further creation of religious art either of a specifically ecclesiastical and public or of a more generally devotional and private character. By denying the theological propriety of such works of art and thereby prohibiting their commission, he had excluded the artist

3. For photographs of the statue consult Hans Hoffmann, "Baugeschichte bis zur Reformation," in *Das Grossmünster in Zürich,* Mitteilungen der Antiquarischen Gesellschaft in Zürich, 32, Part III (Zurich, 1941), plate 60.

from the service of the Church. On the other hand, he had permitted to the artist secular areas, primarily those of the decorative arts, in which the Zurich artisans had been so active before his arrival in the city.

In acceding to Commander Schmid's request for an order regulating the preaching of the Gospel in the canton, the Council had acted with alacrity. Its second decision, made with equal speed immediately after the disputation, was to establish a special committee to investigate ways eventually to remove all images from the city churches. Zwingli, Jud, and Engelhard naturally were appointed to it, as were four representatives each from the Small and Great Councils; serving also were the Prior of Embrach, the Abbot of Cappel, and Commander Schmid.[4] The representatives from the Small Council doubtless were loath to make any suggestions toward immediate action, because the burgomaster did not want the images removed at all; indeed, the very idea "was inimical to Herr Marx Roist, and a great burden upon him."[5] On the other hand, the three people's priests, together with the Prior, the Abbot, and Commander Schmid, were agreed that the images should be abolished as soon as possible, a conviction with which the representatives of the more evangelical Great Council were generally sympathetic. Yet it must not be forgotten that originally, Schmid had pled for the retention of images, and this earlier point of view, together with the conservatism of the Small Council and the iconophile influence of Roist generally, led now to an initial policy of great caution. The committee's first recommendation, returned to the Council sometime before November 11, was simply to leave the images standing while the faithful were further instructed on the subject of their removal. One procedural decision only was reached: those who had donated statues and paintings to the city churches could personally withdraw them now if they wished to do so.[6] What Kleinbrötli had insisted upon the very day of Jud's iconoclastic sermon had finally been adopted by the Council.

But the first interim solution quickly proved unsatisfactory. There was, in fact, such resentment among the canons of the Great Minster over the com-

4. Z, *8*, 129, 5–9.
5. Wyss, *Chronik*, pp. 40–41.
6. Z, *8*, 130, 11–12.

mittee's decision that by Thursday, December 10, the Council had requested Zwingli's advice.[7] He submitted the following memorandum, prepared in collaboration with Engelhard and Jud:

> First it is our opinion that the paintings should be immediately closed and not opened again until further notice. They are, after all, closed during periods of fasting and the other images are covered over. But the silver, gold, and other ornamental images shall not be carried again, either on festival or on other days, but the greatest treasure of the Word of God shall be carried in the hearts of men, not the idols before their faces.   [814, 4-10]

Zwingli's acquiescence to the Council's policy of moderation is here clearly evident. All paintings with moving panels which could be closed were to be shut—though, it must be noted, not necessarily permanently. The other images, such as the reliquaries or the silver gilt busts of Saints Felix and Regula, were never again to be carried in procession. On that point alone, if on no other, Zwingli had arrived at yet another procedural decision. All works of art were nonetheless to be allowed to remain in the churches temporarily. With respect to their final disposition, the memorandum read simply:

> Let us therefore leave the matter as [it stands] in the orders last given out, so that no one shall place any images either within or outside the churches, unless he has put them therein previously, or unless an entire congregation, with a majority, has decided to do this, and that without any shame, ridicule, and mischief and anything that may wantonly annoy anyone.   [814, 11-15]

The Council accepted Zwingli's suggestions in their entirety and at once prepared a briefer version of his memorandum to be issued publicly.[8] It was read aloud in the city churches three days later, on Sunday, December 13.[9]

The decree had hardly been promulgated before the more conservative canons of the Great Minster began again to protest any action, no matter how cautious, regarding images and the Mass. Indeed, their objections were so vociferous and so persistent that by the end of the week they had persuaded the Council to call another disputation on the two subjects, but one

7. Egli, doc. 456.
8. Ibid., doc. 458.
9. Ibid., doc. 456.

that was severely restricted. Invitations were sent out on Sunday, December 19, only to the members of the chapter of the Great Minster and the clergy within the city proper:[10] no one in Canton Zurich or any other canton was summoned. Furthermore, rather than inviting, as before, the Bishops of Constance, Chur, and Basel, as well as representatives of the University of Basel and the Confederacy, the Council decided to ask them for their written opinions on Zwingli's *A Brief Christian Introduction*. The debate itself was set for Monday, December 28.

On that day, only two months after the Second Zurich Disputation had been concluded, the canons of the Great Minster, the members of the Great and Small Councils, and all the clergy of the city met once more in the Town Hall to discuss the problem of images and the Mass. Unlike its predecessor, this debate, such as it was, played itself out by the end of the very first day. Both parties simply decided to hold yet a further disputation on the two questions early in the following year, and until then the canons reluctantly agreed to abide by the Council's interim measures of December 13.[11] Thus as the year 1523 ended, the images remained still in the Zurich churches, the people of the city were waiting still for a final decision on their removal by the Council, and Zwingli was preparing himself not only for the written opinions of the episcopal and Confederate authorities on his *A Brief Christian Introduction* but also for the forthcoming verbal opposition from the canons of the Great Minster.

THE FOURTH DISPUTATION: JANUARY 19–20, 1524

The debate with his own colleagues came first. If the Third Zurich Disputation had been considerably smaller than the second in size, the fourth was even more so.[12] The cathedral chapter chose five of their number, led by Conrad Hofmann. The Council in turn selected six of its ablest members, among whom was Commander Schmid. Together with Zwingli, Jud, and Engelhard, these fourteen men, representing the "old believers" and the "right believers,"[13] respectively, met in private on Tuesday and Wednesday, January 19 and 20, to discuss the problem of images and the Mass yet again.

10. Ibid., doc. 460.
11. Ibid.
12. Ibid., doc. 483.
13. See Egli, docs. 483, 484, 485, 486, 489, for the contemporary records of the Disputation. The phrase "old believers" is taken from Egli, doc. 483, "right believers" from Bullinger, *I*, 175.

The argument for the propriety of images was quite unlike that offered by Lüti in October of the preceding year. Here there was neither acting nor devil's advocacy; the canons must have realized that they were making a last stand. It was, on the whole, a lame one. Conrad Hofmann, the first to speak, failed to move his opponents despite the length and occasional petulance of his statement. Two of his colleagues decided to leave the matter to the decision of the Council. Another expressed the hope that he would not be compelled to dispute; then he, too, acquiesced to the Council. Only Rudolph Hofmann made any real attempt to defend the iconophile position.

Hofmann tried at first to rebut his opponents from Scripture alone, but fell back more and more on ecclesiastical tradition. His final statement was a document consisting of twenty-three theses drawn from a wide variety of sources, almost all of them nonscriptural.[14] So, for example, in the fourth thesis he cited Bonaventura's threefold argument for the necessity of images, and in theses 6, 7, and 14 simply repeated the evidence from Saint Augustine and Saint John of Damascus given by Bonaventura. Elsewhere he drew on Aquinas, Gabriel Biel, Saint Basil, Saint Anthony, Vincent of Beauvais, the decisions of Church councils, and Canon Law. In addition to all these he even adduced the sort of miraculous evidence so prevalent in the literature of popular piety, such as the Veronica at Rome, or the following:

> Likewise it stands written in a pious book called the *Fasciculus Temporum,* under the year 1214 after the birth of Christ: That a great stone cross had come down from heaven and the image of Christ had been set or painted on it. And thereupon was written in golden letters: *Jesus Nazarenus, Rex Judeorum.* And a blind man was made to see by this cross and crucified one.

Hofmann's defense rarely rises above the intellectual level of that quotation. In contrast to the brevity, conciseness, and power of Hätzer's pamphlet, Hofmann's theses are loose, rambling, and disorganized, giving the impression, ultimately, of intellectual bankruptcy. Consequently, after two days of fruitless discussion, the disputation was terminated.

With regard to images, the old believers among the canons had made their final attempt and had failed. Their disagreement with and resentment toward Zwingli and the Council continued; it could hardly be extinguished at

14. Egli, doc. 486. Hofmann's source for much, if not all, of his evidence was probably Gottschalk Hollen, *Praeceptorium divinae legis, clero et vulgo deserviens* (Nuremberg, 1497); cf. the description in Hermann Siebert, *Beiträge zur vorreformatorischen Heiligen-und Reliquienverehrung* (Freiburg im Breisgau, 1907), p. 22.

once, nor could it ever be entirely. Yet never again did they openly attempt to oppose or interfere either with Zwingli's recommendations or the Council's decisions on the question of images. The right believers had successfully concluded a most significant contest.

THE SECOND INTERIM DECREE: MAY 14, 1524

While Zwingli was waiting to hear from the Confederate and episcopal authorities beyond Zurich in regard to his *A Brief Christian Introduction,* the city was still awaiting the Council's closing action on the removal of the images. The people were fully conscious that the latter had been deferred only until Pentecost; [15] they must have been aware, too, that Zwingli had been privately debating the question with the cathedral chapter. Now that he had overcome this last opposition, curiosity and anticipation over the forthcoming decision grew apace. There had been no open iconoclasm in the city during the months intervening since the Second Disputation; on the other hand, there were still undercurrents of dangerous tension in Zurich. The possibility of a recurrence of open iconoclasm had by no means disappeared, and that the Council was quite aware of the fact is demonstrated by its action on Saturday, May 14. On the very eve of the great Pentecostal feast, the following decree was issued:

> Many people know how our lords have determined among themselves concerning images and the Mass, and commanded that the people should stand firm in this matter until now, that is to say, until Pentecost, and no one is to have done anything nor taken up anything. And since Pentecost is now here, unrest may consequently occur right away and our lords wish very much to be foresighted in this matter. And thus they command anew concerning these two matters, that is to say, images and the Mass, that still no one, be he woman or man, young or old, religious or lay, shall take up anything or do anything; but rather to wait for our lords who will take action in this matter as they think necessary and good.[16]

The candor of the document is revealing. Although the Council ran the not inconsiderable risk of "unrest" occurring "right away," it was forced nonetheless in public to imply that its members had not yet arrived at a final

15. Egli, doc. 530.
16. Ibid., doc. 530, sec. 7.

decision on the image question. The interim measures proposed first by the commission and seconded by Zwingli were apparently to continue in operation.

Less than twenty-four hours later, some incidents of iconoclasm were reported in Zollikon.[17] The fears of the Council were confirmed. If, despite the decree of May 14, iconoclasm had actually taken place on Pentecost itself, and in a small country village, how long could order be maintained in the city? Clearly, a final solution had to be found as rapidly as possible. Accordingly, on Monday, the sixteenth, the committee was requested to investigate the matter of procedure again.

> J. Jakob Grebel, M. Binder, M. Berger, M. Setzstab, M. Wegmann, Konrad Escher, Hans Usteri, and Heinrich Werdmüller shall obtain advice from the three people's priests of Zurich, the Abbot of Cappel, the Commander of Küsnacht, and the Prior of Embrach as to "what now their pleasure may be concerning images and the mass, how one shall act further therein, and what their opinion and that of the eight of my lords of the committee may be herein." These recommendations shall come in writing to the Great and Small Councils and the Burgomaster for further final measures.[18]

THE DECREE OF MAY 1524

At some time after May 21 the committee submitted its private report, written by Zwingli himself,[19] to the Council, and shortly after that, probably during the last week of May, the following decree, based on the committee's recommendations, was made public throughout the city:

> 1. Particular persons who have made [images] or who have had images made and set them up in churches shall, within one week, take these images from the churches and keep them at home. And if they are not taken out of the churches within one week, the church warden shall then take them out of the church and keep them among the other church possessions.
>
> 2. But where images, tablets and the like have been made from

17. Egli, doc. 535; cf. Heinrich Bruppacher and Alex. Nüesch, *Das alte Zollikon: kulturhistorisches Bild einer zürcherischen Landgemeinde von den ältesten Zeiten bis zur Neuzeit* (Zurich, 1899), pp. 49–56, esp. p. 55.

18. Egli, doc. 532.

19. Z, 3, 120, 1–123, 10.

[funds provided by] the members of the church as a group, then no single person shall take such things away, neither a few nor many, neither secretly nor openly, but let the decision if they wish to have them stay or not remain with the church membership as a whole, or the majority of them. And whatever the whole membership of the church or a majority shall clearly decide shall stand thereby as long as it is pleasing to them.

3. And whatever a church congregation shall decide concerning this shall thereby remain, and about or concerning this decision no congregation or single person shall speak to the others, entice them, disdain them, or irritate them, either with words or with deeds, but be quiet and peaceful. And whoever does not do this should be severely punished. In addition, no one shall make any more images in order, out of his own wish, to put them in churches, and no sculptor shall carve them on pain of heavy punishment.

4. And if a congregation shall have decided that they will let their images and tablets stand and remain in the churches, they should burn no candles before them, nor have any incense therein, nor burn incense before such images, nor do them any other reverence, but direct everything to the honor of God and Our Redeemer Jesus Christ alone.

5. And since the crucifix of Our Lord signifies no deity, but only the humanity and sufferings of Christ, and is also a sign for Christians and for the whole of humanity, such crucifixes of Christ shall remain everywhere in the churches and on the streets, in wayside niches and wherever they may be, and for this reason no one shall impiously break, tear out, or commit any wantonness with them on pain of heavy punishment.[20]

In its clear and powerful wording, this decree definitely represents an improvement over the temporizing decree of May 14. Moreover, the explicit ban on the creation of any more works of art intended for church use was definitely a new move forward, as was also the explicit prohibition of all reverence to the images then in the churches. And yet, these innovations notwithstanding, the decree, in effect, simply restated the basic provisions of the interim solution: privately or communally owned or commissioned statues, paintings, and votive tablets could be withdrawn from the churches by their donors; otherwise all works of art had to be left where they were. All that was new here with regard to procedure was the addition of a specified time-

20. Z, 3, 115, 16–116, 30; cf. Egli, doc. 543.

limit of one week for removal. Official commitment to a full-scale plan for the final and complete removal of the images was doubtless still being deferred by Burgomaster Roist.

THE FINAL DECISION: JUNE 15, 1524

Exactly one month after Pentecost, Marcus Roist suddenly died.[21] That it was indeed his personality and his influence more than anything else which had so prolonged a solution to the image problem is demonstrated by the fact that on Wednesday, June 15, the very day of his death, the Council issued still another decree, this one the long-awaited announcement of the removal of all the remaining images from the Zurich churches:

> Concerning the written recommendations of the committee on images, be it known "that one shall do away with images and idols with such good behavior that the Word of God will be given its due." The three people's priests and one man from each guild are to carry out this business, but are "to prevent the idols from being smashed wantonly." And if someone has made his own idols, he may with the permission of the committee take them into his own hand.—"Hereon there is added again that if from true, evangelical Scripture anyone can bring forward anything more true and divine against this, this same we will await, and thereinafter cordially be advised." [22]

The sudden change of tone in this brief and blunt text is extraordinary. Above all, the decree reveals that the Council did, in fact, have a plan for the removal of images and could act swiftly to implement it, granted the proper circumstances. The members of the committee on the problem of images may have devised it sometime after May 16; if so, it probably had not been used, because of Roist's objections. If prepared then, it may not even have been shown to him. Or it may have been formulated hastily on the day of his death. In any event the specific references in the decree to the three people's priests and one man from each guild indicate that beyond doubt a solution to the problem of removal was ready. That later on the same day the Council issued an even more strongly worded decree,[23] emphasizing and reaffirming the contents of the first, is further indication of the Council's preparedness.

21. Wyss, *Chronik,* p. 40.
22. Egli, doc. 544.
23. Ibid., doc. 546.

THE REMOVAL OF THE IMAGES: JUNE 20–JULY 2, 1524

Now that the solution had been found and approved, the Council continued to act swiftly. A committee of twelve men from the Council was chosen,
each one a member of a different guild.[24] To this initial group of twelve
cited in the decree, the city constable, also a member of the committee, added
the senior city architect and an unspecified number of stonemasons, smiths,
locksmiths, carpenters, and workmen of his choice.[25] The entire body of
men was headed by the three people's priests, Jud, Engelhard, and Zwingli.
Only five days were required for this preliminary organization, so that by
Monday, June 20, the final stage was at hand. The gap between intention
and action was at last to be completely closed; all was ready for what
Bullinger aptly called "the war against the idols."[26]

The committee as a body went into every church in Zurich. Once inside,
they locked the doors behind them, and then, free from all disturbance from
the curious crowds without, began to dismantle the church. The work was
done quietly and efficiently by the various experts who had been selected by
the constable for that purpose, and as a result no unnecessary damage or useless destruction was reported. Every standing statue was removed from its
niche or its base and, together with the base, taken out of the church. It was
then either broken up by the masons, if made of stone or plaster, or burned,
if made of wood. Every painting was taken down from the altars and
burned outside. All murals were chipped away or scraped off the walls. The
altars were stripped of all images and vessels, all votive lamps were let down
and melted outside, and all crucifixes were removed.[27] Even the carved choir
stalls were taken up and burned.[28] Then the walls were whitewashed so that
no traces whatsoever of the old decorations and appointments might be
seen.[29] That done, the whole group went on to another church and repeated
the process. The entire operation took only thirteen days, from Monday,

24. Ibid., doc. 552.
25. Wyss, *Chronik*, p. 42.
26. Bullinger, *1*, 175.
27. Wyss, *Chronik*, p. 42. Evidently the Council decided to revoke the fifth section of its
May decree, which may, indeed, have been simply a concession to Roist.
28. Ibid., p. 43. This was done in the Great Minster, for example, on the afternoon of
Thursday, June 30.
29. Only the altars remained. They were removed during July, August, and September
1526; cf. Wyss, *Chronik*, p. 70; Bullinger, *1*, 367; and Edlibach, *Chronik*, p. 279.

June 20, through Saturday, July 2.[30] By Sunday, July 3, 1524, scarcely a statue, a painting, a crucifix, a votive lamp, a reliquary, a shrine, or image or decoration of any sort was to be seen anywhere in the Zurich churches. When the pious Hans Stockar, he who had journeyed to Compostela and the Holy Land, came from Schaffhausen to Zurich and entered the Great Minster, he reported that "there was nothing at all inside and it was hideous." The "corporeal things" had disappeared, so that Zwingli could exclaim triumphantly: "In Zurich we have churches which are positively luminous; the walls are beautifully white!"[31] The idols had been vanquished.

30. Rudolph Staehelin, *Huldreich Zwingli: Sein Leben und Wirken nach den Quellen dargestellt, 1* (Basel, 1895), 377, gives the dates for the removal as July 2–July 17. All contemporary sources, however, give June 20–July 2. Farner, *3,* 602, accepts them and suggests that Staehelin's error derives from a misinterpretation of the dating of Egli, doc. 552. The reconstruction of the dismantling of the churches is based on Bullinger, *1,* 173–76; Wyss, *Chronik,* pp. 40–44; and Zwingli's own account, *Z, 4,* 150, 1–152, 7; also Oskar Farner, *Heinrich Bullinger am Grossmünster in Zürich* (Zurich, 1942), pp. 6–7, and Farner, *3,* 485–88.

31. Both quotations from Farner, *3,* 490.

8. THE ANSWER TO VALENTIN COMPAR

*Do you suppose we conceal our object of worship because
we have no shrines and altars? What image can I make of
God when, rightly considered, man himself is an image of
God? What temple can I build for him, when the whole
universe, fashioned by His handiwork cannot contain him?
Shall I, a man, housed more spaciously, confine within a tiny
shrine power and majesty so great? Is not the mind a better
place of dedication? our inmost heart of consecration?*

Minucius Felix

Early on the second day of the Second Disputation Zwingli had remarked in
passing that by comparison with the question of the Mass, that of images
was a "childish matter" (2, 733, 8–9). Nevertheless, he was unable thereafter to dismiss those images so lightly. Unprepared as he had been to give
Myconius genuinely effective advice in December 1522, he had found himself
similarly unprepared for the September demonstrations of 1523. Of his extant works, the section on images in *A Brief Christian Introduction* marks
his first attempt to deal systematically with the visual aspects of the cult of
the saints. From November 1523 until July 1524, when the images were
finally removed from the city churches, the practical problem of ecclesiastical
art had been ever with him. Against the immediate background of their removal, he prepared a defense of his iconoclasm, published August 18, 1524,[1]
in reply to the judgment of *A Brief Christian Introduction* by the Bishop of

1. Z, *3*, 155, 28–184, 31.

Constance. For the remainder of that year he was absorbed in work on his great *Commentary on True and False Religion*.

He had not yet done with the problem of images. At some time late in 1524 or early 1525 [2] Valentin Compar, the land-secretary of Canton Uri, sent to Zwingli a critique of the Reformer's theology centering around four fundamental articles: his doctrine of the Gospel, his understanding of authority, his iconoclasm, and his denial of Purgatory. This document, unhappily lost, must have been restrained in tone as well as judicious in temper, for Zwingli later acknowledged publicly in his *Answer* that Compar has "more good grace in his writing than all those who write against one another at this time" (*4, 53,* 10–11).[3] He determined, therefore, to reply to Compar as soon as the *Commentary* was completed.

It is of considerable significance that in the latter work Zwingli had intended originally not to discuss images at all, perhaps because he thought that what he had written on that subject in his reply to the Bishop of Constance was sufficient. Yet the pressure was such that he acquiesced, explaining the brevity of his discussion in the *Commentary* by stating that he would thereafter write a book devoted entirely to the subject (*3,* 900, 2–6).[4] Compar's critique must thus have inspired him to think through again, and formulate on a larger scale, the theological reasons for his rejection of ecclesiastical and liturgical art. Although the separate book was never published, what would have been its contents must have been incorporated into Zwingli's reply to Compar's third article, since of the four parts into which the *Answer* is divided, that on images is the longest and most carefully wrought; it is indeed, as Zwingli confessed, his "complete opinion" (84, 15) on the subject. The phrase is important: on this occasion he produced a synthesis of all that he had thought and written on ecclesiastical art since his arrival in Zurich. Moreover, inasmuch as the *Answer* opens with a double salutation, one to the Confederacy and one to Compar, Zwingli clearly intended the document to be something more than a local polemic. The *Answer to Valentin Compar* must thus be understood as a defense and an explanation to the rest of Switzerland of the whole Reformation as it had thus far affected the visual arts in Zurich.

2. K. D. Kluser, *Der Landschreiber Valentin Compar von Uri und sein Streit mit Zwingli,* Historisches Neujahrsblatt herausgegeben von der Gesellschaft für Geschichte und Alterthümer des Kantons Uri, 1 (1895), 38.

3. Unless indicated to the contrary, all references in the text are to Vol. 4 of Zwingli's works.

4. Z, *3,* 900, 1 to 906, 5. This section on images and that in the reply to the Bishop of Constance will not be analyzed, since all the arguments contained in them are incorporated and refined in The *Answer to Valentin Compar.*

THE DEFINITION OF TRUE BELIEF

The massive indictment of images in the *Answer to Valentin Compar* rests entirely on Zwingli's radical discrimination between a true Christian belief and a false Christian belief. He begins by putting the question: what is the ultimate object of Christian belief—that is to say, how is the Christian properly to understand the content of the word God? The word is defined here as "that good from which all things arise and come, in which all things exist, and are sustained, to whom all men should go in all their evil and vileness" (86, 22–25). It must follow, then, that true Christian belief can consist only in a reliance on this absolute unconditional good, for God "calls Himself our father, helper, solacer, and protector, so that we will erect no other father, helper, solacer, and protector" (86, 28–30). That, in fact, is why "Jesus Christ has, when He taught us to pray, first told us to say Father, that is: that we should recognize Him as our Father without a doubt, not only with our mouths, but profoundly in our hearts" (88, 12–15). The Christian is confronted first with the uniqueness of God as the ultimate object of his belief, and second, with the fact that his belief must consist in a response to this uniqueness which recognizes no qualification:

> Only those are believers who know truly in their hearts that they should go to God alone in all their affairs. For they know that power over all things is in His hands alone, and that such power can be in the hands of no one else except in His. For they know that there can be no God except Him. Thus help, protection, grace, death, and life may rest in no one's hands except His. [88, 23–28]

This is the first of the two superintending frames of reference within which Zwingli's discussion of images will fit: on the one hand, the uniqueness of God as the object of man's true belief; on the other, man's unconditional response to that object of true belief. "The believer is one who trusts in God alone" (97, 7–8).

THE DEFINITION OF FALSE BELIEF

But men have never put their whole belief and trust in God. They have merely professed to do so, while turning actually to other people and other things in His stead. Zwingli is acutely conscious of this defect in human nature, just as he is aware of man's inclination to hypocrisy in public worship. The failure to rely ultimately on God alone is a persisting fact of man's spiritual life. People "may well be believers, but not in the true God" (89, 21). Thus what should be the sole object of man's belief has everywhere been fragmented into multiple responses to a congeries of substitutes for Him. All substitutes, however, are immediately recognizable and easily reduced to a single common denominator—namely, anyone or anything to whom man "goes for help, who is his sole comfort and treasure" (89, 18–19); in other words, anyone or anything placed between God and man by man himself: "They are not believers who go to anyone else for help other than to the one, true God. For thus are the believers differentiated from the unbelievers in that the believers, or those who are trusting, go to God alone; but the unbelievers go to the created [*den gschöpften*]" (88, 29–33).

THE DYNAMICS OF FALSE BELIEF

What, then, is the source of *den gschöpften?* How are they to be identified specifically as substitutes for God? And in what way do they intervene between God and man? To these three interlocked questions Zwingli returns one answer: all substitutes for God, regardless of their virtually infinite variety, are the inevitable result of a single dynamic process peculiar to man, a process which Zwingli understands and interprets in psychological fashion.

In turning away from God as the sole object of his ultimate belief, man has either consciously or unconsciously put his real trust in creatures and created things. He may, for example, regard his doctor as the one who is alone responsible for the state of his health; he may rely ultimately on political power, or social prestige; he may trust completely in the power of wealth, so that, as Zwingli says, "his gold or possessions are god" (97, 13–14; cf. 14–24). To these manifestations of false belief, all of which are internal and initially unconscious thought-processes, Zwingli assigns the single word *Abgott,* "strange god." His use of *Abgott* is precise and virtually consistent throughout the essay. Whenever he uses the word, he intends to convey the notion of a psychic process in which someone or something important in a man's interior life, regardless of its external form, is displacing God as the object of that man's real faith. What Zwingli had understood loosely as "temptation" (2, 710, 9) in 1523 has deepened by 1525 into a specific pattern of estrangement. Indeed, the word *Abgott* itself designates the process of becoming-estranged-from-God, and must be interpreted as Zwingli's final development of the implications of the phrase "inward idols" (*inneren götzen*) to which he had referred but once in the Second Disputation (2, 710, 7) and only partially explored in *A Brief Christian Introduction* (2, 655, 21–25).

Increasingly as these strange gods make themselves felt, and as man becomes more conscious of his reliance on them, he must try eventually to give to them some specific form; the mental process must be pictured. Zwingli is aware that an instinctive need as well as an instinctive capacity for imagining things is so deeply rooted in the human psyche that "what the mind of man takes in hand for himself runs always to phantasy and makes an image [*verbildt*] of the same" (96, 30–31). In fact, "there is no one," he asserts, "who, as soon as he hears God spoken of, or any other thing which he has not already seen, does not picture a form [*gstalt*] for himself" (96, 24–26). Furthermore, the experience of the senses is as ineradicable a need of human existence as the imaginative faculty: "by nature man falls upon those things which are placed in the realm of the senses" (92, 15–16). Thus the movement from an invisible, subjective process, existing initially within man's mind, to a visible, objectified image, is inevitable. The internal strange gods must sooner or later be externalized, and to all forms of such externalization, regardless of their variety, Zwingli assigns the single word *Götze,* "idol." Anyone or anything within man's mind estranging him from true belief in God, thereby initiating false belief, constitutes, as an internal, spiritual phenomenon, an *Abgott,* a strange god; as an external, material phenomenon perpetuating false belief, it is a *Götze,* an "idol" (cf. 96, 10–11). "Where one has strange gods, there one begins to honor them with idols and outward reverence" (106, 13–15). It may be a creature, a human being already existing, or it may be an object brought into existence by man's hands. The *Götzen* are thus defined as "portraits of the *abgötten*" (99, 2); they are the final results of an endless process of human invention (cf. 137, 3), for "the strange god [*der abgot*] always comes before the idols [*dem götzen*]" (133, 27–28). Consequently, "service to idols follows only afterward, when the strange god is already set up in your hearts" (105, 18–19; cf. 132, 6–7). For Zwingli idolatry is therefore not to be understood conventionally. He replies to the iconophiles that if men "have their hope in creatures, then they are idolaters, *although these same creatures are not idols*" (89, 22–23; italics mine). Idolatry thus interpreted, as opposed to true belief, constitutes the second superintending frame of reference for Zwingli's discussion of images.

In 1523, when he had dealt with the problem of music in the *Interpretation and Substantiation of the Conclusions,* Zwingli found himself confronted by a fundamentally irreconcilable tension between the ideal of a truly private prayer such as Christ commanded, and the reality of the spiritual and psychological dangers inherent in any form of public worship. In dealing with the problem of the visual arts, he faces a comparable tension. True belief consists in a continuing, single relationship between man and his *creator* God. False belief consists in discontinuous, multiple relationships between man and his several self-*created* substitutes for God (cf. 88, 32–33; 89, 28–29). True belief must be of such an abiding intensity "that it cannot be diminished *by any visible thing*" (92, 14; italics mine). Pressing continually against this assertion, however, as Zwingli recognized, was the fact that men naturally turn to visible things, so that all men are in fact idolators by nature (96, 26–27). He thereby discloses his acute awareness of the tension never absent from the *Answer*—namely, the conflict, as irreconcilable as that between private prayer and common prayer, between the ideal condition of true belief, permanently beyond human realization, and the reality of man's ever-present idolatry.

Against the tension between the two, Zwingli turns then to the problem of the images themselves: "We are arguing only against those images which have lessened belief in the one God, such as those to this or that saint as a helper, and against the images to which one does reverence" (94, 21–24). Thus Zwingli's discussion is to be conducted on two distinctively different grounds: on the one hand, the relationship which the image holds to those who are in some way or another affected by seeing it; on the other hand, the relationship which the image bears to the person or persons represented or suggested by it. He deals with the first as the central manifestation of popular piety—that is, with the ceremonial and spiritual abuses which the images have induced in the faithful.

POPULAR PIETY

God commanded men neither to worship images nor to serve them. The iconophiles interpret the commandment to mean merely "that one should not kneel before images because that is an outward thing; and because it is only a ceremony it therefore has nothing to do with the New Testament" (101, 7–10). Zwingli rejoins simply by pointing to the incontrovertible fact that churches everywhere were choked with statues and pictures which the faithful worshiped (cf. 107, 8–109, 30). They bowed to them, knelt before them, burned incense before them, prayed to them; they had even come to believe that certain statues or images in some places or shrines were holier than others. What is this, he argues, if not worship: "why do you bow before idols in church and not bow before images [*bilden*] in your room, but drink, swear, gamble or do even worse before them" (101, 18–21)? Where paintings or statues induce no false hopes and are not thereby revered, where they are simply images (*bilder*), "the likeness [*glychnussen*]" (96, 11–12) of anything that is visible but gives no cause for a religious response, then these cannot be regarded as idols. But paintings and statues in churches do, in fact, induce an immediate religious response. The "danger here is that everything which is in the church becomes from that moment on so great and holy in our eyes that we think it cannot be touched, so dear has it become" (101, 29–32; cf. 104, 12–14; 122, 27–29). Consequently, such images are idols, either because "you hold those in the church to be holier than those elsewhere, or, on the other hand, that you honor them for a purpose other than that which they signify" (101, 22–24). Reverence for the image may thus be induced on two interrelated but distinguishable grounds: first, the physical setting itself, and second, that significance popular piety reads into the images. But for Zwingli architecture cannot confer sanctification; the shrines and churches housing statues and paintings of the saints are simply buildings. Furthermore, the faithful worship statues and images even when they are erected outside churches, because they have come to believe that any statues and paintings can accomplish miracles. A local example was the statue of St. Anne at Ober-Stammheim to which miracles were attributed. It stood in the open and was much frequented for at least one year, if not two, before a chapel was built to house it. Thus the response of uneducated people to the sight of saints' images was sufficient ground for denying their propriety and for abolishing them. Zwingli bluntly reiterated Sebastian Hofmeister's argument during the Second Disputation: "Take the image of St. Anne at Stammenheim. Did men go there before it was made? No. And now that it has been burned do men go there so much? No" (102, 21–24). The behavior of the people was proof sufficient of their idolatry, of their captivity to the senses.

LEARNED PIETY

Zwingli objected to images also with regard to the relationship which they bore to the person represented or suggested. The learned iconophiles were more sophisticated in their false belief, for they denied that they worshiped the images. Following Bonaventura, Aquinas, and the precepts of the

Summa Rudium, they maintained that "we honor the images for another reason; the image of Saint Peter for his sake, who is in heaven" (104, 16-17). "I honor no image," they argued; "I also burn no candles before it, except to him whom the image signifies" (104, 17-19). To this traditional argument Zwingli insists first of all that saints, far from being desirous of such veneration, in fact abhor it. "If they were living still today, they would cry out against us: Why do you attribute to us that which is God's alone?" (90, 9-11). Zwingli first proposed this idea in the *Interpretation and Substantiation of the Conclusions* (3, 95, 29-34); Hätzer had taken it up in the second of his Answers; Commander Schmid had made it prominent during the Second Disputation. Now Zwingli returns to the theme with even greater vehemence, adducing the example of Paul and Barnabas (Acts 14:8-20), who, because they had healed a cripple, were worshiped by the citizens of Lystra:

> They tore their clothes and fell among the people, crying: "You men! What are you doing? We are mortal men, just as you also, and we teach you so that you may turn from such foolishness (namely, that they had attributed to a creature that which was from God alone) to the living God who has created heaven and earth, the sea and all that is therein," and so forth. [91, 4-9]

Zwingli stresses the fact that Paul and Barnabas were possessed by no "inward idols of temptation"; they had no "strange gods"; they permitted nothing whatsoever to impinge on the exclusiveness of their belief and trust in God. So he reiterates the argument he had advanced earlier in *A Brief Christian Introduction:* How could such true believers approve of being worshiped or venerated because they were presumed to possess powers which belonged to God alone, powers which had been attributed falsely to them by their fellow men? For that, Zwingli argues, is what men have done to the saints:

> We have heard that we shall have no other god before our God and Father . . . although we look immediately for a blessed end with St. Barbara and seek a healthy stomach with St. Erasmus, yet we know well that the only god is the true God. But God has given much of this power to the former and the latter pious believers. Yet we have said this without foundation in the Word of God, and we have attributed to these pious, departed Christians that which is God's alone.
>
> [89, 36; 90, 1, 4-9]

The inevitable psychological process of seeking to imagine and picture God, which Zwingli had earlier described, has led men to distribute, as it were, portions of God's power among men and women such as Saint Paul or Saint Barbara, believing them to be saints for false reasons, and thence, because of those false reasons, making them, in effect, gods themselves, because they are worshiped for the special attributes which men have accorded them (cf. 132, 19–21; 136, 34).

It is at this point that the dynamic process by which a strange god eventually becomes externalized is given concrete illustration:

> We all know that one has set up service to idols only because one therefore hopes to get something thereby . . . this one in St. Peter's name that he guard him from despair, that one in St. Niklaus' name that he not drown, and so forth, just as each has his own fear and trouble. But notice: was it right, therefore, that you sought for this or that help from Saints Peter, Niklaus, Gertrude, or Barbara? No. You should not have made them into such idols. [105, 2–3, 6–11]

If Zwingli's distinctions between strange god, idol, and image are borne in mind, this passage is central for an understanding of the role that religious images play within his dynamic of false belief. A man, for example, is mortally afraid of drowning. When this fear grips him, rather than relying wholly on God's omnipotence he turns to Saint Nicholas to intercede for him with God. The choice of saints was doubtless, by and large, arbitrary at first, depending on the tales told of them.[5] Gradually, however, a relationship between the man's fear of drowning and Saint Nicholas became fixed in his mind to the degree that he removed from God the power to save him from drowning and attached that power permanently and specifically to the Saint. As Zwingli said elsewhere of Saint Christopher, "I do not mean that he is an idol, but that you are allotting to him that which is God's alone" (99, 26–28; cf. 100, 8–10; 132, 19–21). In such fashion true belief was replaced by false belief, the unique union of faith between man and God was broken, and Saint Nicholas, as the estranging element, had become—*against his own will* as well as against God's—an *Abgott*, a strange god within the

---

5. Cf. Erasmus' Colloquy, The Franciscans; or, Rich Beggars, *The Whole Familiar Colloquies of Desiderius Erasmus of Rotterdam,* trans. Nathan Bailey (London, 1877), pp. 187–88: "This town abounds with swineherds, by reason of a large wood hard by that produces plenty of acorns, and the people have an opinion that St. Antony takes charge of the hogs, and therefore they worship him, for fear he should grow angry if they neglect him."

man's mind. Then as the man's instinct to picture things, to make a *gestalt*, became operative and was joined to his need to give to this *gestalt* a sensible form, the process of becoming-estranged-from-God was externalized and objectified in a painting or statue of Saint Nicholas. The decision to make a visible artistic representation of Saint Nicholas was initially idolatrous, however, because it was inspired not by a saint but by an *Abgott*. Thus the whole process of externalization and objectification into an image was idolatrous. Even before the image had been made, it was an idol.[6]

These, then, are the two arguments with which Zwingli rebuts the doctrine that "the honor rendered to the image passes to the prototype": first of all, the saints themselves do not wish to be so honored, and, second, owing to the dynamics of false belief, to represent a saint by any kind of image is in fact to create an idol, even when the image is neither worshiped nor venerated. Both were suggested in the brief commentary on Exodus 20:3-4 which he wrote for *A Brief Christian Introduction*. Now, after two years of deepening reflection on the problem—not so much against the background of local iconoclasm as in 1523 but rather in the context of systematically defining true Christian belief, what "has to do with the greatest part of our salvation" (95, 1-2)—he had come to the conclusion that God prohibited the making of all images "of all gods, that is: all those that anyone could himself choose for his own solace" (92, 26-27).

IMAGES OF CHRIST: THE DIVINITY OF CHRIST

Zwingli turns next to the refutation of what he considers "the greatest counter-objection which the idol protectors make" (113, 20)—namely, images of Christ. That objection was, in fact, the crux of the iconophile argument which Compar stated as follows: "Christ is God and man; one may therefore portray Him according to His human nature" (114, 23-24). Zwingli's rejoinder consists in an extended discussion of the two natures and their unity, but although he affirms the unity of Christ, he greatly empha-

---

6. Zwingli points out that the individual process described above is exactly paralleled in the religious history of the pagans: "they came to the point where they realized that a God must exist. But that they serve God alone was not enough for them; they gave a portion of the divine power to many and thought these same to be the sun, the moon, Jove, Mercury, and others. That was not enough. After that they also portrayed these same imagined gods of theirs and thus split the one God into many gods (see how the strange god always comes before the idol!), and thereafter also portrayed these gods in all sorts of forms and finally have served and honored the created more than the creator" (Z, 4, 133, 21-30).

sizes His divinity, to the point, in fact, of depreciating His humanity. Such an emphasis is characteristic of Zwingli's Christology, for he always tended to stress the distinction of the two natures as against their unity, especially as the controversy with Luther over the Real Presence deepened. God is the author of Redemption, and Christ's humanity, even on the Cross, plays, as it were, an auxiliary role. It is the divinity rather than the humanity of Christ that saves mankind: "Redemption is through the deity, although the death is of man" (118, 25–26). Consequently, since even the iconophiles are agreed that God may not be portrayed, then "it follows that one should not and may not portray Christ. For the divinity of Christ may not be portrayed because the deity may and should not be portrayed" (119, 2–5). The propriety or even the possibility of any visible representation of Christ in His divinity is completely denied.

IMAGES OF CHRIST: THE HUMANITY OF CHRIST

Equally emphatic, however, is Zwingli's toleration of images of Christ in His humanity: "Where anyone has a portrait [*bildnus*] of His humanity, that is just as fitting to have as to have other portraits. . . . No one is forbidden from having a portrait of the humanity of Christ" (119, 15–17, 24–25). Thus men may, after all, make images of Christ as man, but with two major qualifications.

First of all, under no circumstances are they to be offered reverence of any sort (118, 14–15; 119, 25–26). If an image of Christ's humanity is made and reverenced, it becomes, like images of the saints, an idol. Moreover, the idolatry thus induced is of the worst possible sort, because man would be putting his faith in a creature rather than the creator. In Zwingli's specialized vocabulary man would be turning Christ Himself into an estranging and separating element from God. Everyone, therefore, "who now has the image of Christ in his house should take care that he not make it into an idol; for as we have already said, with us no pictures become idols faster than those of Christ" (119, 27–28; 120, 1–2).

The second qualification is that such images or portraits of Christ are under no circumstances to be designed for churches, or placed within them. Above all, the crucifix must everywhere be removed, for as Zwingli bluntly observed: "I have never seen in churches a cross displayed without one making it into an idol . . . we call the golden, silver, stone, and wooden crosses our Lord God; we embrace them as if we received solace and comfort from them. As soon as that happens, away with them (120, 2–3; 119, 19–22). On this point Zwingli is adamant. He has abandoned completely the theoretical latitude of the May decree of 1524, just as the Council had abandoned it in practice in June; neither in churches nor in private homes could a symbolic representation of Christ be tolerated longer. But outside the churches, in private homes or public places, images of Christ in His humanity could be displayed. In *A Brief Christian Introduction* Zwingli had said with regard to images that "if someone places representations of historic events [*geschichteswyss*] outside the churches, this may be allowed so long as they do not give rise to reverence" (2, 658, 19–20). It had appeared, then, that the word *geschichteswyss* might exclude all possibility of religious art. Both the word and its context were ambiguous, however, and it is quite possible that in 1523 Zwingli was undecided on the question whether such an art was possible. Two years later his position is clear. An art with Christian content is permissible, but only within the severe qualifications on which he insisted. The persons and events of Christian history, its central figure not excluded, are portrayable in visual form only, *geschichteswyss,* purely historical phenomena. Christian representational art is thus voided entirely by Zwingli not only of any liturgical and ecclesiastical content or purpose but also of any spiritual dimension.

REPRESENTATION AND THE WORD

"The portrait of Christ teaches the simple, unlettered man, and incites him to devotion which he would not have if he had not seen the portrait of Christ" (120, 10–12). Compar in that single sentence brought forward the two principal arguments which had sustained the use of images in the medieval West, the didactic one stemming from Pope Gregory and the hortatory one stemming from Saint Bonaventura. To both Zwingli replies with a devastating series of parallel comparisons of the value of the Word and the worthlessness of images, the whole revolving now around the pedagogics of faith.

To begin with, men can learn nothing of the content of God's Word from an image. "Why," Zwingli rhetorically asks, "do we not send images to unbelievers so that they can learn belief from them?" (120, 18–19). Precisely because we would be required to explain what they mean, which in turn requires knowledge of the Word. "If now you show an unbelieving or unlettered child images, then you must teach him with the Word in addition, or he will have looked at the picture in vain" (120, 22–25). For if "you were newly come from the unbelievers and knew nothing of Christ and saw Him painted with the apostles at the Last Supper, or on the Cross, then you would learn nothing from this same picture other than to say: 'He who is pictured there was a good-looking man in spite of it all' " (121, 18–22). Zwingli's witticism is a particularly telling index to his contempt for the Gregorian defense of images. One may have images of Christ, but they are powerless; the "story must be learned only from the Word, and from the painting one learns nothing except the form of the body, the movements or the constitution of the body or face" (121, 26–29).

In 1523 Zwingli had excluded all music from the service of worship on the basis of a threefold argument drawn from Scripture: (1) God had not explicitly commanded it; (2) Christ had instructed men to pray individually and in private; and (3) Saint Paul had urged men to pray to God in their hearts. Two years later Zwingli adduces now virtually the same threefold argument for the denial of any pedagogical value to images: (1) "God has not told us to teach from pictures, but from His Word" (122, 3–4); (2) "If teaching with images assists toward a knowledge of faith, then there is no doubt that Christ would have taught us to make images" (122, 9–11); and (3) "the holy apostles have forbidden us to have idols" (122, 12–13).

Paintings and statues, therefore, as visible, palpable forms appealing to the eye, cannot be the bearers either of spiritual or of educational effects. By the same token, the sensuous experience stimulated in the beholder cannot have a spiritual or educational character. The arts of the eye can neither teach the Holy nor express the Holy. They can portray only the accidents, not the substance, of Christianity, as they are given in the relativities of time and history. Men have thought that they could acquire the substance of true belief from pictures and statues only because for centuries the Papacy taught with them rather than with the Word. In saying that, Zwingli discloses what is for him one of the most important and urgent reasons for the removal of images—namely, that they constitute a barrier to the proper religious education of Zurich. Once they were entirely removed, then Zwingli's goal would be attained: "the hunger for the divine Word would become greater in men, and men would call more earnestly on God for preachers and workers than otherwise occurs" (127, 32–34).

REPRESENTATION AND TIME

Another traditional argument on which Compar earlier drew for the retention of images had been that enlightened Christians in the sixteenth century could not possibly worship images as had the pagans or even the Israelites when they prostrated themselves before the Golden Calf. Zwingli retorts by maintaining that there is essentially no difference between the pagan idol and the Christian "image," so called, because the latter, as he has demonstrated, is, in fact, an idol too: "The objection that those idols were of gods, and ours not, has long been superseded. Ours are just as much strange gods as theirs" (141, 31–32). Indeed, the only distinction which he can find at all between pagan and Christian practice with regard to images is the fact that "the heathen idols insulted only the true God, but our idols insult the true God and His chosen saints" (111, 16–17).

On the other hand, in countering Compar's objection Zwingli stresses that true belief, as he has defined it, existed in the time of Moses as it does now in sixteenth-century Zurich, and so likewise with false belief. The nature of either, in other words, cannot be transformed or bound by time. He presses the argument now against the following statement by Compar:

> A Christian goes across the field. He finds there the Passion of Christ, once, twice, or three or more times in image-niches along the way; whenever he sees them he does honor to Christ's Passion. . . . But when he finds no such images on his path, then he never thinks either of God or His saints. Therefore images are good for us and never evil.
>
> [124, 25–28; 125, 12–14]

Whereas the extraordinary extent to which late medieval piety was captive to the senses is perhaps nowhere better epitomized than in Compar's admission, Zwingli's rejoinder is no less devastating. Service to God is "to be busy in the will of the heavenly father" (125, 22), and that is not a matter of occasion. It is, to the contrary, a life service. "Right, true, brave, and steadfast reverence for God is when a man carries his God with him in his heart, God willing, wherever he goes, even if he nowhere sees a piece of wood with a saint's picture on it" (126, 13–15). The false believer is one whose belief is, in fact, bound by time. He is one who by "looking at images or idols induces devotion for no longer than one sees them and mumbles a meaningless word" (125, 31; 126, 1–2). For such isolated and haphazard moments of false belief and false devotion Zwingli has nothing but scorn, dismissing them contemptuously with the proverb "out of sight, out of mind" (126, 4–5). True belief knows no such passing moments.

Zwingli interrupts his argument with a significant brief excursion on the Sabbath in order to demonstrate that it, too, is not simply an appointed time, but an inner and continuing process. It would be only "an outward thing if we thought the day of the Lord—that is, Sunday—is bound therefore to that day" (129, 3–5). When the Sabbath is not properly understood as an interior spiritual phenomenon with neither beginning nor end, then Zwingli condemns it as a ceremonial, "bound to time [*zyt gebunden*] which is an element of this world, that is, an outward thing" (129, 2–3). And so it is with images because they, too, are ceremonials (130, 1–3). There is no other single passage in the *Answer* which concentrates so intensely in one sentence all the aspects of false belief against which he is so vehemently protesting. The two diametrically opposed structures of true belief and false belief which have served as referents for the image problem are incomparably illumined. The prime symbol of true belief is the Word, invisible and heard; the prime symbol of false belief is the image, visible and seen.

THE SACRAMENTAL PROBLEM

The difference between these two forms of belief points finally to the most fundamental reason for Zwingli's opposition to images. The liturgy of the Mass had not always been conducted with the visual splendor of the late Middle Ages. The primitive Church seems not to have regarded such material aids as necessary or important. Yet the attractive power of the image eventually proved irresistible, and its admission by the Church was indeed momentous, not alone for the history of art but also for the history of Christian worship. Piety and worship grew so sensuous that as early as the twelfth and thirteenth centuries a "dominant motif" of the religious life of the people had become "the desire to behold sacred reality with bodily eyes." [7] To that desire the Church had responded by proclaiming, above all else, the dogma of Transubstantiation, and it can scarcely be fortuitous that the authoritative formulation of the Real Presence of Christ and the elaboration of so much of the Mass liturgy should occur in the same centuries.

Both are expressions of that drive toward the palpably real, that insistent demand for the concrete in faith and worship, that attempt to bind the spiritual to the material, which is so profoundly characteristic of the high and late Middle Ages. Within the structure of the liturgy itself there began in this period an intensification of everything that would appeal to the sensibility. Before the twelfth century, for instance, the priest had kissed the altar

7. Otto von Simson, *The Gothic Cathedral: Origins of Gothic Architecture and the Mediaeval Concept of Order*, Bollingen Series, 48 (New York, 1956), xx.

twice only, upon approaching it and upon leaving it; by 1300 the kiss "was performed every time the celebrant turned around at the altar." [8] Until the eleventh century, altars had been rarely more than three or four feet square; from that time onward, they grew steadily in size, until by the fifteenth century some could be found which were twelve feet long. In the thirteenth century altars became more and more elaborately decorated: the austere *mensa* was gradually giving way to the great reredos-altar of the fourteenth and fifteenth centuries.[9] Altar crosses and candles made their appearance in the twelfth century,[10] and there were significant alterations in the vestments of the priest. Under Innocent III the symbolism of their colors was codified and elaborated. Those which the priest wore to the altar had customarily been interpreted as signifying Christ's Passion. During the thirteenth century an actual cross appeared on the back of the chasuble, a development which meant that "the allegorical presentation of the Crucified could be imaged even in the external figuration." [11] Nor was it enough to satisfy the sense of sight: in the same period the extension of the priest's hands after the consecration came to be understood as an imitation of the arms of Christ stretched out upon the cross, so that the sense of movement, too, was symbolically gratified.[12] Finally, this period saw everywhere conscious efforts to amplify and enrich the musical aspects of liturgical drama.[13]

The climax of such multiplication and intensification of all that was sensuous in the liturgy of the Mass was the Elevation of the Host.[14] The faithful of the Middle Ages knew that Christ was really present in the consecrated elements. But they knew, too, that they could actually see only the sacramental appearance of bread and wine, of which the substance was Christ's body and blood. Their insistence upon actually seeing the elements is, perhaps, the supreme expression of the medieval drive for visualizing the sacred. Thus the custom arose toward the close of the twelfth century of elevating the Host so that, although only for a moment, the people might see it. The Lateran proclamation on Transubstantiation served not only to answer this longing to see God, but to intensify it as well. Greatly increased impor-

8. Joseph A. Jungmann, S.J., *The Mass of the Roman Rite: Its Origins and Development*, trans. Francis A. Brunner, C.SS.R. (New York, 1951), *1*, 107.
9. Ibid., pp. 109, n. 37; 109–10.
10. Ibid., p. 109, n. 37.
11. Ibid., p. 112.
12. Ibid., p. 107.
13. Ibid., pp. 123–27.
14. Ibid., pp. 119–21.

tance was attached to the Feast of Corpus Christi, first officially instituted by Urban IV in 1264,[15] when the people could see the Host not just for a brief moment in a dimly lit church but for a much longer period. In the brightness of day they could follow it with their eyes, and adore it as it was carried through the streets in solemn and splendid procession.

Thus the liturgy of the Mass in the high and late Middle Ages gave rise to an intensely emotional and sensuous experience, the substance of which was mediated by the arts. First of all, the Church was in itself a representation of supernatural reality. Although a structure of stone and wood and glass, its reality lay in the fact that, by virtue of the language employed in the ritual of dedication, the church was, "mystically and liturgically, an image of heaven." [16] Inside the building the worshiper entered another world. The more splendid the interior, the richer the vestments, the more glorious the music, the more elaborate the liturgy, with all its attendant magnificence of sight and sound, of processional movements and odors of incense and burning candles, the nearer the worshiper came to an intimation of heaven itself. And when the priest, the *creator creatoris,* at length raised the Host on high, the worshiper saw Christ: "See the Son of God who, for your sakes, shows His wounds to the Heavenly Father; See the Son of God who, for your sakes, was thus lifted on the Cross; See the Son of God who will come to judge the living and the dead." [17] A more dramatic climax to a sufficiently dramatic spectacle could scarcely be imagined, and this threefold repetition of the exhortation to "see" in Berthold of Regensburg's sermon on the Mass emphasizes the overwhelmingly visual aspect of the religious experience.

Such a spectacle, in the exact sense of the word, was for Zwingli the apogee of idolatry. Christ's human body was something specifically defined and delimited; it was in Heaven, invisible and incommunicable. There was no possibility of a corporeal, material eating of Christ in the bread. He rejected both the Transubstantiation of the medieval church and the Consubstantiation of Luther.[18] The presence of Christ at the Lord's Supper in Zurich could be only a spiritual one, for Christ could be an object of faith only and solely through His divinity, just as His divinity rather than His

15. Ibid., p. 122.
16. Von Simson, *The Gothic Cathedral,* p. 8.
17. Jungmann, *The Mass of the Roman Rite,* p. 121.
18. The literature on Zwingli's eucharistical doctrine is large, controversial, and complex; cf. the magisterial survey by J.-V.-M. Pollet, "Zwinglianisme," *Dictionnaire de Théologie Catholique, 15* [2] (Paris, 1950), cols. 3825–42.

humanity redeemed mankind. As a result, the spiritual realm was sundered from the material. The faith and worship of the medieval Church had sought to bring the two always closer and closer together. Zwingli strove to divorce them completely. For the faithful in the Middle Ages, viewing the celebration of the liturgy of the Mass was to undergo a multiple sense experience in which sight and sound, smell and movement all were profoundly aroused and implicated. The Zwinglian Sermon Liturgy and the celebration of the Lord's Supper stand in irreconcilable opposition to such a religious experience. Insofar as it was possible, Zwingli eliminated everything sensuous from worship. Music, vestments, incense, ritual gestures, and images—all were of no avail to man precisely because his faith, the only reality, the invisible action of the Holy Spirit in men's hearts, had nothing whatsoever to do with the senses. To the triple exhortation to "see" of Berthold of Regensburg, he would thus have replied: "Faith is from the invisible God and it tends toward the invisible God, and is something completely apart from all that is sensible. Anything that is body, anything that is of the senses, cannot be an object of faith" (*3*, 798, 14-17). On those two great affirmations— with respect at least to images—rested Zwingli's *Answer to Valentin Compar*.

EPILOGUE: *The Broken Wheel*

Do not hesitate, my beloved son, believe with a whole faith that the spirit of God has filled thy heart when thou hast adorned His house with so much richness and variety of ornamentation.

Roger of Hellmarshausen (Theophilus)

Undoubtedly there is no religion where there is a picture.

Lactantius

The *Answer to Valentin Compar* of 1525 was indeed Zwingli's "complete opinion" on the subject of ecclesiastical and liturgical art, just as the *Substantiation* of the three *Conclusions* on prayer in the *Conclusions* of 1523 had been his definitive statement on liturgical music. From 1525 on the Liturgy of the Sermon and the Liturgy of the Lord's Supper were celebrated in the austere whiteness of the Zurich churches amid the awesome stillness which the Reformer had so ardently desired. His achievement was scrupulously maintained by his friend and successor as religious leader of the city, Heinrich Bullinger. Nothing illustrates more vividly the stubborn continuity of the setting[1] for the Zurich liturgy than the Second Helvetic Confession which Bullinger drafted in 1562 and published in 1566. Zwingli's great affirmation of the invisible God from his *Commentary on True and False Religion* is virtually repeated in the very first sentence of the chapter on images: "And because God is an invisible Spirit, and an incomprehensible

---

1. Changes in the formal structure of the liturgy had been made as early as 1535; cf. Julius Schweizer, *Reformierte Abendmahlsgestaltung*, pp. 115–27.

Essence, he cannot, therefore, by any art or image be expressed." [2] Shortly thereafter Bullinger summarized and reaffirmed the long chain of argumentation against images which had begun with Hätzer's pamphlet and ended with Zwingli's reply to Compar: [3]

> And seeing that the blessed spirits and saints in heaven, while they lived here, abhorred all worship done unto themselves (Acts 3:12, 14:15; Rev. 19:10, 22:9), and spake against images, who can think it likely that the saints in heaven, and the angels, are delighted with their own images, whereunto men do bow their knees, uncover their heads, and give such other like honor? [4]

With respect to the absence of music, Bullinger the musician defended the silence of the Zwinglian liturgy in the chapter on prayer. "If there be any churches," he wrote, "which have faithful prayer in good manner, without any singing, they are not therefore to be condemned, for all churches have not the advantage and opportunity of sacred music." [5] Over three decades after his death, the integrity of Zwingli's intent for the setting of the liturgy was thus staunchly and faithfully guarded by Bullinger.

The first celebration of the Lord's Supper on Maundy Thursday, 1525, had been a triumph for Zwingli; it was the climax of his reconstruction of the liturgy. It was also an event of the greatest significance for the artistic and musical history of sixteenth-century Zurich, for that new form of worship necessarily marked a revolution in the life of any artist or musician living in the city. Its dimensions can be gauged when one reflects upon the fact that for centuries the Church and its liturgy had been at once the patron and the source of inspiration for artists of all sorts. Luther had put it most compactly: "There is scarcely one of the handicrafts in all the world, which does not contribute a great part of its activity to, and derive its gain from, the Mass." Architects had designed the buildings for its celebration, modest village chapels as well as great cathedrals. Stone masons and carpenters had built them. Sculptors had pierced their walls and ceilings with infinitely

---

2. "The Second Helvetic Confession" in *The Creeds of Christendom,* ed. Philip Schaff (4th ed. New York, 1919), *3,* 836.

3. The ultimate source for the idea may be Luther: see his remarks in "An Open Letter to the Christian Nobility of the German Nation" in *Three Treatises* (Philadelphia, 1947), p. 57; for notions of idolatry in Luther similar to Zwingli's cf. Philip S. Watson, *Let God Be God! An Interpretation of the Theology of Martin Luther* (London, 1954), pp. 85–86.

4. "The Second Helvetic Confession," p. 837.

5. Ibid., p. 898.

various carvings: in niches inside and out they had set countless statues; they had raised rood screens and decorated choir stalls; they had fashioned the altars. Painters had covered walls and altars with pictures; glassmakers had filled the windows with color. Seamstresses had prepared the varied and resplendent vestments of the clergy. Goldsmiths, silversmiths, jewelers, enamelers, and metal workers of all sorts had provided the furniture for the altar, the crucifixes, candlesticks, chalices, monstrances, censers, basins, reliquaries. Musicians had composed music for the liturgy. All these men and women played an indispensable role within the life of the medieval Church; working with every available material substance, they were ever extending and enhancing the sensuous splendor of its liturgy.

But Zwingli's concept of faith and true belief, and the form of worship he had created by which the community could express that faith, no longer required such manifold activity. The visual arts, like music, could no longer function as bearers of spiritual effects. The painter and the sculptor were as powerless to aid the worshiper or assist him in belief as the musician. The visual arts were, in fact, like music, positive hindrances to true faith and true worship. Just as Zwingli had sought to divorce the spiritual realm from the material in his understanding of the Presence of Christ in the Lord's Supper, so had he also in his understanding of how the Supper should be celebrated severed all creative relationships between the artist and the Zurich Church.

That is not to say that the possibility of a religious art was completely denied. Zwingli had maintained that pictures of Christ in His humanity, as well as representations of scenes and events from Scripture, could be allowed in private homes, even in public places. So long as they were not intended for use by the Church or as devotional aids, so long as they did not give rise to any feeling or expression of reverence, so long as they were merely *geschichteswyss,* historical representations, such pictures could be made. But a religious art thus circumscribed, must become more and more open to secular influence. Zwingli's opposition to any liturgical or ecclesiastical art contributed to the gradual secularization of religious art—a trend already apparent in the ecclesiastical art of the city before his arrival.

Deprived of the patronage of the Church, released from any responsibility to the authority of the Church, the artist turned now for his patronage to the wealthy burghers. Here the immediate impact as well as the lasting influence of the Zwinglian reformation is decisive. Though it did not by any means initiate such activity, it promoted and greatly intensified a development in the secular arts that had become increasingly evident in Zurich during the four decades prior to 1519. Interior decoration, for example, gradually became more important and elaborate. The goldsmiths turned to making table plate for the various guilds. Slowly at first, then more rapidly as the century wore on, their work grew progressively more ornate as utility and simplicity retreated before the exaggerated splendor of huge ceremonial goblets and salvers. The interest in topographical accuracy disclosed by Hans Leu the Elder in his panel for the Chapel of the Twelve Apostles continued to be cultivated. Indeed, when the panel was removed from the Great Minster in 1524, it was not destroyed: Christ and the city saints were simply painted over with reproductions of those parts of the city which their images had concealed. This concern for a combination of literal realism and art naïvely presaged by Leu reached its climax toward the end of the century when Josias Murer completed his extraordinary bird's-eye view of the city in 1576.[6] The portraits of the city, in increasingly accurate maps as well as paintings, found their counterpart in portraits of its inhabitants, for portraiture as it was practiced by Hans Asper and the great Tobias Stimmer, representations not of saints but of real men and women, "living images made by God and not by the hands of men," [7] was the major visual art of reformed Zurich after 1532.

Nor was music neglected. It, too, continued to flourish, but again, as with the visual arts, within primarily secular conditions. Before 1519 the musical culture of Zurich had been centered almost entirely around the ecclesiastical institutions of the city. After 1532 it was centered in the home and in the school. Zwingli's influence here is as decisive as it was for the visual arts. He was, in fact, one of the most enthusiastic proponents of the domestic cultivation of music, both spiritual and secular, as is certainly revealed by his reply to Faber in 1526. One of the major directions of music instruction in the schools also reflects the pedagogical thrust of the northern musical humanism in which he had been educated: the young boys of Zurich were taught Latin under the tutelage of Johannes Fries the Elder by singing choral settings of the Horatian Odes, just as Zwingli had learned at Vienna under Celtis. The choral drama, such as the *Plutos* for which Zwingli had composed the music, became more and more popular in the city after 1535, but its subject matter, unlike the humanistic dramas of Vienna, was biblical. These Passion plays, Nativities, re-enactments of the tale of Joseph or of Job were a reflection on a public and communal scale of the Plague Song and

6. Zürcher, *Die künstlerische Kultur*, p. 106.
7. *Leo Jud, Katechismen*, ed. Oskar Farner (Zurich, 1955), p. 263.

the Cappel Song: their content was religious but not liturgical. And this same distinction which Zwingli had so pointedly drawn was maintained not only in these dramas but in the home and the school. From 1532 on, the children of Zurich were required to sing hymns and spiritual songs three times a week at the end of the school day; on other days their instruction was to be concluded with the singing of a psalm. Again, the intent of such singing was primarily pedagogical. But as more and more hymnals and collections of spiritual songs were published, and as the silence of the Zurich liturgy became more and more the notable exception among the reformed cities of Switzerland, it became increasingly difficult to maintain, as Zwingli had done in 1523, that such religious music had a valid place in school and in the home but none whatsoever in the public communal worship of God. To the pressure of arguments running counter to Zwingli the Zurich Church finally succumbed, and in 1598, twenty-three years after the faithful Bullinger died, congregational singing was introduced into the Great Minster on June 4, 1598, ironically enough the Feast of Pentecost.[8]

Its introduction into the liturgy was a violation of Zwingli's theology of worship. It is at the same time a singularly illuminating illustration of the consequence for the arts of his radically spiritualized concept of faith. Images were not admitted to the church; music was. The liturgy of Zurich in 1598, just as that of 1525, was open witness that the Zwinglian reformation had shattered the unity of art and religion which for centuries had been the greatest single source of higher culture in Western Europe. The great wheel of the Church, encompassing and enriching all artistic activity, inspiring it and encouraging it to contribute to the liturgy of the Mass at its center, had been broken.

8. Hannes Reimann, *Die Einführung des Kirchengesanges in der Zürcher Kirche nach der Reformation* (Zurich, 1959), p. 88.

BIBLIOGRAPHICAL NOTE

This study has been based primarily on the works of Huldrych Zwingli in the Corpus Reformatorum, *Huldrych Zwinglis Sämtliche Werke* (Berlin–Zurich, 1905 ff.). *Heinrich Bullingers Reformationsgeschichte,* ed. J. J. Hottinger and H. H. Vögeli (Frauenfeld, 1838–40), has been indispensable, as has Emil Egli, *Actensammlung zur Geschichte der Zürcher Reformation in den Jahren* 1519–1533 (Zurich, 1879). The most useful of the contemporary chronicles has been *Die Chronik des Bernhard Wyss,* ed. Georg Finsler, Basel, 1901. There exists, to my knowledge, no book on the subject of Zwingli's attitude toward the visual arts and music prior to this one. The Reformer's attitude to the visual arts was first dealt with directly by Hermann Spörri in chapter 5, pp. 111–31, of his *Zwingli-Studien* (Leipzig, 1866). He understood the significance of the concept of faith for the *Answer to Valentin Compar* (p. 116), but he did not develop the implications of the idea any further. Hans Lehmann, "Zwingli und die zürcherische Kunst im Zeitalter der Reformation," *Ulrich Zwingli: zum Gedächtnis der zürcher Reformation, 1519–1919* (Zurich, 1919), touches briefly on Zwingli's critique of images but is much more helpful for the art history of Zurich.

Indispensable for the art historical background have been the detailed studies of Walter Hugelshofer, *Die Zürcher Malerei bis zum Ausgang der Spätgotik,* Mitteilungen der Antiquarischen Gesellschaft in Zürich, 30, Number 4 (Zurich, 1928), Number 5 (Zurich, 1929); Richard Zürcher's survey, *Die künstlerische Kultur in Kanton Zürich: Ein geschichtlicher Überblick* (Zurich, 1943); and, for the Great Minster, *Das Grossmünster in Zürich,* Mitteilungen der Antiquarischen Gesellschaft in Zürich, 32 (Zurich, 1937–42). *Zürcher Bildnisse aus fünf Jahrhunderten* (Zurich, 1953) has been most helpful for the history of portraiture; and, for the architectural history of the city, *Die Stadt Zürich,* Die Kunstdenkmäler des Kantons Zürich, Die Kunstdenkmäler der Schweiz, 4, Part I (Basel, 1939), and 5, Part II (Basel, 1949), is an inexhaustible mine of information. The only extended study of Zwingli's criticism of images known to me is the excellent recent one by Hans Freiherr von Campenhausen, "Zwingli und Luther zur Bilderfrage," *Das Gottesbild im Abenland* (Witten und Berlin, 1959), pp. 139–72, an expansion of portions of his earlier article "Die Bilderfrage in der Reformation," *Zeitschrift für Kirchengeschichte, 68* (1957), 96–128.

A great deal more has been written on the subject of Zwingli's attitude to music, but much of it is inconsequential. Most useful for the musical history of Zurich have been Antoine-E. Cherbuliez, *Geschichte der Musikpädagogik in der Schweiz* (Zurich, 1944), Hannes Reimann, *Die Einführung des Kirchengesanges in der Zürcher Kirche nach der Reformation* (Zurich, 1959), and the older but still valuable study by Arnold Geering, *Die Vokalmusik in der Schweiz zur Zeit der Reformation* (Aarau, 1933). Leo Weisz, "Kirchengesang und Kirchenmusik im alten Zürich," *Schweizerische Musikzeitung und Sängerblatt, 73* (1933), 1–11, 45–50, is the only close study known to me of the musical history of the city before the Reformation. Julius Schweizer, *Reformierte Abendmahlsgestaltung in der Schau Zwingli* (Basel, n.d. [1954]), and Fritz Schmidt-Clausing, *Zwingli als Liturgiker* (Göttingen, 1952), have both been extremely helpful. Finally, the brief portions on Zwingli in the essay by Oskar Söhngen, "Theologische Grundlagen der Kirchenmusik," *Die Musik des Evangelischen Gottesdienst, Leiturgia, 4* (Kassel, 1961), have independently confirmed most of my major conclusions. I have not attempted beyond this to list here other, less important background books, articles, or dictionaries.

INDEX

Only names of saints, places (*Zurich* excluded), and names of sixteenth-century persons (*Zwingli* excluded) cited in the text are indexed below.

187